Accession no.
00984423

Professional development
education management

D0513040

COMPANION VOLUMES

The companion volumes in this series are:

Educational Management: Strategy, Quality and Resources, edited by Margaret Preedy, Ron Glatter and Rosalind Levačić

Organizational Effectiveness and Improvement in Education, edited by Alma Harris, Nigel Bennett and Margaret Preedy

Leadership and Teams in Educational Management, edited by Megan Crawford, Lesley Kydd and Colin Riches

All four of these readers are part of a course, Effective Leadership and Management in Education, that is itself part of the Open University MA Programme.

THE OPEN UNIVERSITY MA IN EDUCATION

The Open University MA in Education is now firmly established as the most popular postgraduate degree for education professionals in Europe, with over 3,500 students registering each year. The MA in Education is designed particularly for those with experience of teaching, the advisory service, educational administration or allied fields.

Structure of the MA

The MA is a modular degree, and students are therefore free to select from a range of options the programme which best fits in with their interests and professional goals. Specialist lines in management and primary education are also available. Study in the Open University's Advanced Diploma and Certificate Programmes can also be counted towards the MA, and successful study in the MA programme entitles students to apply for entry into the Open University Doctorate in Education programme.

COURSES CURRENTLY AVAILABLE:

- Management
- Child Development
- Primary Education
- Curriculum, Learning and Assessment
- Special Needs
- Language and Literacy
- Mentoring
- Education, Training and Employment
- Gender
- Educational Research
- Science Education
- Adult Learners
- Maths Education

OU supported open learning

The MA in Education programme provides great flexibility. Students study at their own pace, in their own time, anywhere in the European Union. They receive specially prepared study materials, supported by tutorials, thus offering the chance to work with other students.

How to apply

If you would like to register for this programme, or simply find out more information, please write for the *Professional Development in Education* prospectus to the Central Enquiry Service, PO Box 200, The Open University, Walton Hall, Milton Keynes, MK7 6YZ, UK (Telephone 01908 653231).

Professional development for educational management

Edited by
LESLEY KYDD, MEGAN CRAWFORD
AND COLIN RICHES
at The Open University

OPEN UNIVERSITY PRESS
Buckingham · Philadelphia

·1184258

LIBRARY

ACC. No. 00984423 DEPT.

CLASS No.
371· 201 KYD

UNIVERSITY
COLLEGE CHESTER

Open University Press
Celtic Court
22 Ballmoor
Buckingham MK18 1XW

email: enquiries@openup.co.uk
world wide web: http://www.openup.co.uk

and 325 Chestnut Street
Philadelphia, PA 19106, USA

First published 1997
Reprinted 1998 (twice)

© 1997 Compilation, original and editorial material, The Open University

All rights reserved. No part of this book may be reprinted or reproduced or utilized in any form
or by any electronic, mechanical, or other means, now known or hereafter invented, including
photocopying and recording, or in any information storage or retrieval system, without
permission in writing from the publishers.

A catalogue record of this book is available from the British Library

ISBN 0 335 19812 0 (hb)   0 335 19811 2 (pb)

Library of Congress Cataloging-in-Publication Data

Professional development for educational management / edited by Lesley Kydd, Megan
    Crawford and Colin Riches.
        p.   cm. — (Leadership and management in education)
    Includes bibliographical references and index.
    ISBN 0-335-19812-0   ISBN 0-335-19811-2 (pbk.)
    1. School administrators—In-service training—Great Britain.   2. School
administrators— Training of—Great Britain.   3. School management and organization—
Great Britain.   I. Kydd, Lesley, 1950–   .   II. Crawford, Megan, 1957–   .   III.
Riches, Colin R.   IV. Series.
LB1738.5.P76   1996
371.2'01—dc20   96-32328
                                                                                                                  CIP

Typeset by Type Study, Scarborough, North Yorkshire
Printed and bound in Great Britain by Redwood Books, Trowbridge

Contents

Acknowledgements

The chapters listed below come from the following sources, and Open University Press would like to make grateful acknowledgement for permission to reproduce it here.

1 Whitaker, P. (1993) 'The personal dimension' Chapter 3 from *Managing Change in Schools*, Buckingham, Open University Press 1993.
2 Jarvis, P. (1994) 'Learning practical knowledge', *Journal of Further and Higher Education*, published by NATFHE – The University and College Lecturers Union.
3 Eraut, M. (1993) 'The characterisation and development of professional expertise in school management and in teaching', *Educational Management and Administration*, 21(4): 223–32.
4 Bullock, K., James, C. and Jamieson, I. (1995) a version of 'An exploratory study of novices and experts in educational management', *Educational Management and Administration*, 23(3): 197–205.
5 Bennett, N. (1996) 'Analysing management for personal development: theory and practice' (commissioned article).
6 Ouston, J. (1993) 'Management competences, school effectiveness and education management', *Educational Management and Administration*, 21(4): 212–21.
7 Cave, E. and Wilkinson, C. (1987) 'Developing managerial capabilities in education' in *Teaching and Managing: Inseparable Activities in Schools*, Croom Helm.
8 Møller, Jorunn (1996) 'Reframing educational leadership in the perspective of dilemmas' originally written for *School Administration: Persistent Dilemmas in Preparation and Practice*, Stephen L. Jacobson, Edw. S. Hickcox and Robert B. Stevenson, (eds). (Praeger Publications, an imprint of Greenwood Publishing Group, Inc., Westport, CT, USA, November 1996). Reprinted with permission, all rights reserved.
9 Kydd, L. (1996) 'Issues surrounding teacher professionalism and managerialism' (commissioned article).
10 Morgan, C. (1996) 'Selection – predicting effective performance' (commissioned article).

11 Oldroyd, D. and Hall, V. (1991) 'Identifying needs and priorities', Chapter 4 in *Managing Staff Development: A Handbook for Secondary Schools*, Paul Chapman Publishing Limited, London.

12 Poster, C. and Poster, D. (1993, 2nd edn) Chapter 1 'What is appraisal?' in *Teacher Appraisal: Training and Implementation*, Routledge, London.

13 Hutchinson, B. (1995) 'Appraising appraisal: Some tensions and some possibilities', *Higher Education*, 29: 19–35 with kind permission from Kluwer Academic Publishers.

14 Hall, D. (1994) 'Professional development portfolios for teachers and lecturers', *British Journal of In-Service*, 18(2).

15 O'Sullivan, F., Jones, K. and Reid, K. Chapter 1 'The development of staff' from *Staff Development in Secondary Schools* reproduced by permission of Hodder and Stoughton Educational.

Introduction

LESLEY KYDD

Increasingly professional development is being recognized as crucial not only to the individual but also to the promotion of effective and efficient organizations. This book considers professional development in two ways – from the perspective of the individual and from the perspective of the organization. Educational management is a diverse and complex range of activities calling on the exercise of considerable knowledge, skill and judgement by individuals, but its practice is dependent on the culture of particular organizational settings. It is this constant interplay between individual capability and organizational requirements which makes professional development for educational managers both challenging and exciting.

These chapters consider how the concepts, skills and insights gained through professional development can be applied by educational managers to specific organizational tasks and systems. They have been selected on the premise that the greatest resource of any organization is its human resource. The assumption is made that organizations will function more efficiently and effectively if the people who work in them are encouraged to develop professionally themselves and to use that approach to undertake organization tasks. One of the crucial tasks for educational managers is to apply the principles of professional development not only to themselves but also to the people and tasks that they manage.

Professional development for educational management is too often considered both in the literature and practice as a highly individualistic process focused on the needs, aspirations and careers of teachers who are potential managers, ignoring the need for organizational development. Conversely, it is too often supposed that institutions exist by themselves and for themselves, with less consideration being given to the developmental needs of the people within them. This book assumes that individual and organizational development are not separate and discrete but co-exist in a mutually supportive relationship. Although individual development may not necessarily have tangible outcomes for the organization, a developing individual is likely to make a richer contribution to it. Conversely, organizational development will only happen if the individuals within it are developing. Professional development and organizational effectiveness are then inextricably linked. This is not to suggest that the integration of personal and organizational needs is always a simple and straightforward resolution; often the task is difficult and complex.

This collection of readings proceeds from the perspective that professional development, either individual or organizational, begins from a process of reflection on where things are, where we would like to get to and how we can get there. Reflection on practice is not a simple process. It relies on the application of conceptual tools which will centre that practice on enlightened self-thinking. Reflection on practice is not simply about knowing how or having the 'knack' to manage a particular situation or set of tasks. It requires self-knowledge and conceptual frameworks which shape the reflective process. It is continuous and constantly needs new knowledge and frameworks. Part 1 of the book contains chapters which deal with the reflective process in individuals; Part 2 looks at some of the tasks and systems which contribute to the developing organization.

Part 1: The individual and professional development

Few writers on professional development explore what could be called the components or conceptual tools of reflection. This part of the book looks at some of these issues, beginning with the individual and the acquisition of self-knowledge, as well as how people learn and, most importantly, do not learn from their own experience. The contribution of humanistic psychology and the notion of self-actualizing (or realizing human potential) to the processes of self-development are discussed. The skills and knowledge needed to become more effective managers are considered as well as the learning processes which educational managers go through at different points in their careers. We also discuss the role of competences as a mechanism for moving forward the professional development of managers. Finally, professional development is not only about acquiring knowledge and skills, it is also about the values which underpin our actions and the difficult and very real dilemmas involved in decision making for educational managers.

The chapter by Whitaker introduces and overviews the relationship between individual and professional development and the importance of organizational culture and environment to the release of human potential. It draws on a broad range of concepts and literature, beginning from the premise that an enhanced view of personhood and human potential on the part of managers will lead to more effective management in organizations. He suggests that one of the key roles for managers is to recognize that all human beings are different and have different aspirations both personally and in their careers. Managers should work towards creating organizational cultures which recognize these diversities and differences and support the development of human potential. Much of this hinges on recognizing and providing safe psychological conditions for the achievement of organizational change. From this starting point we are made aware of just how complex managing people can be.

The chapter by Jarvis is particularly important for the professional development of the individual since it looks at the nature of knowledge and its acquisition. He considers three areas: the location of practical knowledge within an epistemological framework; the learning process; and, finally, the process of learning practical knowledge. The process of learning is described in the typology of a learning cycle, which is particularly useful for examining the acquisition and outcomes of knowledge in behaviour patterns. Jarvis argues that knowledge 'how' and 'tacit' knowledge acquired from practice are most likely to lead to the acquisition of expertise. The difficulty is that many of us fail to learn from experience – in other words non-learning is a barrier to personal professional development which in turn can hinder organizational development.

Michael Eraut moves us into a discussion about the nature of professional knowledge and the interplay between personal and professional knowledge and expertise. There has always been debate over exactly what the knowledge base of educational expertise might be; he suggests there is a need for a new approach to characterizing professional expertise. He argues that public knowledge is necessarily explicit whereas personal knowledge may be explicit or tacit. Eraut suggests that four processes are involved in the nature of professional work itself: acquiring and interpreting information; skilled behaviours; deliberative processes such as planning; and meta-processes concerned with direction/controlling one's own behaviour. As well as providing valuable insights into experiential learning and management training he also draws attention to two principles which should pervade the meta-processes of any profession – those of client-centredness and the moral obligation to improve one's own professional performance.

So far, then, we have considered the self and how the development of human potential can be helped or hindered by an unsympathetic organizational culture. We have discussed the acquisition of practical knowledge and the role of learning and not learning in organizations. For managers and indeed anyone working in a learning context it is important to know how and why people learn and why people often fail to learn from experience. This failing may not necessarily be deliberate so much as an inability to recognize tacit knowledge – the things we do without thinking about them or that we are unaware we do – in particular situations and interactions. We have then added an analysis of the role and acquisition of professional knowledge to the development of educational managers. So personal insights, knowledge and skill acquisition form components of professional development.

The next chapter details a piece of empirical research by Bullock *et al.* about the nature of the learning which supports the development of educational managers. The researchers looked at three groups of educational managers: those established in post; those new to post and those new to management. They report a number of interesting findings. As might be expected, those established in post displayed greater confidence and tended to have a more sophisticated and considered view of such management skills as delegation and decision making. They had clearly moved away from a view of success which derived from the classroom to one where management was of the most importance. In contrast, those new to post prioritized establishing success in the classroom before concentrating on the management role. The issue of teaching and managing, and career progression largely through the management line is interesting; it emphasizes once again that the professional development of educational managers is not unproblematic.

Nigel Bennett's chapter is wide ranging and moves us on to consider questions of what is educational management and what makes good management practice. Bennett takes the view that good practice rests on our understanding of what a particular job should entail when compared with what we actually do. Therefore, we develop a theory about our job which informs our judgements about the quality of our practice. Having outlined two traditional theories of management, drawing on the work of Taylor and Mintzberg, he goes on to look at ways in which good and bad management are characterized by questions of values and how crucial these are to the judgements we make. Finally, he considers the competency-based models of management development, pointing out that competency models of management skills are increasingly influential. The two models compared draw an important distinction between identifying satisfactory performance and superior performance.

The competency debate is picked up in the next chapter by Janet Ouston which considers the literature linking management competence and school effectiveness. She argues that there are a number of approaches to competence and that what is needed is a balance between skills, qualities, personal effectiveness, knowledge and understanding. This chapter confirms Bennett's concerns that the Management Charter Initiative approach to competence does not address questions of philosophy and, particularly, of values. Ouston argues that the competence movement tends to see the development of management skills as hierarchical, whereas management is an integrated rather than a sequential activity and must take into account questions of the values which underpin decisions and actions.

The next chapter moves on to consider competency in a different way and introduces the concept of capability. It reports on a research project carried out at the University of Ulster to identify and distil the essential capacities which educational managers need. Cave and Wilkinson again emphasize the complexity of the management task, arguing that effective management performance also involves activities and qualities which are difficult to explain and measure. This picks up one of the themes which runs through these last three articles, that measures of competence are not sufficient either to measure a person's ability as a manager or to account for the complexity involved in management activities. Cave and Wilkinson identify three elements which they suggest constitute capability. These are knowledge, skills and higher-order capacities similar to Eraut's meta-processes. They argue strongly that the latter are vital to the effective exercise of knowledge and skills. They suggest that managerial capability is exercised in key management areas through generic managing processes, and they consider the implications of this for management development programmes. These should be conducted through small group peer interaction over a period of time. These groups should be clearly focused and use reflective practices and review to maximize the learning opportunities available.

Having suggested that management development is an integrated activity which is about more than acquiring skills and knowledge and which has to do with making decisions and judgements based on values, in the last chapter of Part 1, by Møller, we consider the question of ethics. Møller argues that above all education and educational management are moral activities and that the decisions made by managers are necessarily moral ones. She describes an action research project which frames the activity of educational leadership within a perspective of dilemmas. Here Møller captures not only the diversity of decision making, she also presents the very difficult decisions which managers have to make, by means of a series of vignettes describing typical situations. For example, how does an educational leader build a shared vision of the school when a member of staff does not subscribe to this vision and yet their views and behaviour are in no way anti-educational or harmful to the children in their care? Thus the chapter frames a series of dilemmas for educational managers.

Part 1 understands the professional development of the individual as a series of steps, and highlights issues of the knowledge, skills and values which educational managers need. It looks at what can be called the components of professional development for educational management. The chapters follow the premise that professional development has something to do with the realization of self-potential – a process which needs to be informed through the acquisition of knowledge, skills and relevant theoretical perspectives.

Part 2: The organization and professional development

The second part of the book moves on to consider the professional development of educational managers and teachers in an organizational context. The chapters are arranged to provide a number of perspectives on systems within educational organizations which may help or hinder the professional development of those who work within them. Part 2 argues that organizations should be characterized as *developing* organizations and that the role of educational managers in determining the organizational climate for development is crucial to the effectiveness of the organization. The systems within an organization, their structure and management and the purposes they serve will all influence the culture of the organization and contribute to the ways in which it develops. Educational managers face a difficult task in reconciling the disparate needs and priorities within the organization to ensure organizational effectiveness. This issue is exemplified in discussions about appraisal and staff development as well as in the increasing use of professional development portfolios in the development of reflective practices.

The first chapter by Kydd looks at two issues, professionalism and managerialism, which permeate educational organizations. Professionalism is often used to explain particular behaviours and to justify our actions. However, as this chapter describes, a number of policy initiatives in the last 15 years have contributed to the emergence of 'managerialism' as a way of conducting the management activities not only of schools and colleges but also of other public services. Managerialism has led to the systematization of management activities and to the emergence of clear lines of accountability for those working in educational establishments. This chapter suggests that there may be a conflict between the values and ethics of professionalism and those espoused through the more tightly controlled managerial agenda. It also picks up on one of the important dilemmas not only for educational managers but also for the education profession as a whole – between teaching as a valued activity and advancement through taking on a management role.

Colin Morgan provides a comprehensive overview of the literature and practices of selection in educational organizations. He argues strongly for the application of management skills to rational approaches to selection. The chapter addresses the vagaries of traditional selection practices and argues that job selection should be about evidence tied to occupational performance, past and expected, rather than qualities approved of for wider reasons. Selection should be an act of prediction rather than some kind of gamble. It is crucial to effective organizations and is, therefore, a critical management activity.

Having selected the right staff, another key area for those concerned with enhancing the professional development of individuals within the organizational context is to consider that educational organizations do not exist discretely within a vacuum. They are complex organizations which must seek to reconcile a diversity of needs generated both internally and externally – from government and local authority policy initiatives, from staff, students and the community. Oldroyd and Hall look at the problem of needs identification and setting priorities from the perspective of reconciling differences in the process of school development planning. They argue that teachers' needs should be identified in relation to the school development plan. This raises an interesting dilemma in terms of need perceived by the individual and need perceived by the school, and suggests that the question of individual and organizational need is not always easily resolved. Oldroyd and Hall also consider the question of reconciling different priorities expressed by different groups and argue that the involvement of teachers in the processes of needs analysis and school development planning promotes self-reflection. Their chapter also has a number of useful checklists and exercises which will help those of you who are involved in this kind of management activity. What this chapter demonstrates above all for educational managers is the multiplicity of needs at all levels within an organization and the difficulties which are involved in making sense of them.

The next two chapters move on to consider the questions of staff development and appraisal. Much debate surrounds the meaning of these terms and the systems which operationalize them within organizations. Appraisal can be seen as a means of promoting staff development and professional expertise, or it can become a bureaucratic exercise driven by form filling and some kind of judgement about the quality of performance. Poster and Poster draw a distinction between performance review (which focuses on the setting of organizational goals and the review of performance against these goals) and staff development review (which focuses on improving the ability of the individual through the identification of personal development needs). They consider that appraisal is much more crucial to successful organizations than might be implied by its characterization as bureaucratic form filling. They suggest that appraisal can help individuals to know about and make sense of organizational management styles, expectations and ways of behaving. They also discuss the effects and differences of various organizational cultures and climates and how these can be communicated to the individual through appraisal systems. Thus systems such as appraisal serve important organizational functions and are one of the mechanisms by which individuals are socialized into and maintained within the organization's purposes, values and outcomes.

Hutchinson looks at the introduction of appraisal systems into higher education. He draws out two lines of development in appraisal systems very similar to those identified by Poster and Poster. The first of these he characterizes as the managerialist form of appraisal, where efficiency and equality are to be assured through rigid procedures, and the power to effect change is seen as coming from 'using the systems'. The second form of appraisal he sees as 'professional development', where there is a shared commitment to improvement, where formal attention is given to the context in which an individual works and where self-appraisal is an integral part of the whole process. This discussion is followed by the reporting of a research project which examined the universities' appraisal procedures and attempted to provide feedback, particularly on the crucial area of the appraisal interview.

One of the outcomes of needs analysis, identification of priorities and appraisal is that these activities generate a great deal of self and organizational knowledge and insights that fall outside the terms of reference of particular systems and measures. The chapter by Hall reports on an interesting project at the University of Greenwich which introduced the keeping of professional development portfolios by teachers. A professional development portfolio is a collection of material made by a professional that records and reflects on key events and processes in that professional's career. Hall suggests that interest in portfolios has increased partly through the recognition by award-giving bodies that professional development rests on the integration of theory and practice through the use of reflection. Portfolios are ideal vehicles for the documenting of professional development for the purposes of accreditation. He suggests that what distinguishes a professional development portfolio from a professional diary or a record of achievement is this emphasis on reflection. Among the benefits to be derived from putting together a portfolio are that it can help teachers prepare for job applications and for appraisal interviews. Such an approach can, therefore, provide a key means towards promoting professional development both in an individual and organizational context.

The final chapter in the book, by O'Sullivan *et al.*, once again addresses our two themes of the professional development of the individual and developing organizations. These authors consider the issue of staff development and how it can be made to work in practice. They usefully distinguish between the broader concept of professional development as an individual and personal process which is continuous, and staff development, which relates to the development of an individual teacher as a member of staff in a particular school. They provide some useful checklists for all of those involved in staff development and helpfully outline a school-focused staff development cycle.

The book as a whole takes educational managers through a process of professional development as an individual and as an organizational activity. Throughout, the focus is on the development and improvement of performance of people – the greatest resource of any organization. I hope that you enjoy working through them.

PART 1

The individual and professional development

1 | Changes in professional development: the personal dimension*

PATRICK WHITAKER

Personhood

One of the key contributing factors to an enhanced view of personhood and human potential has been the emergence over the past fifty years of humanistic psychology with its concern for the fully functioning person. The key pioneer was Abraham Maslow, who by asking about the psychology of the healthy and happy person sought to go beyond a preoccupation with personality dysfunction and the limitations imposed by attending only to behaviour, to discover a more comprehensive understanding of the human condition. In *Motivation and Personality*, Maslow (1970) set out his theory of the hierarchy of needs, the concept of self-actualization and important insights into the nature of happiness, love and learning. His pioneering work laid the foundations for further research and developments which have found practical expression in counselling, psychotherapy, self-help groups and the assertive alternative in interpersonal relationships.

It was Carl Rogers who led the way in translating Maslow's idea into practicalities. He took Maslow's concept of self-actualization as the pinnacle of the needs hierarchy and placed it in a broader context.

> The mainspring of creativity appears to be the same tendency which we discover so deeply as the curative force in psychotherapy – man's tendency to actualize himself, to become his potentialities. By this I mean the directional trend which is evident in all organic and human life – the urge to expand, extend, develop, mature – the tendency to express and activate all capacities of the organism, or the self. This tendency may become deeply buried under layer after layer of encrusted psychological defenses, it may be hidden behind elaborate facades which may deny

*This chapter has been edited and abridged from Chapter 3 'The personal dimension' which appears in Patrick Whitaker's book *Managing Change in Schools*, published in 1993.

its existence; it is my belief however, based on my experience, that it exists in every individual, and awaits only the proper conditions to be released and expressed.

(Rogers 1967)

One of the exciting developments in management theory and practice is the way that the notion of self-actualization is now being recognized in organizations and there is a new emphasis on the processes necessary to enhance human potential and capability – in other words to create the right conditions to release the actualizing tendency in all individuals, whether it be in families, schools, business organizations or in society as a whole.

[. . .]

Theories X and Y

One of the most useful contributions to our understanding of organizations has been provided by Douglas McGregor, who in *The Human Side of Enterprise* (1960), highlighted the powerful effect that assumptions about personhood can have on work and motivation. McGregor posed two contrasting sets of assumptions about people in organizations, referred to as Theory X and Theory Y.

Theory X

People dislike work and try to avoid it. They have to be bribed, coerced and controlled and even threatened with punishment to perform adequately. Most people lack ambition, prefer to be led and wish to avoid responsibility. By nature people are resistant to change.

Theory Y

People do like work and don't have to be forced or threatened. If allowed to pursue objectives to which they are committed most people will work hard and not only accept responsibility, but actively seek it. People have a natural ability to change and adapt.

Managers and leaders proceeding from a Theory X position will tend to build management structures and systems designed to: direct the efforts of staff; control their actions; modify their behaviour to fit organizational needs. They will also adopt interpersonal behaviour towards staff that is characterized by: persuasion; reward or punishment; instruction and command.

Managers and leaders who espouse Theory Y assumptions will tend to build management structures and systems designed to: make it possible for people to develop; seek responsibility; take risks; set ambitious targets and challenges.

Clearly these are polarized positions but they do help us to place our own experience within a powerful theoretical framework (see Figure 1.1).

For many of us, past experience in families, schools and the workplace has been – unless we are exceptionally lucky – predominantly of the Theory X kind. As a result of this, part of our career path into senior positions may be motivated by a desire to avoid the controlling forces of Theory X being exerted on us, and perhaps also to be among a smaller group in society who hold power to control others. An important element in the

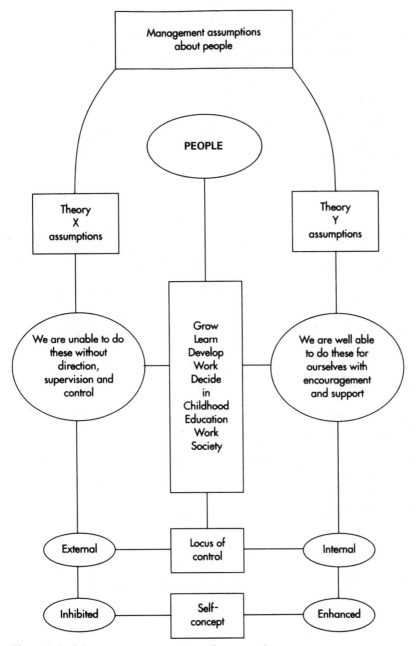

Figure 1.1 Management assumptions about people

development of managers and leaders is a capacity to develop an awareness of the way that Theory X experiences have affected us and formed our behavioural tendencies as managers. For many, the greatest challenge is balancing an intellectual commitment to Theory Y with an experience that has conditioned us in the dynamics of Theory X.

A less polarized view of people and work has been offered by Schein (1980) who argues that complexity is the key characteristic of people and that they tend not to behave consistently and predictably. No single style of management can be regarded as relevant to all situations. What is needed is behaviour appropriate to the needs and circumstances of varying situations.

One of the problems of traditional management practice has been an assumption of simplicity – that consistency and predictability in human affairs can be relied upon by leaders. As we become more attuned to notions of complexity, uncertainty, unpredictability and untidiness in human affairs we will learn to realize the importance of choice and appropriateness in the face of differing circumstances and situations.

It is important to recognize the power of assumptions when a new job is taken on. The new colleagues we work with, particularly those in junior positions are likely to assume that any procedures or behaviours you adopt are motivated by the same assumptions and reasons as your predecessor. If you follow a Theory X manager and wish to inculcate a Theory Y culture you may be disappointed and frustrated to find that new colleagues greet your suggestions with some scepticism and mistrust – they may well assume that it is yet another device to control and contain them. To gain support it is necessary to overcome this powerful inheritance factor first by explaining your beliefs, concerns, assumptions and expectations and then making your interpersonal style as consistent as possible with these.

[. . .]

Multiple intelligence

One of the obsessions of the education system is intelligence, and the debate about inheritance and environment continues. An enhanced perception of human potential requires that we develop a more holistic view of intelligence and its contribution to human achievement and personal effectiveness. Some interesting alternative definitions are emerging.

In *Inside Organizations* (1990), Charles Handy offers a working list which has several different types of intelligence:

Logical those who can reason, analyse and memorize.
Spatial those who can discern patterns in things and create them.
Musical those who can sing, play or make music of all sorts.
Practical the person who can pull a carburettor to bits but might never be able to spell the word or explain how they did it.
Physical the footballers, athletes and dancers among us.
Intra-personal the sensitive people who can see into themselves, the quiet perceptive ones.
Inter-personal those who can make things happen with and through people.

This offers an altogether new and richer view. As Handy observes:

It is the tragedy of much of our schooling that we are led to think that logical intelligence is the only type that matters. Any observation of our friends and colleagues in later life will prove that the other intelligences are at least as important, if not more so.

(Handy 1990)

We should, he argues, train ourselves not to ask how intelligent people are, but which type of intelligence do they have most of?

The traditional view of intelligence emphasizes 'cleverness', mental agility and intellectual strength. During recent years a more balanced view has begun to emerge with an enhanced view of human intelligence. Denis Postle (*The Mind Gymnasium*, 1989) describes four types of intelligence:

1 Emotional intelligence
   - radiating warmth
   - awareness of own feelings
   - sensitivity to feelings of others
   - creating harmony and goodwill
   - dealing with emotional issues openly
   - empathizing with the experience of others

2 Intuitive intelligence
   - 'gut' feelings
   - hunches
   - speculating about the future
   - using imagination
   - willingness to take risks
   - capacity for change

3 Physical intelligence
   - concerned with fitness and health
   - enjoyment of physical activities
   - pride in manual skills and dexterity
   - sensible and balanced diet
   - love of the outdoors
   - good at household tasks

4 Intellectual intelligence
   - reasoning
   - problem solving
   - analysis
   - calculation
   - handling information
   - abstract ideas

Personal effectiveness draws on all four of these intelligence types and it is important not to over-value intellectual capacities at the expense of the others. Increasing evidence suggests that managers are perceived by others as effective when they behave sensitively in interpersonal situations, have a capacity to handle emotional situations well and are seen to be able to relax and enjoy a full and satisfying life outside the workplace.

A third view considers intelligence in the context of leadership and change in educational institutions. Management and leadership capability can be considered in relation to three distinct but interrelated areas of intelligence: professional intelligence; personal intelligence; managerial intelligence.

1 Professional intelligence

This is the type of intelligence we acquire and develop through professional training and experience. It generates qualities, skills and knowledge of a specialist and technical nature, specific to particular occupations and professions. Engineers have a different sort of occupational intelligence from nurses and lawyers. This type of intelligence is often the key focus in job related training within organizations.

2 Personal intelligence

This is an intelligence acquired and developed through the process of socialization. It generates personal qualities, skills and knowledge that enables us to develop and sustain relationships. It determines the capacity to get on well with other people in both professional and social settings.

Until fairly recently personal intelligence rarely featured in the formal educational process although it is constantly referred to by adults in the socializing of the young. Although it is crucially important in management it has rarely been the subject of training and development. It is often our relationships with others that cause our most difficult and emotionally painful moments. It is not surprising then that the additional pressures that work involves can increase the challenge and stress in our own relationships. Success in the management role requires us not only to be aware of this but to improve our own qualities, skills and knowledge in order to manage our relationships effectively and sensitively.

3 Managerial intelligence

This is an intelligence needed to work with and through other people. The following classification of managerial abilities provides a useful starting point for consideration:

1 Creating
   - having good ideas
   - finding original solutions to common problems
   - anticipating the consequences of decisions and actions
   - employing lateral thinking
   - using imagination and intuition

2 Planning
   - relating present to future needs
   - recognizing what is important and what merely urgent
   - anticipating future trends
   - analysing

3 Organizing
   - making fair demands
   - making rapid decisions
   - being in front when it counts
   - staying calm when the going is difficult
   - recognizing when the job is done

4 Communicating
   - understanding people
   - listening

- explaining
- written communication
- getting others to talk
- tact
- tolerance of others' mistakes
- giving thanks and encouragement
- keep everyone informed
- using information technology

5 Motivating
- inspiring others
- providing realistic challenges
- helping others to set goals and targets
- helping others to value their own contributions and achievements

6 Evaluating
- comparing outcomes with intentions
- self-evaluation
- evaluating the work of others
- taking corrective action where necessary

One of the ways of creating an enhanced view of human potential in the management of change is to proceed on the basis of a wider view of personal aptitude and capability. An integrated, holistic and systemic view of intelligence helps to change the concept of management from one of channelling limited capability to one of realizing and empowering unlimited potential.

The brain

One of the problems with traditional education and particularly traditional methods of teaching is the understanding of the way the brain works. As educators we have radically misperceived the nature of the brain. During the last fifteen years or so research has discovered that the brain is infinitely more complex than we had ever assumed. One of the main discoveries is that we have two upper brains rather than one and that they operate in different ways with different purposes (see Table 1.1).

Traditional teaching methods have placed an almost obsessive emphasis on the functions that are located in the left hemisphere – giving greater attention to the memorizing of facts, the search for single correct answers and an attention to logical

Table 1.1 Upper parts of the brain

Left hemisphere	Right hemisphere
language	rhythm
logic	music
number	images
sequence	imagination
linearity	daydreaming
analysis	colour

sequence. Research has also shown that where learners are encouraged to utilize a mental area, particularly those located in the right hemisphere, this improves performance in other areas (Buzan 1982). In other words, where learners are encouraged to engage in the brain functions of imagery, imagination and rhythm in the pursuit of knowledge and understanding then learning is more successful. [. . .] Clearly this has fundamental implications for the way in which we organize learning in formal educational settings. It gives added emphasis for the creation of both a liberally balanced curriculum and also broad and varied teaching methods. [. . .]

Another crucial consideration is the fact that we have also hugely underestimated the power of the brain and the capacity of the young to achieve far more than we ever thought possible. This awesome potential also improves with age and the belief that mental activity declines as we get older is not supported by the evidence. We know that if the brain is stimulated, no matter at what age it will continue to increase its capacity.

Motivation

[. . .]

Attention to motivational factors is an important starting point for the selection of appropriate management styles. This process involves a sensitive understanding of staff needs and aspirations. These are likely to be complex and somewhat difficult to define explicitly. Each person involved in a work team or section is also likely to have a different pattern of needs and aspirations. Among the needs likely to be present in almost any group are the need to be:

- supported
- heard
- noticed
- encouraged
- trusted
- appreciated and valued
- informed
- helped to clarify ideas
- helped to develop skills and abilities
- challenged and extended

When the culture of the organization satisfies these particular needs people tend to work harder, with greater commitment and with a more purposeful sense of direction. Leadership can be said to be effective when staff consistently experience these motivational factors. Creating the culture which satisfies these needs is vital to the success of an organization and the quality of service it provides. Further insight is provided by Frederick Herzberg (1966) who has observed that in organizations workers are highly motivated when:

1 The work itself is intrinsically satisfying and challenging.
2 Workers have a decision making role and are involved in the co-management of the organization.
3 Successful work leads to recognition and the possibility of career advancement.

He also observed that workers are badly motivated when:

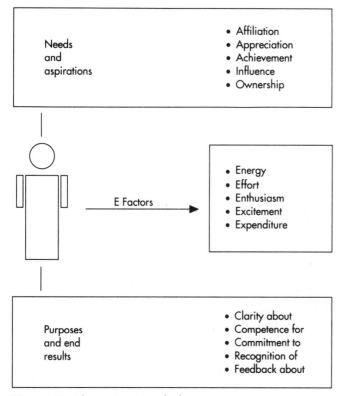

Figure 1.2   The motivation calculus

1 They are over-supervised and there are too many rules and regulations governing personal as well as professional activity.
2 Workers have difficult relationships with senior staff and when 'bossy' attitudes cause frustration and anxiety.
3 There are poor relationships with co-workers, low staff morale and divisive attitudes.
4 The working conditions are poor.

[. . .]

Handy (1976) emphasizes the importance of acknowledging individual choice and decision making in motivation.

The 'E' factors shown in Figure 1.2 represent the amount of energy, effort, enthusiasm, excitement and expenditure an individual decides to invest in any activity. The motivation calculus is the mechanism by which we decide how much 'E' to invest.

This model highlights a number of key elements that need to figure in management behaviour at the interpersonal level, and in the development of a culture supportive of human potential, endeavour and achievement.

1 The work that we do needs to respond to deep needs for satisfaction within ourselves.
2 The work we do needs to provide opportunities to satisfy aspirations and achieve results.
3 Energy, effort, enthusiasm, excitement and expenditure are decisions of individuals, not the inputs of managers or leaders.

Managers are in the business of helping to satisfy needs and this demands a sensitive attention to the thoughts and feelings of the staff involved. Effective managers are those who have a capacity to sense a pattern of needs in those they work with and to adapt their working style accordingly. Motivation is a key consideration in management and it is useful to be aware of three components: the needs to be satisfied; the aspirations to be achieved; self-esteem.

In managing, treating all people the same is a recipe for difficulty and disappointment. The guiding principle should be to treat people appropriately according to their perceived needs and aspirations and with a sensitivity to their self-esteem. This involves a careful combining of the professional, personal and managerial skills discussed earlier.

Human potential

Organizations do not have a good track record of creating conditions of trust in which people are able to give their best. Coercive and controlling styles of leadership and management do little to create commitment or to release locked up skills and abilities. Some understanding of the concept of human potential is important.

This concept suggests that living is a process of becoming – a gradual unfolding of personhood. Leading humanistic psychologists such as Abraham Maslow and Carl Rogers have argued that individuals have within themselves vast resources for healthy and successful living. These resources become minimalized and suppressed during the process of socialization but can be rekindled if a supportive psychological climate is created. Such an actualizing tendency is a characteristic of human beings but is also present in all organisms. Traditional styles of management have tended to reinforce the suppression of potential, and senior staff in organizations have tended not to concern themselves with building the psychological climate in which this directional tendency can be promoted. Leaders need to consider to what extent the current culture and climate of their organizations provides conditions for human growth and development, and the extent to which supposed under-performance can be attributed to the undernourishing quality of the human environment. Successful leadership is very much a process of activating potential and of providing the space and conditions in which it can be creatively expressed. A key aim for leaders is the cultivation of the actualizing tendency in themselves and in each and every member of staff. This emphasizes the processes of releasing and empowering, rather than those of controlling and supervising.

Self-concept

Two ideas very relevant to the process of change are that of psychological success (Argyris 1964) and the future focused role image (Singer 1974).

Psychological success is vital to the healthy survival and growth of a positive self-concept. It helps us to feel a strong sense of both competence and self-confidence in relation to those aspects of our lives in which we expend energy and effort. Change, particularly where externally imposed can pose threats to psychological success and consequently to the self-concept. Managers and leaders can reduce this threat, and support change in individuals by helping them to:

1 Understand the challenges involved in change and the nature of expected end results.
2 Formulate personal goals for the journey of change.
3 Determine their own methods for reaching those goals and producing the desired end results.
4 Assimilate and incorporate new elements into the self-concept.

This is a delicate process requiring skill and sensitivity.

In times of rapid change the difficulty of envisioning future role images can cause confusion and anxiety. One of the key characteristics of personal growth and development is the formation within our minds of an anticipated self – how we want to become, or what we need to be. This is often most noticeable in the formation of career aspiration – three years as head of department, then deputy headship and then headship in about ten years time. The trouble is that the world will be somewhat different when that career plan is fulfilled. How different the current educational reality is from that anticipated ten years ago by many recently appointed headteachers, and how many are now reflecting, having successfully achieved their aspirations – 'This is not what I came into headship for.'

In striving to support educational and organizational change it will be necessary to give increased attention to the issue of the future focused role image in order that long-term goals based on present realities do not become too fixed too early, leading to disappointment and frustration when they cannot be realized as hoped. Managers and organizations will need to accept that professional development will have to place personal goals alongside professional ones to help in the creation of appropriate temporal orientation and a more integrated and holistic self-concept where there is a more healthy relationship between the personal and the professional.

Locus of control

A further insight into behaviour within organizations is offered by the concept of 'locus of control'. Rotter (1966) suggests that it is possible to distinguish two particular control dynamics. The first of these identifies those people who feel very much in charge of themselves and agents of their own destinies as 'internals' – their locus of control is within themselves. Those who feel that they have very little control over what happens to them are referred to as 'externals' – their locus of control is perceived as being external to themselves. Evidence by Phares (1976) makes it very clear that those who operate their lives with an 'internal' dynamic are better able to make choices in their lives, take responsibility for their own actions and the consequences of them and are better able to cope with failure and learn successfully from it. In particular Phares discovered that 'internals':

1 have greater self-control
2 are better at retaining information
3 ask more questions of people; notice more of what is happening about them
4 are less coercive when given power
5 see other people as being responsible for themselves
6 prefer activities requiring skill than those involving chance
7 have higher academic achievements
8 are more likely to delay gratification

9 accept more responsibility for their own behaviour
10 have more realistic reactions to their own successes and failures
11 are less anxious
12 exhibit less pathological behaviour

The clear implication from research work in this area is that when people accept responsibility for themselves and their own behaviour and recognize their own power to affect and influence the way that circumstances develop, they will be likely to work more creatively and cooperatively to the benefit of both themselves and the organization as a whole. Within the school setting there is a clear need to identify and cultivate an 'internal' dynamic both within the classrooms of the school but also within the management culture itself.

Empowerment

This is a concept closely related to the actualizing tendency referred to above. It concerns the capacity of individuals to take increasing responsibility for the satisfying of their personal and professional needs. It differs from motivation in that empowerment places emphasis on the individual for creating his or her own conditions for growth, for defining challenges and for setting goals and targets. Central to this concept are a number of key assumptions and values (Hopson and Scally 1981). These include:

1 Each person is a unique individual, worthy of respect.
2 Individuals are responsible for their own actions and behaviour.
3 Individuals are responsible for their own feelings and emotions and for their responses to the behaviours of others.
4 New situations, however unwelcome, contain opportunities for new learning and growth.
5 Mistakes are learning experiences and are seen as outcomes rather than failures.
6 The seeds of our growth are within us. Only we ourselves can activate our potential for creativity and growth.
7 We can all do more than we are currently doing to become more than we currently are.
8 Awareness brings responsibility and responsibility creates the opportunity for choice.
9 Our own fear is the major limiter to our growth.
10 Growth and development never end. Self-empowerment is not an end to be achieved but a constant process of becoming.

Within organizations those who operate in a self-empowered way are characterized by:

1 An acceptance that change and development are the natural order of things and that change is to be welcomed rather than shunned and avoided.
2 Having skills to initiate change and the capacity to learn new skills and ideas.
3 Taking personal responsibility for actions and behaviour.
4 Making clear goals for themselves and developing action programmes to meet them.
5 Being action biased.

6 Frequently reviewing, assessing and evaluating their own progress and seeking feedback from others.
7 Being concerned to see others taking greater responsibility for their own lives.

In the effective organization many staff will be operating in self-empowering ways. Attempting to create a climate which is person centred, motivating and empowering is a vital challenge to those involved in educational management and leadership. [. . .]

Life cycles

An effective change agent is one who in the process of promoting and supporting professional change is able to recognize and understand the complex processes of personal adaptation that inevitably accompany it. Some understanding of developmental psychology is very useful in making connections between the personal and the professional in the change process. Knowing how best to help someone in the professional domain requires an appreciation that individual and personal factors will also contribute to the stance that an individual assumes.

Change is a common and constant feature of our personal lives. The process of growth, development and aging attend everyone and our relationships continually develop and modify in the light of experience. During the course of an average lifetime a person passes through a number of phases and stages. The developmental psychologist Erik Erikson (1977) has identified eight of these, as shown in Table 1.2.

This scheme offers a series of critical periods in the human life cycle. Each phase presents the individual with crucial development work to undertake – represented in the scheme by a pair of alternative orientations or stances towards life, the self and other people. If the surrounding environment provides sufficient opportunity and support for the polarities to be resolved, individuals acquire psychological sturdiness and social competence as they develop. For most people the resources available for support are variable and there is a tendency to move into successive phases with 'unfinished business' from the previous stage. Thus individuals are unable to bring to the work of the new phases the full range of psychological attributes necessary. The struggle into young adulthood is especially hazardous and most reach it with a surface ability to cope and make their way in the world but their inner lives can be characterized by psychological uncertainty and emotional confusion. In difficult relationships and under organizational pressure these inadequacies can be exposed and coping behaviours can often be

Table 1.2   Erikson's stages of human development

Infancy	0–2	trust v. mistrust
Early childhood	2–4	autonomy v. shame and doubt
Play age	5–7	initiative v. guilt
School age	6–12	industry v. inferiority
Adolescence	13–19	identity v. role confusion
Young adulthood	20–30	intimacy v. isolation
Maturity	30–60	generativity v. stagnation
Old age	60 plus	integrity v. despair

accompanied by feelings of guilt, anger, resentment and despair. Many people travel through life deeply disappointed with the quality of their lives and their seeming incapacity to find effective and lasting strategies to life's difficulties and challenges.

Those involved in work as agents of change need to appreciate that the personal lives of individuals are characterized by a struggle to survive and find fulfilment. The ways that individuals behave in organizations and react to change and new expectations may be determined as much by the development struggles described by Erikson as by the particular details of the organizational issues at stake. A curiosity about human behaviour and a sensitivity to the psychological struggles of human living are an important part of being an effective manager and leader. [. . .]

In his analysis of teacher development, Leithwood (1990) has identified the following career cycle:

1 Launching the career.
2 Stabilizing: developing mature commitment feeling at ease, seeking more responsibility.
3 New challenges and concerns, diversifying, seeking added responsibilities.
4 Reaching a professional plateau: re-appraisal, sense of mortality, ceasing striving for promotion or stagnating and becoming cynical.
5 Preparing for retirement: focusing, disenchantment, serenity.

Bolam (1990) identifies five job stages:

1 Preparatory stage: when wishing to apply for a new job
2 Appointment stage: when selected or rejected
3 Induction stage: first two years in post
4 In-service stage: 3–5, 6–10, 11+ years in post
5 Transitional stage: promotion, redeployment

Most organizations, even quite small ones are likely to contain people at different stages of these cycles. Clearly, the relationship to change will depend upon where in this cycle particular individuals have reached. A probationary teacher will want to establish some basic classroom stability and confidence before having to face a significant change in methodology. Teachers in mid-career, with promotion aspirations to the fore, may well look upon change as an opportunity to demonstrate improved competence and gain leadership experience. A deputy head in professional plateau, having decided against further promotion may look upon an early retirement as preferable to managing major change. Too often the issue of life and career patterns in a staff is not something that is easily brought into general staff discussion, yet a common acceptance of patterns of professional diversity is essential if change objectives are to be met and the change process is to be managed appropriately and as comfortably as possible.

Life and career cycles are essential cultural issues that need to be acknowledged and responded to. The links between the personal and the professional will be blurred and they are not easily separated. Only by making our needs and aspirations clear and explicit can we create the pool of information from which sensible and appropriate decisions can be made and in order for managers and leaders to build a sensitive awareness of developmental needs and differences.

References

Argyris, C. (1964) *Integrating the Individual and the Organization*. Chichester: Wiley.

Bolam, R. (1990) Recent developments in England and Wales, in B. M. Joyce (ed.) *Changing School Culture through Staff Development – 1990 Yearbook of the Association for Supervision and Curriculum Development*. Alexandria, VA: ASCD.

Buzan, T. (1982) *Use Your Head*. London: Ariel Books/BBC Books.

Erikson, E. (1977) *Childhood and Society*. London: Triad/Granada.

Handy, C. (1976) *Understanding Organizations*. London: Penguin.

Handy, C. (1990) *Inside Organizations*. London: BBC Books.

Herzberg, F. (1966) *Work and the Nature of Man*. New York: Staple Press.

Hopson, B. and Scally, M. (1981) *Lifeskills Teaching*. London: McGraw-Hill.

Leithwood, K. A. (1990) The principal's role in teacher development, in B. M. Joyce (ed.) *Changing School Culture through Staff Development – 1990 Yearbook of the Association for Supervision and Curriculum Development*. Alexandria, VA: ASCD.

McGregor, D. (1960) *The Human Side of Enterprise*. New York: McGraw-Hill.

Maslow, A. (1970) *Motivation and Personality*. New York: Harper and Row.

Phares, J. (1976) *Locus of Control in Personality*. New Jersey: General Learning Press.

Postle, D. (1989) *The Mind Gymnasium*. London: Macmillan.

Rogers, C. (1967) *On Becoming a Person*. London: Constable.

Rotter, J. R. (1966) Generalized expectancies for internal versus external control of reinforcement, *Psychological Monographs*, 80(1).

Schein, E. H. (1980) *Organizational Psychology*. Hemel Hempstead: Prentice-Hall.

Singer, B. D. (1974) The future focused role image, in A. Toffler *Learning for Tomorrow: the Role of the Future in Education*. New York: Random House.

2 | Learning practical knowledge*

PETER JARVIS

[...]
This chapter falls into three parts – the first examines knowledge and skill and seeks to locate practical knowledge within an epistemological framework; the second looks at the learning process and discusses both learning knowledge and learning skill; the final section analyses the process of learning practical knowledge. Finally, some of the implications of this are discussed.

Knowledge, skill and practical knowledge

Epistemological studies have been quite central to philosophy for the past few centuries, but it is impossible to review this vast field here. However, some questions about knowledge are crucial to these considerations. Precisely what is knowledge? How can people be sure that what they know corresponds with the 'real' world out there? How can they be sure that the knowledge is true? These are but some of the major questions that confront any philosopher. They cannot all be answered in this chapter, but these are some of the questions that need to be explored if practical knowledge is to be understood.

Scheffler (1965) sought to respond to the questions about knowledge as truth propositions when he distinguished between three ways of verifying knowledge: rational-logical, empirical and pragmatic. Rational-logical knowledge is that form of knowledge that is acquired when a mathematical problem is solved since the logical rules have been followed and a conclusion has been reached. Empirical knowledge is that which people gather through their senses. Pragmatic knowledge is experimental and actors have it when they know that something they know actually works in practice – in

---

*This chapter has been edited and abridged from an article by Peter Jarvis in the *Journal of Further and Higher Education*, published in 1994.

this sense it is scientific. If that knowledge is not capable of producing the types of results that are expected, then it is rejected and new knowledge sought that works. Herein lies the idea of the human being as scientist, seeking always to understand and experiment upon social reality (Kelly 1963).

However, this idea of experimentation is also quite crucial to understanding something of the relationship between personal knowledge and action – perhaps, between theory and practice. It is always a probability situation. Heller (1984: 166) suggests that the 'pragmatic relationship denotes the direct unit of theory and practice'. People almost always act upon the probability that the action will achieve the desired results, and they act with 'sufficient ground' (p. 169), that is that they have some knowledge that enables them to act in a certain way and that they believe that their action will have specific results, or else they will not so act. Pragmatic knowledge is a form of scientific knowledge that should underlie a great deal of professional practitioners' actions. Because they know it works, it is necessarily conservative in nature – why should actors change their behaviour when they know what they are doing works? It is no good the theoretician trying to convince them they are wrong, because they have proved to themselves that what they know works. However, they cannot necessarily control all the circumstances within which their actions occur – hence every situation is one of probability.

This is probably a weakness in Habermas' (1972) formulation of technical-cognitive knowledge. Habermas also has three forms of knowledge or, as he calls them, processes of enquiry: the technical-cognitive, the historical-hermeneutic and the emancipatory – with the technical-cognitive being about practical knowledge. He (p. 309) regards this as being about 'control over objectified processes', and whilst this control may well refer to human action itself, the possession of knowledge does not necessarily mean that those who possess it must necessarily have control over the processes, only that they understand them. Hence, Habermas' discussion seems deficient here, although his inclusion of the idea of interest is important in order to begin to explain why people do act in certain ways, and not others.

It was Ryle who raised this question of practical knowledge in a seminal study in 1949. He (1963) distinguished between knowledge how and knowledge that and suggested that in everyday life 'we are more concerned with people's competences than with their cognitive repertoires' (p. 28). In this he was attacking the intellectual emphasis upon cognitive knowledge, and yet he oversimplified the problem by adopting a behaviourist solution and he suggested that when 'I am doing something intelligently . . . I am doing one thing and not two' (p. 32). Here Ryle has actually confused three things – the skill, the knowledge how to perform an action and the monitoring of an action. However, Ryle implicitly raises two sets of inter-related problems: firstly, he implies that 'knowing how' and 'being able' are synonymous, which is incorrect; secondly, he demonstrates quite clearly that when people perform an action they cannot necessarily always articulate the theory underlying the action.

Scheffler (1965) also points out that knowing how and being able are not synonymous concepts. He provides the illustration of a person who might know how to drive a car but is prevented from doing so for a variety of reasons, e.g. having a broken leg. There are contingencies that cannot always be controlled. Hence, the difference between having the knowledge and being able to perform the skill still remains crucial to this discussion. However, this illustration does not probe deeply enough and another question emerges – when people say 'I know how to . . .' are they really using a term that has a cognitive orientation at all? Would it not be more correct to claim that 'I am able to . . .'? In other words, the possession of a skill does not necessarily always mean that people have all the knowledge how, although there may well be other occasions when they actually have or have had that knowledge. There are no doubt times when a skill is learned and only as it is being acquired do the actors gain any knowledge how – but there are other occasions when they learn the rules and perform the actions, but as they habitualise their actions, so the rules play a less significant part and they begin to forget them. There is further reference to this throughout the remainder of this chapter.

This discussion about not being able to articulate what people actually know has come to the fore again in a recent study about practical knowledge and expertise. Nyiri (1988: 20–1 – all quotes are from Feigenbaum and McCorduck 1984) writes:

> One becomes an expert not simply by absorbing explicit knowledge of the type found in textbooks, but through experience, that is, through repeated trials, 'failing, succeeding, wasting time and effort . . . getting to feel the problem, learning to go by the book and when to break the rules'. Human experts thereby gradually absorb 'a repertory of working rules of thumb, or "heuristics", that, combined with book knowledge, make them expert practitioners'. This practical, heuristic knowledge, as attempts to stimulate it on the machine have shown, is 'hardest to get at because experts – or anyone else – rarely have the self-awareness to recognise what it is. So it must be mined out of their heads painstakingly, one jewel at a time'.

Ryle may well be correct that some of the original rules are forgotten through constant practice, but Nyiri is suggesting another element – that through continuous experimentation new knowledge is gradually absorbed from experience which might never have been articulated. Practical knowledge, then, is hidden in the practitioner, or as Polyani (1967) suggests, it has become tacit knowledge, i.e. knowledge that cannot necessarily be expressed in words. The nature of that knowledge is pragmatic, i.e. it is accepted because it is known to work. But because it is known to work practitioners are loathe to change it, and so it is essentially conservative.

It is therefore maintained here that practical knowledge has two inter-related dimensions: knowledge how and tacit knowledge. Both of these are in the cognitive dimension and both relate to the ability to perform an action, the skill; although neither of them are synonymous with it. However, tacit knowledge requires a little more understanding and there appear to be at least two processes of acquiring it: the first is about forgetting and the second is about learning. The former is the one upon which Ryle and others have focused: that as practitioners gain expertise in practice, they tend to forget the original rules upon which that practice is based. The latter is that form of learning which was called pre-conscious learning in an earlier study (Jarvis 1987), and it is one which Marsick and Watkins (1990) call incidental learning. This is learning from experience without being conscious of the learning that is occurring in the ordinary processes of daily living. The exact constitution of these two elements will differ in different people, although for the purposes of this chapter there is no need to develop it further here. It is necessary, however, now to understand the process of human learning, and this constitutes the second part of this analysis.

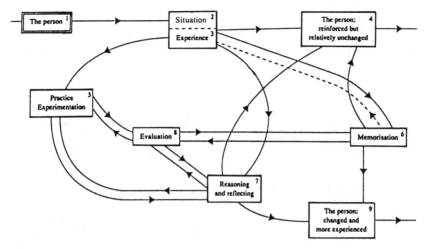

Figure 2.1   A learning cycle

Human learning

In a previous study on learning (Jarvis 1987) it was demonstrated that learning occurs in a number of different forms and ways. Figure 2.1 (Jarvis 1987: 25) indicates something of the complexity of the process, in which it may be seen that while all learning begins with experience, there are a number of routes from that through the learning process: one route is entirely practical while the others are cognitive. Now this is significant for any understanding of both knowledge how and tacit knowledge.

From Figure 2.1 it might be claimed that all learning is a response to an experience however that experience is induced. Basically, it is suggested that there are at least nine potential learning responses to an experience and that they may be classified into three fundamentally different categories: non-learning, non-reflective learning and reflective learning (Table 2.1). Each of these three categories contains three types, although in reflective learning there are two forms of each of the three types. In the following analysis these types are discussed.

Table 2.1   A typology of learning

Category of response to experience	Type of learning or non-learning
Non-learning	Presumption
	Non-consideration
	Rejection
Non-reflective learning	Preconscious
	Skills
	Memorisation
Reflective learning	Contemplation
	Reflective skills
	Experimental/creative

(Each of the reflective forms of learning can have two different outcomes, conformity or change)

It is possible to think of situations where more than one of these forms of learning occurs simultaneously, although in the next three sections of this part of the chapter each of these types is discussed individually, and in each instance one suggested route through Figure 2.1 is indicated.

Non-learning

It is very clear that people do not always learn from their experiences, and this is a feature of everyday life that is peculiarly poorly researched. [. . .] Three non-learning responses to experience are now discussed: presumption, non-consideration and rejection.

Presumption: This is the typical response to everyday experience, and Schutz and Luckmann (1984: 7) describe the experience thus:

> I trust the world as it is known by me up until now will continue further and that consequently the stock of knowledge obtained from my fellowmen and formed from my own experiences will continue to preserve its fundamental validity . . . From this assumption follows the further and fundamental one; that I can repeat my past successful acts. So long as the structure of the world can be taken as constant; so long as my previous experience is valid, my ability to operate upon the world in this and that manner remains in principle preserved.

While this appears almost thoughtless and mechanical, it is suggested here that this is the basis of a great deal of social living since it is totally meaningful to the actors. Practitioners might well presume upon their practice quite frequently. A great deal of life is lived on the basis of the stock of knowledge gained from previous learning experiences, which is the life-world, and presumption is a typical response to an everyday experience; it is the situation of being in harmony with the social world in which individuals live and move and have their being, and it is a point to which we shall return in the final part of this chapter.

(The route through Figure 2.1 is 1 through 4)

Non-consideration: For a variety of reasons people do not respond to a potential learning experience; maybe because they are too busy to think about it or maybe because they are fearful of the outcome, or even because they are not in a position to understand the situation within which they find themselves. Hence, the potentiality of learning from the experience might be recognised, but practitioners may not be able to respond to it. This is another response that occurs quite commonly in everyday life, and the effect that it has upon the actors may vary in accord with the reasons why no response was made.

(The route through Figure 2.1 is 1 through 4)

Rejection: Some people have an experience, think about it but reject the possibility of learning from it. For instance, think of a person experiencing the complexity of the modern city and exclaiming, 'I don't know what this world is coming to these days!' Here is a possible learning experience, an experience of the complex world but instead of probing it and seeking to understand it, some people reject the possibility. Equally the illustration could have been with the professional practitioners who accuse the theoretician of being too far removed from reality to offer practical advice. Rejection may actually serve to confirm the actors in their already held position.

(The route through Figure 2.1 is 1 through 3 through 7 to either 4 or 9)

Non-reflective learning

These forms of learning are those which are most frequently socially defined as learning. The three that have been isolated in this research project are: pre-conscious, skills learning and memorisation. The factor above all else what enables them to be placed within one stratum together is that they do not involve reflectivity.

Pre-conscious learning: This is a form of learning about which there is little research. It occurs to everybody as a result of people having direct experiences in the course of their daily life about which they do not really think, nor about which they are even particularly conscious. It occurs when individuals are monitoring their actions, albeit with a low level of consciousness, but which the mind is actually committing to memory. These forms of learning occur at the periphery of the vision, at the edge of consciousness, and so on. This type of learning is often called 'incidental learning' but the term is not employed here because it does not convey the idea of a learning process that passes into the mind without the learner being conscious of it. A full discussion of this approach occurs in the work of Marsick and Watkins (1990), but further reference is also made to this in the final section of this chapter.

It is significant that the research project discussed here was not itself aimed at analysing this type of learning, although a number of the respondents mentioned it during the research itself.

(The route through Figure 2.1 is 1 through 3 through 6 to 4)

Skills learning: This type of learning is traditionally restricted to such forms of learning as training for a manual occupation, or drill, or the acquisition of physical skill through training. However, some learning in preparation for a physical occupation is certainly not non-reflective, so that this has to be restricted to the learning of simple, short procedures that somebody on an assembly line might be taught. These skills are also often acquired through imitation and role modelling.

(The route through Figure 2.1 is 1 through 3 through 5 to 8 to 6 either 4 or 9)

Memorisation: This is perhaps the most commonly known form of learning; children learn their mathematical tables, their language vocabularies, and so on. Adults, when they return to higher education, sometimes feel that this is the type of learning that is most expected of them and so they try to memorise what such and such a scholar has written, and so on, in order to reproduce it for an examination. Hence, the authority figure speaks and every word of wisdom has to be learned and memorised. Memorisation can also occur as a result of past successful acts, the results of which are stored away and form the basis of planning for future action, or even of presumption in action.

(The route through Figure 2.1 is 1 through 3 to 6, then possibly to 8 to 6 and then to either 4 or 9)

Reflective learning

Thus far it has been shown that learning tends to be culturally reproductive, simply because that is the way that it is frequently defined socially. It is suggested that non-reflective learning can do no other than to reproduce the structures of society, but this is not true of reflective learning. Three forms of learning involve the process of reflection, contemplation, reflective skills and experimental learning, and thinkers such as Argyris (1982 *inter alia*), Boud *et al.* (1985), Gadamer (1976), Kolb (1984), Mezirow (1990, 1991 *inter alia*) and Schön (1983) have all examined the process of reflection. Because of Freire's work it might be assumed by some people that all reflective learning has to be revolutionary or critical, but this is certainly not always the case, for the outcome can be conformity, criticality, or creativity.

Contemplation: This is a common form of learning for which the behaviourist definitions make no allowance and yet, in many ways, this might be viewed as a most intellectual approach to learning because it involves pure thought. This is the process of thinking about an experience and reaching a conclusion without reference to the wider social reality. It is, for instance, the process of mathematical reasoning without reference to the physical reality beyond the mathematical problem. However, it is in reaching a conclusion that differentiates contemplative learning from just thinking. The religious type of terminology was carefully chosen since it allows for meditation, as well as the thought processes of the philosopher, the activities of the pure mathematician, and even everyday thinking and learning.

(The route through Figure 2.1 is 1 through 3 to 7 to 8 to 6 to 9 – with the two-way processes operating throughout the latter part)

Reflective skills: This was called reflective practice in an earlier publication (Jarvis 1987: 34–5). It is one of the forms of learning that Schön (1983) concentrates upon when he points out that professionals in practice think on their feet. In the process they often produce new skills as they respond to the uniqueness of their situation. It is not only learning a skill but learning about the knowledge undergirding the practice and, therefore, knowing why the skill should be performed in a specific manner.

(The route through Figure 2.1 is 1 through 3 to 5, 7, 8 loop, as many times as necessary in both directions, out from 5 to 8 to 6 to 9)

Experimental learning: That is that form of learning in which theory is tried out in practice and the end-product of the experimentation is a new form of knowledge, creative thinking, that relates fully to social reality. This approach to learning relates very closely to Kelly's (1963) understanding of human beings as scientists, seeking always to experiment on their environment and learning new knowledge from it.

(The route through Figure 2.1 is 1 through 3 to 7, 5, 8 loop, as many times as necessary in both directions, out from 7 to 8 to 6 to 9)

Having examined the concept of practical knowledge and the complex process of learning, it is now possible to seek to understand the process of learning practical knowledge.

Learning practical knowledge

In the first part of this chapter practical knowledge was shown to consist of two dimensions: knowledge how and tacit knowledge, with the latter having two elements – one of forgetting and the other of learning. The acquisition of knowledge how is also more complicated than it might appear on the surface and four different processes are discussed here. Six aspects in the acquisition of practical knowledge are, therefore, analysed here: learning knowledge how; learning how in practice; acquisition of tacit knowledge by forgetting; acquisition of tacit knowledge by learning pre-consciously; acquisition of knowledge how by reflective learning; continuing learning and education relating theory to practice. Throughout the following discussion all the types of learning mentioned in the previous section occur, although no attempt is made here to illustrate this precisely. These six processes can occur in sequence, but many of them are simultaneous, so that the order below does not exclude other possible sequences.

Learning knowledge how: This is the type of preparation that occurs in initial professional, or vocational, education. Students attend a training school and are instructed in the knowledge about how to perform in practice, and they also learn some of the knowledge that. The learning knowledge how may consist of traditional lectures and demonstrations. Academic knowledge, as Young (1971) has so forcefully pointed out is abstract. But there is a sense in which the type of knowledge taught in the classroom should be abstract and generalised for it is only when it is put into practice that it can be concrete and specific. The teaching and learning is often a matter of memorisation of material taught and, sometimes, also the opportunity to practise some of the skills following demonstrations. Ideas like reflective learning and critical thought are espoused, although they may often be rhetoric rather than reality, or espoused theories rather than theories in use. Indeed, knowledge how should be pragmatic and so the opportunity to criticise it should actually occur when it is tried out in practice.

This raises an interesting, but significant issue, about critical thinking; if the knowledge taught is pragmatic then the criteria for criticism must lie in the practicality of that knowledge and curricula should be constructed in such a manner as to allow for critical debate, after having provided the opportunity to practise the knowledge that has been taught in the classroom and reflected upon it.

Learning how in practice: It was claimed earlier that a relationship between theory and practice was one of pragmatism since no actors can possibly control all the possible exigencies that surround an action. Mackenzie (1990) sought to show how district nursing students (public health type nurses) learned in their practice setting. Using ethnographical methods she studied district nurse students undertaking practice and noted that there are three stages in the process: the first she called 'fitting in', which is the process of observing how the practice functions and learning from colleagues and senior practitioners – both their strengths and their errors – and devising strategies that enable them to fit in; the second stage she called 'trying and testing out' and during this stage the

students move from dependency upon their senior practitioners to a level of indepen-
dency; finally, there is a third stage which she called 'reality of practice' in which the
student learns to become a practitioner and during that time there is an integration of the
knowledge learned in the classroom with that learned in practice, where this is possible.
Naturally enough some contradictions are also discovered and some of the rules are
found not to be practicable. This final stage is the beginning of the professional
practitioner.

Acquisition of tacit knowledge by forgetting: As Nyiri pointed out, the independent
practitioner begins to forget the original rules. Other writers, such as Ryle (1963) and
Benner (1984) make precisely the same point, that with the growth in expertise the
original rules tend to play a less conscious part in professional practice. But there is a
danger here because it is also the beginning of the process of habitualisation, which can
also result in bad practice. [. . .] In this process the theoretical and abstract rules play a
less significant part in practice and so they tend to be forgotten. Hence, the knowledge
has become internalised, tacit and difficult for the practitioner to articulate.

Acquisition of tacit knowledge by learning: This is the second element in the process of
acquiring tacit knowledge and this starts from two basic assumptions: that practitioners
do monitor their performances and that they adapt them to different situations. Through
this process of conscious action the actors are learning pre-consciously from their
practice and skill performance. This process of monitoring and retrospecting upon
action is totally different from reflective practice, which is discussed in the next
sub-section; this is a natural process of being consciously aware – even at a very low level
of consciousness – of the total situation within which the actions are performed. The
results of monitoring and retrospecting both the actions and any slight adjustments in the
performances in order to adapt the specific situations are frequently internalised without
conscious awareness. Hence, pre-conscious learning occurs through these processes of
thinking about actions, which result in the development of a body of tacit knowledge
within practitioners; knowledge that they would find almost impossible to articulate.

Reflective practice and knowledge how: Actors plan, monitor and retrospect upon
actions in the normal cause of events, but sometimes the action has not produced the
desired results, sometimes disjunction occurs between expectations and achievements. It
is here that the idea of probability is important, for practitioners cannot always be sure of
acting in an almost taken for granted manner; they are sometimes confronted with
disjuncture and they are forced to re-think the whole situation. At this point practice is
the situation from which a reflective learning experience occurs, and if the practitioners
do reflect upon the situation and learn from it, then they add to their body of knowledge
how. But if they are too busy, or they reject the opportunity, then non-learning occurs
and their practice will be impoverished because they failed to learn from their experience.

Knowledge how and continuing learning and education: Through continuing learning
[. . .] and continuing professional education practitioners can and do continue to add to
their body of knowledge how. During this process practitioners have opportunities to
read journals and magazines; there are libraries and learning resource centres available
and there are experts who can be consulted. In addition, there are continuing
professional education courses, and these are becoming increasingly available as the

growing awareness about human resource development results in more opportunities for further training. However, the extent to which continuing education, in the more formal sense, relates to the specific learning needs of the practice as undertaken by practitioners, remains an area in which more research is needed.

Thus it may be seen that both knowledge how and tacit knowledge develop through the process of learning from practice, and implicitly the point at which non-learning occurs was also highlighted and it is this to which further reference is made below.

Concluding discussion

Benner (1984), following Dreyfus and Dreyfus (1980), traces five stages in the process from novice to expert: novice, advanced beginner, competent, proficient and expert. This seems to be a natural progression but if it were natural and almost inevitable, then every practitioner who stayed in practice for a long time would automatically be classified as an expert. However, this is not actually the case in practice, and the point raised earlier about the failure to learn from experience becomes crucial to this discussion. Those long-term practitioners who are not experts may never have achieved that state because they failed to learn from their practice experiences, and the reasons for non-learning become increasingly important if human resources are to be developed fully.

But those who are the experts are those who have acquired both knowledge how and tacit knowledge from their practice. It is perhaps even more significant in this age of managerialism that only those who are in practice can ever be the experts, for those who leave it cease to be in a position to increase their knowledge how and, above all, their tacit knowledge. Not only is this a lesson for managers, it is also one for teachers. It is only through doing something that a fully developed understanding of it can be acquired, or as Pentti Havukainen (1991: 60), an elderly Finnish thinker, wrote: 'The best way to understand the tango is to dance it, not analyse it'!

References

Argyris, C. (1982) *Reasoning, Learning and Action*. San Francisco: Jossey-Bass.

Benner, P. (1984) *From Novice to Expert*. Menlo Park, CA: Addison Wesley.

Boud, D., Keogh, R. and Walker, D. (eds) (1985) *Reflection: Turning Experience into Action*. London: Kogan Page.

Dreyfus, S. E. and Dreyfus, H. L. (1980) 'A five stage model of the mental activities involved in skill acquisition'. Unpublished report. University of California at Berkeley.

Feigenbaum, E. A. and McCorduck, P. (1984) *The Fifth Generation*. New York: Signet.

Gadamer, H-G. (1976) *Philosophical Hermeneutics*. Berkeley: University of California Press.

Habermas, J. (1972) *Knowledge and Human Interests*. London: Heinemann.

Havukainen, P. (1991) Auto-Education by Bike, in *Life and Education in Finland*, No. 2, 1991, pp. 59–60.

Heller, A. (1984) *Everyday Life*. London: Routledge and Kegan Paul.

Jarvis, P. (1987) *Adult Learning in the Social Context*. London: Croom Helm.

Jarvis, P. (1992) *Paradoxes of Learning*. San Francisco: Jossey-Bass.

Kelly, G. (1963) *A Theory of Personality: the Psychology of Personal Constructs*. New York: W. W. Norton.

Kolb, D. (1984) *Experiential Learning*. Englewood Cliffs, NJ: Prentice-Hall.

Mackenzie, A. (1990) 'Learning from Experience in the Community, an ethnographic study of district nurse students'. University of Surrey, unpublished PhD thesis.

Marsick, V. J. and Watkins, K. (1990) *Informal and Incidental Learning in the Workplace*. London: Routledge.

Mezirow, J. and Associates (1990) *Fostering Critical Reflection in Adulthood*. San Francisco: Jossey-Bass.

Mezirow, J. (1991) *Transformative Dimensions of Adult Learning*. San Francisco: Jossey-Bass.

Nyiri, J. C. (1988) Traditional and practical knowledge, in J. C. Nyiri and Barry Smith (eds) op. cit.

Nyiri, J. C. and Smith, B. (eds) (1988) *Outlines of a Theory of Traditions and Skills*. London: Croom Helm.

Polyani, M. (1967) *The Tacit Dimension*. London: Routledge and Kegan Paul.

Ryle, G. (1963) *The Concept of Mind*. Harmondsworth: Peregrine Books.

Scheffler, I. (1965) *The Conditions of Knowledge*. Chicago: University of Chicago Press.

Schön, D. A. (1983) *The Reflective Practitioner*. New York: Basic Books.

Schutz, A. and Luckmann, T. (1984) *The Everyday Structures of the Lifeworld*. London: Heinemann.

Young, M. (1971) Curricula as socially organised knowledge, in M. Young (ed.) *Knowledge and Control*. London: Collier-Macmillan.

3 | Developing expertise in school management and teaching*

MICHAEL ERAUT

Part 1: The nature of expertise in school management and in teaching

1 Introduction

Significant debates about the nature of expertise in management and the nature of expertise in teaching have been conducted quite separately over the last two decades, yet they have been addressing many common issues. For example, what are the respective roles in developing expertise of attending courses and learning on-the-job? What, if any, is the role of theoretical knowledge? How do we take into account the significant part played by tacit and personal knowledge? Less well articulated has been a common ambiguity of purpose: has training been directed towards ensuring competence or promoting excellence? If these debates have sometimes been pursued with limited evidence and analysis, they have at least acknowledged the existence of expertise in teaching and in management.

Until quite recently, the expertise of a secondary school teacher was defined in terms of their knowledge of their subject. Teaching itself was not a professional activity but something one learned how to do rather like driving a car. Assuming the role of a schoolteacher was a natural process for a person of good character. Subject knowledge and character were also important in the appointment of headteachers, together with a talent for self-presentation and public relations, and perceived leadership qualities. There was little attempt to discern or develop what today we might call management expertise. [. . .] As teaching and management became more demanding in a less ordered, more rapidly changing society, the importance of good teachers and good managers became more widely acknowledged; but without much agreement on precisely what constituted a good teacher or a good manager. There were of course many distinguished

*This chapter originally appeared as 'The characterisation and development of professional expertise in school management and in teaching' in *Educational Management and Administration*, published in 1993.

books about teaching; and young teachers were recommended to read and ponder those books whose values and approaches appealed to their advisers. But the relationship between such books and classroom practice remained tenuous; and teachers referred to the non-practice components of their training in scathing terms. Books on school management were exceedingly rare, and the literature on general management almost unknown in education.

Knowledge of *education* rather than knowledge of the subjects being taught, did not begin to be taken seriously until it could be defined in terms of discipline-based knowledge acceptable to higher education; and the growth of the social sciences in the 1960s and 1970s provided just such an opportunity. Courses in psychology, sociology and philosophy were presented as providing a new theoretical foundation for the profession of teaching; and long-established child development courses at primary level 'upgraded' to meet new academic criteria. Social science-based courses in management began to proliferate at about the same time, though under strong North American influence and with little participation from the education sector. The level of higher education provision established at that time expanded still further during the 1980s as the original dependency on the social sciences weakened and more practice-oriented courses were introduced under labels such as 'curriculum development', 'evaluation', 'classroom research' and eventually 'educational management'. However, one could also argue that the potential contribution of the social sciences was never properly realised. In rejecting the original adoption of an academic approach which failed to deliver direct application in the classroom, there was often only limited exploration of other ways of bringing discipline-based knowledge to bear on practical situations.

As social science knowledge gained in prestige during the 1960s, educational research was dominated by a positivist approach, through which people hoped to discover empirically the characteristics of a good teacher and/or good teaching. While some useful findings emerged from this work, it was generally disappointing. Thus people have come to accept that empirically-based generalisations are likely to be sparse in education because contextual variations and individual differences have so great an effect on transactions and outcomes. Similar trends can be discerned in the research on management.

However, towards the end of this period of social science hegemony, researchers also began to undertake qualitative studies of how teachers and managers think and work. These revealed that 'good practitioners' had an enormously complex and highly personal knowledge base, constructed from experience but used in a fairly intuitive way. Many traces of discipline-based knowledge could be found but not in their original form. Moreover, much of this complex knowledge-base was tacit rather than explicit, so that practitioners could not readily articulate what they did or how they did it. Teachers and managers were pleased to have this confirming evidence of the level of their expertise; but these new research findings were difficult to apply to training in a positive way. It remained unclear how they could be used to promote the refinement, sharing or learning of what came to be called the 'practical knowledge' of teaching or managing.

This issue became more generally recognised with the publication of Schön's book *The Reflective Practitioner* in 1983, suggesting that the problem of personal, partly tacit, knowledge was common to all the professions. Hitherto, Schön argued, discussion of the issue had been suppressed by two factors: the dominance of codified knowledge within higher education linked to its emphasis on publication; and the prevalence within Western society more generally of a technical-rationality perspective linked to a positivist epistemology. However, while Schön argued his case very convincingly, he did not go very far towards constructing any alternative epistemology (Eraut 1995b)

2 The need for a new approach to characterising professional expertise

There are three main reasons why it is now becoming increasingly urgent to construct such an alternative epistemology. The first is socio-political. The more powerful professions, such as law and medicine, have enhanced their status for some time by claiming a complex knowledge base which is unknowable by outsiders; although there are signs that this is increasingly unacceptable to the general public. But the less powerful professions, such as teaching have suffered from the opposite problem: familiarity rather than mystery has encouraged the belief that any reasonably educated person could do the job without needing to acquire significant additional expertise. Coming from the university which began school-based teacher training 27 years ago, I cannot help suspecting that its recent adoption by government may have been for the wrong reasons. Instead of getting theory and practice into a better kind of relationship through higher education–school partnerships, the ultimate purpose may be to dispense with the higher education element altogether. Similarly, the recommendations of the School Management Task Force could easily be shifted from a proper emphasis on school-based management development to the abandonment of any formal training. Unless the expertise of teachers and managers becomes more clearly articulated, it will be downgraded; and the social history of the professions suggests that abandoning credible claims to a distinctive knowledge base will lead to a process of deprofessionalisation, accompanied by a rapid loss of status and esteem.

My second argument for developing a new epistemology derives from my interest in professional education. Experience is necessary for developing expertise as a teacher or a manager but it is certainly not sufficient. Until we understand more about how people learn (or fail to learn) from experience, we will have little guidance to offer teachers and managers on how to pursue excellence in their work; and we are unlikely to understand *how* people learn from experience if we fail to elucidate *what* they learn from experience. Moreover, such knowledge needs to be widely shared. In order to take control over their own professional learning, teachers and managers need to have some awareness of their own personal knowledge base: what is held in common with others, what is purely personal, what is habit, what is intuitive, what is proven, what is fallible, what is authentic, what they know, what they do not know, how they work, how they evaluate their work, what frameworks and assumptions underpin their thinking.

Thirdly, there is the problem of how a whole profession can improve the quality of its performance. Acknowledging that there is a personal and tacit dimension to much professional knowledge does not deny the advantages of sharing what can be articulated and learning from vicarious experience. The profession as a whole can still learn much from pooling experience, reflecting on it critically and conducting appropriate kinds of research. But without a more adequate epistemology these efforts are likely to be overshadowed by current fashion and undermined by political issues.

3 The relationship between professional expertise and different kinds of knowledge

I have approached the problem of characterising professional expertise from a number of perspectives, which I am now beginning to integrate.

My first approach focused on the problem of knowledge use, a constant preoccupation of those concerned with curriculum implementation. This incorporates both the issue of how theory or indeed any form of book knowledge gets used in practical situations and the issue of how practical knowledge or know-how gets transferred from one context to another or from one person to another (Eraut 1982, 1985).

Then looking at the problem in reverse I addressed the questions of how and what people learn from experience. When does this involve the acquisition of tacit knowledge in the form of recognisable patterns, routines or perceptual frameworks and when does in involve theorising, the creation of theory from reflection or practice (Eraut 1992, 1993). This raised futher issues about both the explicitness and the validity of what was learned from experience.

Combining these two approaches led me to a series of distinctions. First, *public knowledge* is necessarily explicit, whereas *personal knowledge* can be either explicit (and therefore capable of being shared and made public) or tacit (and therefore incapable of being made public without being transformed into some explicit representation). Second, although adopting Gilbert Ryle's (1949) distinction between *propositional knowledge* (knowing that) and *procedural knowledge* (knowing how) I have found it necessary to add a third category, that of *images and impressions*. These are held in the memory but not represented in propositional form, although propositions may be derived from them through reflection. Knowledge of a person, for example, is likely to include images and impressions from a series of incidents held in memory, some public facts and some personal explicit propositions which may well have been first articulated in casual conversation.

Public propositional knowledge comprises facts, case material, concepts, theories, practical principles and conceptual frameworks. It is commonly portrayed as being acquired from books or formally learned on courses; but facts, concepts and practical principles are also acquired informally whenever they are in general use. Such knowledge could be absorbed from one's family and local community or 'picked up' during conversations with fellow-professionals without there being any specific intention to learn about it. Similarly, public knowledge may be used in a conscious, deliberate way or used almost automatically because it has become part of one's normal pattern of thinking. Thus our use of public knowledge is much greater than we usually recognise.

Unless conceptual knowledge is being simply replicated or applied in a routine way, its use is likely to involve considerable thought. Not only does it require thinking about the context of use but also about the particular interpretation to be given to each concept or idea in each particular set of circumstances. As a result of these episodes of use such knowledge becomes personalised. Its specific meaning for any individual depends on this history of use and is also affected by how that person links it into their personal cognitive framework. This process of use incorporates the concept into that person's action knowledge, making it readily available for further use. Whereas public knowledge that has not been used before is unlikely to be used again. Thus both the meaning and the perceived relevance of public knowledge are strongly influenced by the history of its use or non-use.

Personal propositional knowledge can be acquired either by this process of personalising public knowledge or by learning from experience. Most commonly, both sources are interactively involved, but in varying proportions. Discussion of books will usually draw on a range of participants' personal experiences; and learning from experience usually involves some use, albeit intuitive, of public propositional knowledge. Thus personal knowledge is partly tacit and partly apprehended. A significant consequence of this is that people are not aware of everything they know and only partly aware of their own cognitive frameworks. Hence their personal knowledge is not fully under their own critical control, and they should not be confident of its validity. Since all forms of personal knowledge are used in everyday professional work, the need for both public and personal knowledge to be regularly evaluated is apparent.

In addition to the knowledge use perspective and that of learning from experience, I have approached the problem of the nature of professional work itself. My starting point for this has been that professional expertise is embedded in the quality of the processes that constitute such work; and I have distinguished four kinds of process to facilitate discussion of how the different kinds of knowledge discussed above contribute to professional performance.

- Processes for acquiring and interpreting information
- Skilled behaviours
- Deliberative processes, such as planning, evaluating and problem-solving
- Meta-processes, concerned with directing and controlling one's own behaviour.

This classification has the advantage of being common across all person-oriented professions, including education and management. In practice, the performance of almost any professional function will involve processes drawn from several categories; but this does not detract from their usefulness for investigating the nature of professional expertise and the different ways by which it is acquired. In the following sections, I discuss each type of process in turn with particular attention to the nature of the expertise and the ways in which different kinds of knowledge are likely to be involved.

4 Acquiring and interpreting information

Research on perception clearly demonstrates that the acquisition and interpretation of information are linked; and both are significantly affected by pre-existing cognitive frameworks and schemas. People are more likely to notice what they are looking for, and to see what they expect to see. Similarly, interpretations tend to follow rather than challenge accustomed patterns of thinking; unless some prominent problem or issue impinges upon the attention. This 'conservative tendency' is exacerbated in both teaching and management by the conditions under which most acquisition and interpretation of information occurs.

In educational contexts information is rarely acquired by highly systematised methods of inquiry. Tests, questionnaires and interview protocols represent the most systematic approaches, but even they are rarely developed to a high degree of reliability. Informal marking and short discussions are in much more regular use; and most information is probably picked up by observation and casual conversation, as a result of being present in a particular place at a particular time.

The process of information acquisition also differs according to the mode of interpretation: so it is useful to distinguish between three such modes:

- instant interpretation or pattern recognition, as in recognising a person;
- rapid interpretation; as in monitoring one's progress in the middle of a conversation; and

- deliberative interpretation, when there is time for thought and discussion and even for collecting further information.

We should note, however, that habits and pressure of time militate against the frequent use of the deliberative mode. Even the process of reading, which is ideally suited for deliberation, is likely to result in little deliberation unless the context demands it or a special effort is made. When information flows past during real-time incidents in a busy or crowded environment, there is very little time for deliberation. What is remembered will depend on the ability of the perceiver to notice and select the right information rapidly at the time of the encounter. The interpretation may then be refined or modified by reflection after the event, provided that time is found for that purpose.

Another common feature of education is that a great deal of information is acquired piecemeal, then gradually used to build up a picture of a person or a situation. For example, let us consider how a teacher acquires information about individual pupils in her class. Although teachers receive some information from records and comments from other teachers, their knowledge of individual pupils is based mainly on direct encounters in the classroom. These encounters are predominantly with the class as a group, but nevertheless a series of incidents involving individuals in whole class, small group or one-to-one settings are likely to be stored in memory, rather like a series of film clips. In so far as a teacher has made notes, these are likely to serve as aides-mémoire rather than independent sources of information. How is the information then used? Under conditions of rapid interpretation, teachers will respond to situations on the basis of their current images of the pupils; though these images may have themselves been formed by rapid assimilation of evidence with little time for reflection. Under conditions of deliberative interpretation, the most accessible evidence is likely to be carefully considered; but even that may be a sample of remembered encounters selected for their ready accessibility rather than their representativeness.

Psychological research on the information-gathering aspect of human decision-making has shown that a number of errors regularly occur, from which professionals are certainly not exempt (Nisbett and Ross 1980). When retrieval from memory is a critical factor, incidents involving a person are more likely to be recalled if they are more recent and/or more salient. Also sufficient allowance may not be made when a highly atypical sample of incidents provides the basis of the memory record. For example, a headteacher will rarely see teachers at their ordinary work, and a teacher in charge of discipline may only see pupils when they are in trouble. Moreover, because of prior expectations, earlier incidents may affect how later incidents are perceived. Worse still, informal second hand reports or rumours may affect how the first direct encounters with a person are interpreted. People tend to see what they expect to see.

Such experiential learning occurs both during the normal process of maturation from child to adult, when many schemas for understanding people and situations are constructed and during professional practice itself, when further development and modification of frameworks is likely to occur. Even in the professional context this learning may be at best semi-conscious, resulting from experience and socialisation rather than any deliberate learning strategy. Such schemas can easily become biased or ineffective because they are subjected to so little conscious reflection. The problem for professionals, however, is not to exclude such experiential learning, they would be lost without it; but to bring it under more critical control. This requires considerable self-awareness and a strong disposition to monitor one's actions and cross-check by collecting additional evidence in a more systematic manner with greater precautions against bias.

5 Skilled behaviour

Skilled behaviour can be defined as a complex sequence of actions which has become so routinised through practice and experience that it is performed without much conscious thinking or deliberation. Thus teachers' early experiences are characterised by the gradual routinisation of their teaching and this is necessary for them to be able to cope with what would otherwise be a highly stressful situation with a continuing 'information overload'. This routinisation is accompanied by a diminution of self-consciousness and a focusing of perceptual awareness on particular phenomena. Hence, knowledge of how to teach becomes tacit knowledge, something which is not easily explained to others or even to oneself.

Among the more commonly cited examples of skills are swimming and riding a bicycle; but teaching is more like riding a bicycle in busy traffic. Habitual routines are punctuated by bouts of rapid decision-making. For example, Jackson (1968) estimated that a primary teacher might make a thousand decisions a day. These decisions do not involve the deliberative processes discussed below, but are interactive decisions made on the spur of the moment in response to rapid readings of the situation and the overall purpose of the action. Such decisions have to be largely intuitive, so the person concerned will find it quite difficult to provide a quick explanation. This creates a dilemma that characterises large areas of professional work. The development of routines is a natural process, essential for coping with the job and responsible for increased efficiency; but the combination of tacit knowledge and intuitive decision-making makes them difficult to monitor and to keep under critical control. As a result, routines tend to become progressively dysfunctional over time: not only do they fail to adjust to new circumstances but 'shortcuts' gradually intrude. [. . .]

If management is not quite as routinised as teaching, it still involves quite a lot of autospeak when what people say follows familiar pathways. Moreover, managers constantly claim that they are so bombarded with messages and calls for actions that they have little time for deliberation; and in such circumstances behaviour will be at best semi-routinised. Like the information-gathering habits discussed in the previous section, routinised actions are very difficult to change. Not only does change involve a great deal of unlearning and reconstruction but also the adjustment of a 'persona' which is already known to others and taken for granted.

6 Deliberative processes

Deliberative processes such as planning, problem-solving, analysing, evaluating and decision-making lie at the heart of professional work. These processes cannot be accomplished by using procedural knowledge alone or by following a manual. They require unique combinations of propositional knowledge, situational knowledge and professional judgement. In most situations, there will not be a single correct answer, nor a guaranteed road to success; and even when there is a unique solution it will have to be recognised as such by discriminations which cannot be programmed in advance. More typically there will be:

- some uncertainty about outcomes;
- guidance from theory which is only partially helpful;
- relevant but often insufficient contextual knowledge;
- pressure on the time available for deliberation;
- a strong tendency to follow accustomed patterns of thinking;
- an opportunity, perhaps a requirement to consult or involve other people.

These processes require two main types of information: knowledge of the context/situation/problem, and conceptions of practical courses of action/decision options. In each case, there is a need for both information and analysis. What does this mean in practice? We have already discussed the wide range of means by which such information can be acquired; and the phenomena of pattern recognition and rapid interpretation. Here, we consider the more cognitively demanding activities of deliberative interpretation and analysis, for which professionals need to be able to draw upon a wide repertoire of potentially relevant theories and ideas. Also important for understanding the situation is knowledge of the theories, perceptions and priorities of clients, co-professionals and other interested parties. While some may be explicitly stated, others may be hidden, implicit and difficult to detect. Thus one of the most challenging and creative aspects of the information-gathering process is the elucidation of different people's definitions of the situation. Few teachers or headteachers are well prepared for this important aspect of their work.

The other information-gathering task is equally demanding, the formulation of a range of decision options or alternative courses of actions. This depends both on knowledge of existing practice and on the ability to invent or search for alternatives. A particular problem in education is a tendency for even those who are avid networkers to limit their knowledge of practices outside their own school to the level required for conversational facility, which falls far short of that required for making even a preliminary appraisal of its merits. Part of the problem is that most reports refer to work in contexts different from one's own and are written by advocates and enthusiasts of whom one is rightly sceptical. Proper intelligence-gathering is needed, for which the capability to acquire and evaluate information about new ideas and new forms of practice is extremely important. One also needs to avoid ascribing all the responsibility for developing relevant knowledge of practice to one person. It is the combined expertise of the organisation that matters, but how often does anyone attempt to assemble it?

If we confine our attention for the moment to processes like problem-solving and decision-making, much of the literature tends to suggest a rational linear model, in which a prior information-gathering stage is succeeded by deductive logical argument until a solution/decision is reached. In practice, this rarely occurs. Research on medical problem-solving, for example, shows that hypotheses are generated early in the diagnostic process and from limited available data (Elstein et al. 1978). Further information is then collected to confirm or refute these hypotheses. Although described as intuitive, the process is essentially cognitive; but it allows pattern recognition and other experiential insight to contribute at the first stage. In less scientific areas, the need for continuing interaction between information input and possible courses of action is even greater. The information cannot be easily summarised and can usually be interpreted in a number of ways. There is also a need for invention and insight when considering possible actions, so new ideas have to be generated, developed and worked out. The process is best considered as deliberative rather than deductive, with continuing interactive consideration of interpretations of the situation and possible courses of action until a professional judgement is reached about the decision to be endorsed and implemented.

Such deliberation requires a combination of divergent and convergent thinking which many find difficult to handle, especially when working in a team. Some find it difficult to focus sufficiently to be good analysts or are too impatient to think things through, while others feel uncomfortable with any departure from routine patterns of thinking. The need for adopting several contrasting perspectives is also increasingly recognised; and this is one of the arguments for teamwork.

7 Meta-processes

The term meta-process is used to describe the higher level of thinking involved in controlling one's engagement in the other processes discussed above. Thus it concerns the evaluation of what one is doing and thinking, the continuing redefinition of priorities, and the critical adjustment of cognitive frameworks and assumptions. Its central features are self-knowledge and self-management, so it includes the organisation of oneself and one's time, the selection of activities, the management of one's learning and thinking and the general maintenance of a meta-evaluative framework for judging the import and significance of one's actions.

The value of this control process was highlighted by Argyris and Schön (1976) who demonstrated that for many professionals there is a significant gap between their espoused theories (their justifications for what they do and their explicit reasons for it) and their theories in use, those often implicit theories that actually determine their behaviour (see also Day 1982). This gap between account and action is a natural consequence of people's perceptual frameworks being determined by what they want or expect to see, and by people reporting back to them what they think they want to hear. The solution Argyris and Schön recommend is to give priority not so much to objectives – for then one reads situations purely in terms of one's own pre-planned ideas of how they ought to develop – as to getting good quality feedback. Unless one is prepared to receive, indeed actively seek, feedback – which may be adverse or distressing – one will continue to misread situations and to deceive oneself that one's own actions are the best in the circumstances. However, it is not only obtaining good feedback that matters but making good use of it by being open to new interpretations which challenge one's assumptions.

Part 2: The further development of expertise in education

8 The question of quality

One of the most important meta-processes is that of self-development, which provides the focus for the second part of this chapter. However, before proceeding to offer some guidance on how expertise might be developed in each of the four types of process, I want to address the critical issue of quality. My definition of professional expertise is *the capability to perform professional roles*, and, in Part 1, I also argued that *professional expertise is embedded in the quality of the processes that constitute professional work*. This link between capability and quality now needs to be made more explicit.

While recognising that for qualification purposes there has to be some defined cut-off

LIBRARY · UNIVERSITY COLLEGE CHESTER

point at what the NCVQ chooses to call the level of competence, my underlying model assumes that for most professional purposes:

1 there is continuum of capability from very low to very high;
2 capability is partly situation specific and partly transferable;
3 at higher levels of capability in particular, there is likely to be considerable debate about the relative merits of different kinds of performance.

There is plenty of scope for continuing professional learning, transfer should never be taken for granted and there is no universally agreed model of the best teacher or the best manager.

Quality is usually judged by some combination of:

- Stakeholder response, often perceived rather than based on good evidence.
- Connoisseurship, usually based on observation and interview.
- Outcomes, such as documents, test results and pupils' work.

However, the formative judgement of quality is one of the weakest areas of school management. The culture of teaching has traditionally emphasised competence rather than excellence and isolation rather than mutual observation; so connoisseurship has not been well developed. Considerable time and energy gets devoted to the assessment of pupils (this was true even before the 1988 Act) but the information is rarely used for feedback on teaching. The collection of evidence from stakeholders is still an unusual rather than a normal activity.

This problem is exacerbated by the prominence of tacit knowledge, which is mainly developed through experience at times when learning is at best semi-conscious and not under critical control. Some perceptual schemas and interpersonal routines are developed before teachers even begin their training, and some during the early years of teaching: only during training is there much chance of receiving any independent feedback. Likewise many of the perspectives and routines of school managers are developed before they take up their posts. While formal learning opportunities for teachers and managers may be important in developing the quality of their contribution to deliberative processes, they are often ill-suited to developing quality in routinised interpretation and action (see Eraut 1988 for an analysis of the role of management courses). For this it may be better to identify when and where experiential learning is taking place and to try and give it a quality steer.

9 Developing expertise in acquiring and interpreting information

The high reliance put by teachers and managers on informal and experiential methods of acquiring information and rapid interpretations with little deliberation gives considerable scope for misinterpretation. Without significant self-monitoring these processes will be out of critical control, based only on taken-for-granted and largely implicit cognitive and perceptual frameworks. Yet the quality of professional action must necessarily depend on the information on which it is based. The following five suggestions for developing this aspect of professional expertise are derived from the analysis made in section 4.

1 Become aware of one's own constructs, assumptions and tendencies towards misinterpretation.

2 Learn to use additional sources of evidence to counteract any possible bias in one's information base.
3 Find out about the perspectives of the other people involved.
4 Expand the range of one's interpretative concepts, schemas and theories.
5 Make time for deliberation and review.

Deliberation is needed both to ensure a good information base for important decisions, and to maintain critical control through reflective self-monitoring of one's own ongoing, largely tacit, information acquisition and rapid, largely intuitive, interpretations.

10 Improving the quality of skilled behaviour

The main constraints on the further development of skilled behaviour are the natural limits on self-awareness during routinised action, and lack of motivation. [. . .] Nevertheless, there are many possible approaches to improving the quality of skilled behaviour.

1 Get feedback from an independent observer.
2 Make recordings and study them, preferably with some friendly support.
3 Use self-monitoring and collect evidence from others to develop awareness of the effects of one's actions.
4 Observe other people in action.
5 Use the information gained from 1–4 to improve the quality of one's current routines.
6 Expand one's repertoire of routines to meet the needs identified above.
7 Use the information gained to optimise the conditions for effective performance, e.g. timing, grouping, ambience, resources.

Although there is now a tradition, based largely on classroom action research (Elliott 1991) of seeking to improve skilled behaviour in teaching, no such tradition has yet developed in school management. It should be incorporated into the planning of management development programmes to cover such activities as chairing a meeting, leading a working party, or interviewing a parent or counselling a member of staff.

11 Developing expertise in deliberative processes

Section 6 included a number of suggestions; and the quality of deliberation is clearly dependent on the quality of available information (see section 9). However, it is also important to understand the nature of deliberative processes and to know how to handle them, either on one's own or in working groups. The following suggestions are pertinent to developing the quality of professional expertise in deliberative processes.

1 Develop through reading, experience and discussion some knowledge about the various deliberative processes: ways of thinking about them, organising them and making them serve their purpose.
2 Develop appropriate interpersonal skills for contributing to or managing deliberative processes in groups (see section 10).
3 Learn to assemble the appropriate people, expertise and information for production work without incurring too great a cost.
4 Develop a personal and/or group repertoire of concepts, theories, knowledge of practice, thinking skills, etc.

5 Recognise that thinking skills of a high order are needed in tackling practical problems; and get people used to thinking in an action-oriented mode, as opposed to acting in an unthinking mode.

12 Developing the quality of one's meta-processes

Meta-processes have rightly been given a significant emphasis in management education, particularly *self-knowledge* and *self-management*. These last three sections have focused on *self-development*, which critically depends on them both: self-knowledge is needed to give it appropriate direction and self-management to give it sufficient priority. This parallels the need, discussed in the earlier sections, for professionals to make time for deliberation, search for relevant information beyond what has been naturally acquired, and expand their repertoires of routines, schemas, concepts and ideas.

Another important aspect of self-development is understanding the nature of professional knowledge and the different ways in which it is learned. The complexity revealed here should provide a realistic basis for understanding one's own learning.

Also included under meta-processes in section 7, was the conception of a meta-evaluation framework in which values and ethical issues are brought to bear on the direction and control of one's actions. Such a framework is central to any concept of professionalism. I shall conclude, therefore, by stressing two ethical principles which I believe should pervade the meta-processes of any profession (Eraut 1995a). The first is the principle of client-centredness which provides the ethical foundation for the professions; for managers, I would add, the term 'clients' should be expanded to include 'employees'. The second is the moral obligation, with future clients in mind, to improve one's own professional expertise. That principle provides the rationale for this final section, indeed for the whole of this chapter.

References

Argyris, C. and Schön, D. A. (1976) *Theory in Practice: Increasing Professional Effectiveness*. San Francisco: Jossey-Bass.

Day, C. (1982) *Classroom-Based In-Service Teacher Education: the Development and Evaluation of a Client-Centred Model*. Occasional paper no. 9. ICAPE: University of Sussex.

Elliott, J. (1991) *Action Research for Education Change*. Buckingham: Open University Press.

Elstein, A. S., Shulman, L. S. and Sprafka, S. A. (1978) *Medical Problem Solving: an Analysis of Clinical Reasoning*. Cambridge, MA: Harvard University Press.

Eraut, M. (1982)* What is learned in in-service education and how: a knowledge use perspective. *British Journal of In-Service Education*, 9(1): 6–14.

Eraut, M. (1985)* Knowledge creation and knowledge use in professional contexts, *Studies in Higher Education*, 10(2): 117–33.

Eraut, M. (1988)* Learning about management: the role of the management course, in C. Day and C. Poster (eds) *Educational Management Purposes and Practices*. London: Routledge.

Eraut, M. (1992)* Developing the professional knowledge base: conceptions of theory and practice, competence and effectiveness, in R. A. Barnett (ed.) *Learning to Effect* (Proceedings 1992 SRHE Conference), Open University Press.

Eraut, M. (1993)* The acquisition and use of educational theory by beginning teachers, in G. Harvard and P. Hodkinson (eds) *Action and Reflection in Teacher Education*. Norwood, NJ: Ablex.

Eraut, M. (1995a) Developing professional knowledge within a client-centred orientation, in T.

Guskey and M. Huberman (eds) *Professional Development in Education: New Paradigms and Practices*. New York: Teachers College Press.

Eraut, M. (1995b) Schön shock: a case for reframing reflection-in-action? *Teachers and Teaching*, 1(1): 9–22.

Jackson, P. W. (1968) *Life in Classrooms*. New York: Holt, Rinehart and Winston.

Kelly, G. A. (1955) *The Psychology of Personal Constructs* (Vols 1 and 2). New York: W. W. Norton.

Nisbett, R. E. and Ross, L. (1980) *Human Inference: Strategies and Shortcomings of Social Judgement*. Englewood Cliffs, NJ: Prentice-Hall.

Ryle, G. (1949) *The Concept of Mind*. London: Hutchinson.

Schön, D. (1983) *The Reflective Practitioner: How Professionals Think in Action*. New York: Basic Books.

Note

*This material can all be found with other cognate material in Eraut, M. (1994) *Developing Professional Knowledge and Competence*, Falmer Press.

4 | The process of educational management learning*

KATE BULLOCK, CHRIS JAMES AND IAN JAMIESON

Introduction

With devolved autonomy, increased accountability and market forces thrust upon schools in recent years, the field of educational management has become ever more complex. This increase in complexity has been mirrored by a growing realisation of the importance of sound and effective educational management practices in the delivery of the whole curriculum for all pupils (Glatter 1989; Weindling 1990; HMCI 1992). A number of studies (for example, Hoyle and McMahon 1986; Saran and Trafford 1990; Eraut 1993; Southworth 1993) have detailed the skills and qualities that senior teachers require to perform effectively as educational managers, but there have been few published reports of systematic studies of the work of school managers, such as Earley and Fletcher-Campbell (1989), and yet fewer studies that have explored the nature of learning that supports educational management development.

This chapter reports some of the outcomes of an exploratory study of educational managers at different stages in their careers. The study investigated the developmental nature of managerial knowledge and the ways in which that knowledge is acquired. The intention was to reveal the implications for the teaching of educational management which were grounded in the experiences of educational managers, and indicate areas where deeper investigation is warranted.

Research methodology and techniques

The research design concentrated on the use of in-depth interviews to compare the conceptions and experiences of teachers who had just acquired a school management

*This chapter has been edited and abridged. It originally appeared as 'An exploratory study of novices and experts in educational management' in *Educational Management and Administration*, published in 1995.

post with teachers who had substantial experience in similar posts. This technique is supported by other studies into the nature of educational management (Hall *et al.*, 1986; Earley and Fletcher-Campbell 1989) and the process of learning about teaching (Berliner 1987). The groups were carefully selected to represent a range of key variables including seniority, primary and secondary phases, gender and subject area.

Thirteen newly appointed managers were identified through job advertisements in the educational press, and this group was matched closely by experienced managers suggested by colleagues through the School of Education's network of partnership schools. Two teachers who had recently taken on their first post of management responsibility were also included in the investigation. Specific research questions for both novice and expert managers focused on the nature of their educational management knowledge and its development. Discussions concentrated on their prior life and work experiences, the influence on them of particular individuals in schools and other work areas, their conceptualisations of the management role, and individual perceptions and intentions relating to management in an educational institution.

The interviews were carefully analysed for recurring themes and similar phenomena. From this analysis it was hoped that critical factors in the acquisition of educational management skills at different career stages would be identified.

Experience, career paths and progression

This study showed that teachers have the benefit of a wide range of experience, career paths and modes of progression. Thus, learning to become an educational manager takes diverse and idiosyncratic routes. Each developmental opportunity is adapted by educational managers to suit their individual circumstances, personality and needs. The complexity of teachers' espoused theories of, and approach to, management was reflected in their responses to the interview schedule. However, although the transcripts displayed richness and variety, it was possible to identify common trends in the professional development of educational managers.

The original research design sought to explore and compare expectations and experiences of those new to particular management posts with those who were established in similar posts and who were deemed by their peers to be expert. At a very early stage, however, it was realised that the variation and individuality in management development masked any clear demarcation between novice and expert. Few of the so-called novices were wholly new to management, and those in the expert group ranged widely in their experience of management. The data suggested, however, that the development of management expertise could be observed in groups at three career stages. They are those who are:

- educational managers established-in-post;
- educational managers new-to-post;
- teachers new-to-management.

The conceptions and experiences of these three groups have important implications for the development of management skills. Issues which particularly appeared to characterise such growth in expertise were:

- approach to decision-making;
- the practice of delegation;
- views and practice of interpersonal relations.

Educational managers established-in-post

It is, perhaps, not surprising that overall those educational managers who were established-in-post conveyed an impression of being relaxed and secure about the practice of management. There was some agreement that this was a result of the growth in confidence gained through understanding, not only of the organisation and the task, but of personal strengths and weaknesses, and those of colleagues (cf. Eraut 1988). The managers' time in post appeared to have allowed them to take a more holistic and wide-ranging view of their own management tasks in relation to the work of the whole school. These managers tended to be more confident than their less experienced colleagues in their perceptions of the wisdom on which sound management judgements are based.

In their articulations of their principles of educational management, many in this group stressed the importance of taking a considered and inclusive approach to decision-making. One deputy head, in describing his approach to making decisions, enunciated a sophisticated view of the process in relation to his management responsibility:

> It's giving people shared ownership of decisions without giving them the anxiety that things can rebound on them if they go wrong.

This same teacher considered it to be a strength, rather than a weakness, not to make immediate decisions and to take time to consider the available options – also a feature of others in this group:

> If you haven't got the data – you need it before you make a decision. Some people rush into decisions without having the data to make a proper informed and organised decision.

A Head of Mathematics clearly had been influenced by a colleague in this approach to decision-making:

> If you wanted an answer out of him he'd say 'Just give me a bit of time and I'll come back to you' and he always did come back. That's something I've learned.

Knowing when an immediate response is vital and when it is better to pause and reflect may well be a mark of expertise in educational management. Experienced managers have the status and confidence to take time over decisions, but also have the ability to respond more quickly. This may be because they have learned to characterise questions and events into classes of phenomena, and to use schema and principles that have been evolved over time to reach a quick decision. If this is in fact the case, there are similarities between this process and the process of learning to teach (Berliner 1987).

As educational managers became more experienced they were particularly able to inform their decision-making with an overview of the complexity of issues combined with a clarity of purpose and approach which was both perceptive and illuminating. One established primary headteacher in summarising what he had learned from his experience as an educational manager said:

> I come back to the one aspect I feel I have developed over the years which is the ability to relate to people and communicate.

A deputy head gave a clear statement of the overall purpose and priorities of her management practice and how other elements of her practice related to those purposes and priorities:

> The first priority in this school is the children's education. The second priority is staff. I can't see any other way. So it means my concern is the quality of what is going on in the classroom and how things are managed there. If there's a problem with a member of staff that is affecting that then I have a duty to sort the problem out, but the first duty must be sorting out the child. So I'm sympathetic towards staff, but what we do in the class has to be the best we can deliver.

This quotation illustrates another facet of those who are established-in-post. The managers in this group had a sophisticated view of the importance, value and, most significantly, the nature of sound interpersonal skills. One head of faculty explained her concept of interpersonal skills in the following way:

> I think learning different ways of approaching people to do the same task is important. Some of them you can come up front and say 'I'd like you to do that. Can you do it before the end of the week?' With other people you almost have to get them round to thinking it was their idea in the first place and then they'll do it and it will be fine.

In common with the other two groups in this study, a major worry for the established managers was fear of a breakdown in interpersonal relationships with their colleagues. However, while most of those interviewed in this study admitted to disliking – even dreading – confrontations and arguments with colleagues, and stressed that they would much prefer to manage through discussion and negotiation, those established-in-post recognised that confronting issues was a necessary part of their work. Most of the interviewees agreed that they would use similar tactics with staff as they use with pupils, such as allowing room for manoeuvre and avoiding a win–lose situation. This provided an example of the transfer of practice between the classroom and the management role, although, in their descriptions of transactions with colleagues, educational managers appeared to make more use of personal or expert influence rather than positional influence.

It was apparent, however, that antagonistic behaviour from colleagues was encountered infrequently. Major confrontations had not been within the experience of those who expressed most anxiety about them, with only four of all those interviewed recalling such an incident. One difference between those managers who were established-in-post and those in the other groups was that the established managers had come to acknowledge that interpersonal effectiveness in management is not simply about *avoiding* conflict, but is concerned with facing up to it. This group saw the management of conflict as an essential aspect of their role. One Head of Science in describing his management learning in relation to his management of an uncooperative department member reported that:

> One of the characters was generally recognised as being very difficult and I learned to be assertive enough to say 'You're going to do this'.

In the few cases where conflicts had been handled, the anticipation seemed to be worse than the event, with outcomes of learning about sensitivity and diplomacy ensuing for at least one deputy head:

The capability action I had to take taught me if you put your case clearly to staff and explain why you want things to be done, and how you will judge whether they have been done, or not, in a friendly way – then you can see what results you get.

An important developmental step for educational managers is learning to delegate. It can be argued that it is important for the personal and professional development of all teachers, and for organisational effectiveness, that team tasks and responsibilities are identified regularly and shared appropriately. It can equally be argued that the transfer of authority is the key to this process. In schools, the delegation of tasks may be simpler than the delegation of authority, and methods through which authority can be shared may need to be considered. Earley and Fletcher-Campbell (1989) suggest that delegation within school and faculty is an important and complex matter for effective educational managers; and that there are constraints upon the process. Some of the experienced educational managers had been careful to identify areas which could be delegated, and for one, her own learning had enabled her to plan positive staff development tasks:

I started being quite dictatorial and people were very good. But now I've moved round to doing things much more by consensus. We rotate the chair [of department meetings] and I've given people ownership of the meetings and it improved the quality of things that we do.

It may be that both schools and teachers would benefit from a more systematic approach to learning through delegation. This might involve senior colleagues re-linquishing much of their organisational responsibility and final authority to less experienced colleagues, perhaps in a team structure, but offering support by means of theoretical considerations, team discussions and mentoring. It is apparent from this study that the ability to delegate aspects of educational management is complex and not easily acquired; but nonetheless is one of the hallmarks of the expert manager.

Educational managers new-to-post

The educational managers who were new-to-post represented an interesting group. In the original research design it was considered that these teachers would, in many identifiable senses, be starting out on their management learning. This was not so. None of this group was new to management; all had had management experience either at lower levels, or as acting versions of the post which they now held permanently in the same or different organisations. [. . .] As a result of such previous experiences there was considerable overlap with those established-in-post both in conceptions, and experience of educational management. Nonetheless this group did exhibit particular character-istics which are relevant to our understanding of educational management learning.

A general characteristic of this group was that they saw themselves with a task to do. This was often quite specific and it appeared to be seen as a mark of establishing themselves in post. The task may be represented in different ways such as having to 'turn the school around' or simply to establish systems or reorganise a particular function. For one new headteacher this task involved:

organising things like policies for the school, and the National Curriculum, and raising the profile of the school. That's the big priority for this year because unless the children are coming into the school everything else is really irrelevant.

Newly appointed educational managers tended to have targets to achieve and to have clearly explicit criteria for success in a way that those established-in-post did not. There seemed to be an urgency about the 'being new' as though they had only a limited opportunity to achieve. This urgency contrasted with the established-in-post group, although newly appointed managers recognised there was a balance between taking sufficient time for settling in, observing and analysing, and leaving it too long before taking action and making decisions.

Although their identification of specific tasks and success criteria helped to focus choices at a certain level, on the whole the new-to-management group tended to be less relaxed about decision-making than their more experienced colleagues:

> The problem in a meeting is that you want to be able to answer straightaway and I can't necessarily think on my feet very well.

Some new-to-post managers felt that the ability to speak articulately and respond quickly in formal and informal meetings correlated with influence and peer respect, although for many this was not the preferred mode of activity.

In contrast to the established-in-post managers, many in the new-to-post group felt the avoidance of conflict was important. 'Settling in' was couched in interpersonal terms which stressed the importance of establishing good relationships and clear lines of communication in the school and the department. One head of department articulated this very clearly:

> I think the essence of good management, certainly within a school and I would guess elsewhere, is the ability to relate to and communicate with people.

For one manager it was an important concern that the department functioned together – professionally and socially – something which, as a new faculty head, she was keen to facilitate:

> People should begin to find a value, a benefit, in connecting their ideas, rather than feeling threatened by working together and people should seek out opportunities of being together.

The issue of establishing sound interpersonal relations by whatever means is significant for new-to-post managers. They have a task to complete, typically with some degree of urgency, but in an unfamiliar context and working with only recently encountered colleagues. They are anxious not to confront, but equally anxious to complete the task. In a few instances, those new-to-post feared they might experience expressions of obstructive jealousy from their colleagues:

> A particular member of staff was very 'anti' because she wanted the acting headship herself. I knew that was going to be difficult. Even that wasn't on the face of it as difficult as I'd anticipated.

Several of those interviewed in the new-to-post group admitted that they found delegation difficult. Reasons for this seemed to be rooted in an aspiration for status and influence which, at this career stage, was consonant with the leadership of current practice. Certainly, a number of new-to-post managers stressed that they felt they wanted to be seen to be leading from the front. It may be necessary for new-to-post managers to make an acknowledged contribution to the leadership and organisation of the school before being able to identify areas suitable for delegation. Some managers in this group also admitted they did not wish to add to the workloads of colleagues whom they perceived to be already over-stretched. It may also be that new-to-post managers do not have the requisite knowledge of their colleagues and the working context to construct the strategies to support delegation at a comfortable level.

Teachers new-to-management

Two of the teachers who were interviewed in this exploratory study were completely new to management. These two had recently been given a post of first responsibility, and their characteristics are discussed in this survey in order to illuminate the importance of delegation in the early stages of becoming an educational manager.

These teachers who were new-to-management conveyed a sense of the importance for their own self-esteem, and for their standing in the eyes of colleagues, of being wholly responsible for an organisational facility. One of the teachers expressed this very directly:

> I really did want responsibility. When I got my 16–19 responsibility my head of department was off on maternity leave and there was someone else in her place. I was left very much on my own and I liked that. If there was a problem then it was my fault and I was left to get on with it.

The new-to-management group valued being delegated to, and wanted ownership of the tasks. Consequently, delegation was a characteristic of the more senior managers whom they valued. For one teacher, this issue is illustrated by the difficulty she experienced when the teacher, whose responsibility in part she had taken on, returned from maternity leave:

> When X came back she was much more on my tail or doing things just before I was about to do them. She couldn't quite relinquish responsibility.

However, accomplishing or managing that delegated task with the necessary co-operation of others can be difficult, as the following quotation illustrates:

> I have no clout at the moment and I think, if you want to force things through, eventually you just have to do it yourself. I have to prioritise things. When you ask people to do things you obviously have to be very polite and go about it in a roundabout way. If people I'm dealing with are my peers or slightly above me then I *ask* them to do things.

The important issue emerging from these observations is that many schools may not, as yet, be effective in helping teachers who are new-to-management to learn about the practice of delegation. There appeared to be three main reasons for this. Firstly, teachers who are new-to-management are only beginning to learn appropriate interpersonal procedures for delegation. Unless they have work or life experiences in another field which have enabled them to acquire the appropriate skills, they are unlikely to have considered strategies for delegation during their initial teacher education courses. Secondly, being near the bottom of a perceived hierarchy, teachers may be given management tasks but have no power to delegate and no obvious recipient of a delegated task. Thirdly, the new-to-management group are keen to be recognised and acknowledged as the successful generators of activity. All this is in contrast to some well-respected established managers who have expertise in the interpersonal strategies for overcoming barriers to delegation; who understand which responsibilities can be usefully delegated to other members of their managed group, and have the authority to do so; and who, typically, do not need to be seen as generators of activity.

Perhaps not surprisingly, fear of conflict was an important issue for these new-to-management teachers. For one this was expressed as her worst fear. She reasoned that the most appropriate strategy for avoiding conflict and creating appropriate working relationships was to 'be friendly'.

The difficulty in managing others that these young teachers faced is reflected in how they saw their management practice. The management task became central, and efficiency, represented by meeting deadlines, was considered vital. To attain this, the new-to-management teachers tended to carry out the tasks themselves without delegation. They were not managing others; they were achieving tasks for others.

For this group of new managers, management images were characterised by having energy and self-confidence, and by having power and positional influence. The new managers had energy in apparent abundance; but were not overly confident in their interpersonal skills, although they felt that they were carrying out management roles where a high level of interpersonal skill was required. Furthermore, they felt that they had neither the power nor positional influence.

A summary of the issues – and some implications

This exploratory study of novices and experts in educational management has sought to shed light on the complex process of educational management learning. Despite the wide variation between individual educational managers' learning pathways, several issues have emerged. For experienced managers, significant aspects of their expertise centred upon the development of a considered and inclusive approach to decision-making, the delegation of responsibility, and a relatively sophisticated understanding of interpersonal relationships. This contrasts most directly with the characteristics of those new to management. Those new-to-post often face the difficult challenge of being expected to display expertise and achieve important management tasks but typically without adequate situational knowledge nor specific knowledge of the people with whom they have to work. The findings are represented in Table 4.1.

It could be argued that the established educational managers have learned to manage collaboratively (Caldwell and Spinks 1988) and that educational management itself can be viewed as collaborative practice (James 1993). Such a conception of educational management would include a complex view of educational management knowledge and theory as both shared and personal, and open to a wide range of interpretations; a recognition of the importance of reflective practice; a commitment to the autonomy of self and others; and a commitment to continuous improvement. Managing in collaborative cultures may be in sharp contrast to the images of managers and management that some of this group, particularly those new-to-management, may hold. Moving on from those images may well be an important starting point in the management development of new educational managers.

The implications of this study for individuals, schools and continuing teacher education are important and significant. They include the following:

• There is a need for more research into the processes of educational management learning and the influences upon it. There is a need for a greater understanding of the

Table 4.1   Aspects of educational management practice

	Decision-making	Delegation	Interpersonal skills
Established-in-post	Reflective and considered approach; take time if needed; understand the complexity of the system; but have identified the priorities	Clear strategies for delegation; have identified tasks for delegation; will transfer authority	If necessary will face up to, and learn from conflict
New-to-post	Challenged by the need to display expertise without situational knowledge; have identified a priority task to establish themselves in the school	Want to lead from front; uneasy about delegation; may not want to overburden colleagues	Aware of the importance of communication and good relationships; want to avoid conflict and 'settle in'
New-to-management	Have little authority; decisions don't tend to impact on others	Want to be delegated to; but need power as well as task	Fear of conflict; a typical strategy is to be 'friendly'

learning that takes educational managers from novice to expert. This will enable those in schools who are new to management to be managed more appropriately and effectively.

- Management development is necessary for all managers. It needs to be continuous and on-going, and to acknowledge the complexity of management knowledge and the idiosyncratic nature of the individual educational manager's development. Management tasks are now so complex in schools, and the processes required of senior teachers to achieve them so sophisticated, that management development cannot be left to chance, or to ambitious and enthusiastic individuals taking the initiative on their own behalf.
- Early management training is needed. It is clear that teachers begin to take responsibility for management tasks at an early stage in their careers. All teachers should have the benefit of educational management training and there may be a case for including aspects of it in initial teacher training courses.
- Prospective educational managers need to understand the skills of decision-making, and the processes of schematic classification which underpins a well-considered decision. Sharing the decision-making processes in schools might enhance this ability in new managers.
- Delegation has emerged as a significant issue in this study and as an important element in the difference between novice and expert educational managers. This study indicates that potentially a substantial amount of learning can result from delegation. It may be that both schools and teachers would benefit from a more systematic approach to the process of delegation and to the facilitation of the learning which can take place. Such an approach would require senior colleagues relinquishing their

organisational responsibilities and final authority to less experienced colleagues in a more considered way, while offering support, challenge and vision (Daloz 1986) by means of theoretical considerations, individual and team discussions and mentoring.

● Interpersonal skills in the management role, particularly in relation to the issue of conflict, need to be addressed directly in management development. The major concern for both new and experienced managers, in this study, was a fear of a breakdown in interpersonal relationships.

References

Berliner, D. (1987) Ways of thinking about students and classrooms by more and less experienced teachers, in J. Calderhead (ed.) *Exploiting Teachers' Thinking*. Lewes: Falmer.

Caldwell, B. and Spinks, J. (1988) *The Self-Managing School*. London: Falmer Press.

Daloz, L. (1986) *Effective Teaching and Mentoring*. London: Jossey-Bass.

Earley, P. (1992) *The School Management Competences Project: Final Report*. School Management South.

Earley, P. and Fletcher-Campbell, F. (1989) *The Time to Manage*. Windsor: NFER-Nelson.

Eraut, M. (1988) Learning about management: the role of the management course, in C. Poster and C. Day (eds) *Partnership in Education Management*. London: Routledge.

Eraut, M. (1993) The characterisation and development of professional expertise in school management and teaching, *Educational Management and Administration*, 21, 4.

Glatter, R. (ed.) (1989) *Educational Institutions and their Environments*. Milton Keynes: Open University Press.

Hall, V., Mackay, H. and Morgan, C. (1986) *Head Teachers at Work*. Milton Keynes: Open University Press.

HMCI (1992) *The Handbook for the Inspection of Schools*. London: OFSTED.

Hoyle, E. and McMahon, A. (1986) *The Management of Schools*. London: Kogan Page.

James, C. R. (1993) 'Developing reflective practice skills – the potential', invited keynote paper to The English National Board for Nursing, Midwifery and Health Visiting Power of the Portfolio Conference, Nottingham, November.

Saran, R. and Trafford, V. (eds) (1990) *Research in Education Management and Policy*. Lewes: Falmer.

Southworth, G. (1993) School leadership and school development: reflections from research, *School Organisation*, 13, 1.

Weindling, D. (1990) Secondary school headship: a review of research, in R. Saran and V. Trafford (eds) *Research in Education Management and Policy*. Lewes: Falmer.

5 | Analysing management for personal development: theory and practice

NIGEL BENNETT

How do we improve our performance at work? Since the mid-1980s vocational training has moved away from an academic or college base towards a stronger focus on practice which makes more of the skills and abilities of expert practitioners. Often this has involved moving the physical location of training into the workplace.

This is also true of management development. In England and Wales, the School Management Task Force came out firmly in favour of 'on-the-job' or 'close-to-the-job' training (SMTF 1990), with university courses and qualifications being supportive of this work rather than leading it. Clearly visible behind this policy move was a view of teaching and management practice which opposed practice to theory and preached the virtue of the first at the expense of the second.

Such a view is at best naive and at worst dangerous. Practice is not a rag-bag of activities. Good practice rests on our understanding of what a job *should* entail, which we then compare with what we *actually* do. We also consider why our actions have the results they do, and try and find ways of doing better. Thus we have a theory of our job, which informs our judgements about the quality of our practice. The two are inextricably connected. Our theory of our work derives from all kinds of sources, including such knowledge taught to us by our colleagues, what 'worked' in the past, our experience and observation of others doing the same or similar work, our reading and our education and training. One of the most important sources is our own value system: what we believe to be right and good in a given setting.

Discussing this, Young (1981) proposed that in all our actions we are influenced by what he called our 'assumptive world'. This denotes our values and assumptions about how things actually happen and what we ought to do in particular settings. Thus in any given situation, we would create an understanding of what is happening and how we fit into it by turning to our knowledge of similar circumstances (our personal experience and second-hand knowledge such as our reading) and our personal attitudes and values which cause us to regard certain elements of the situation as more important than others. This would enable us to perceive what we could possibly do: we might feel powerless to intervene, or able to influence directly the outcome of the situation. Thus whenever we have to make a decision, we construct a new 'theory of the situation' in order to work out what it is appropriate to do. This is usually similar if not identical to previous occasions, but may become profoundly different on occasions. Argyris and Schön (1978) called their similar concept an individual's 'theory-in-use'. However, they argued that this personal set of beliefs was different from, and might conflict with, the public profession of values and expectation which the person might make, which they christened 'espoused theory'. For example, a headteacher who publicly avowed collaborative decision making, with the staff possessing ultimate authority in the school, might act in practice in an autocratic way, bullying those staff who opposed him or her. The headteacher would have an espoused theory of collegiality and an autocratic theory in use.

If our practice is a reflection of our understanding of our circumstances and our perception of what our job involves, it follows that we can only improve what we are doing if we are clear about that understanding and prepared to put it under review. This involves what Argyris and Schön (1978) call 'double loop learning', in which we reflect not only on what we do but consider the reasons why, and allow for the possibility that those assumptions about good practice may need to be revised. Figure 5.1 shows the nature of double loop learning. You will note that single loop learning explores a problem without attempting to reconsider the assumptions which lead us to define it as that particular problem. Double loop learning allows us to call the very definition of the problem into question, including whether 'it' is a problem at all! If we are to engage effectively in any process of personal development as current or prospective managers, then we have to enter the double loop of examining our assumptions and understandings so as to consider a number of basic questions. What do we understand management to involve? What do we assume about the way people act towards each other? How do we judge what is good and bad management? Only then can we begin to make effective progress towards improving our performance. Although ideally we should develop our answers to these questions in relation to real situations and practical problems needing resolution, this chapter will attempt to give some starting points to inform your own personal reflection.

What does 'management' mean?

Management has become an important activity within education, as with all other public services. Yet it remains unpopular, and is frequently equated with 'them' in everyday speech as the source of most of the problems encountered by teachers and lecturers in going about their work. Under the label of 'the new managerialism' (Deem *et al.* 1995), some educators have claimed that it generates a set of values hostile to the interests of learners and the work of teachers.

Even critics acknowledge that we have to reconcile the diverse interests of people involved in the education of students: distributing limited funds, allocating time and staff resources, and sorting out problems which individuals may not be able to handle, such as major disciplinary issues or health and safety concerns. Balancing all these pressures, setting direction, and ensuring that everything is going well is management's responsibility. This is because most education takes place within organizations, which have to acquire resources and deploy them in order to achieve results. We will not discuss the characteristics of organizations here, but if a school or college exists to bring about

Single loop learning   **Double loop learning**

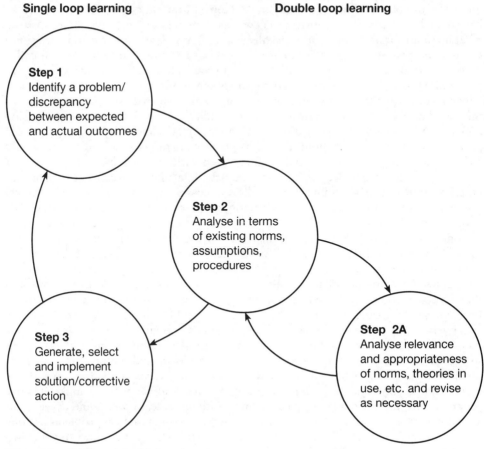

Figure 5.1   Single and double loop learning
Source: Morgan (1986)

education then decisions have to be made which will allow that to happen as successfully as possible. Management is therefore, in principle, a rational activity in that it is concerned with finding the most effective and efficient ways possible of deploying resources in order to achieve the purposes of the organization. However, what represents the best way to manage is itself problematic, for it depends on what assumptions underlie the manager's view of how human beings behave, and what they ought to do and why.

Two basic concepts of management, and their limitations

1 Taylorism

One view, sometimes referred to as Taylorism after the American F. W. Taylor (1911), sees humans as essentially lazy and interested in obtaining maximum reward in return for minimal effort. Consequently, a manager has to exercise close supervision over all aspects of a subordinate's work in order to ensure that each job is completed satisfactorily. This requires a detailed specification of what each job involves, and a separation of each aspect of work into a multiplicity of smaller, tightly bounded tasks, each of which is to be completed repetitively by an individual who would do nothing else. Thus the classic production line was born.

This view of human behaviour within organizations has certain consequences. We must coordinate the various tasks being performed by each individual, and ensure that they all know what they are doing. Their work must be monitored to prevent slacking or unsatisfactory results. Raw materials and other resources have to be obtained in a continuous flow, and organized within the workplace so that each person gets only what is needed for the task, but exactly when required. Thus we arrive from this view of the demands of the production process at the five classic managerial responsibilities which have underpinned most management analyses since the early twentieth century, most succinctly defined by Gulick and Urwick (1937):

> To *plan* means to study the future and arrange the plan of operations.
> To *organize* means to build up material and human organization of the business, organizing both men [*sic*] and materials.
> To *command* means to make the staff do their work.
> To *co-ordinate* means to unite and correlate all activities.
> To *control* means to see that everything is done in accordance with the rules which have been laid down and the instructions which have been given.
> (Gulick and Urwick 1937: 119, emphasis added)

In fact, Gulick and Urwick added two other elements, *budgeting* and *staffing*, since they saw these two key resourcing considerations as being separate from planning and coordination.

This mechanistic view assumes that the world is a stable place. Managers can set up long and complex systems when demand for their product is stable and predictable. It also ignores the needs or interests of the people whose work is being managed. If the world isn't so stable, then it may be appropriate to distinguish between what we might call day-to-day management, in which immediate problems are anticipated and prevented or picked up and solved, and longer-term management, in which the broader direction of the organization and the nature of its work are explored. This latter responsibility, which involves keeping a careful eye on external developments and trying to identify possible opportunities for expansion or areas of work which should be abandoned, is usually seen as a senior management responsibility, and is often referred to as 'strategic management'. Day-to-day management is more typically seen as directly related to the primary task of the organization, and is seen as a 'middle management' responsibility. Both, however, are concerned with creating as stable a set of circumstances as possible within which to plan, organize, command, coordinate and control the work of the people they manage in a rational pursuit of clear goals.

Writers examining management from a feminist perspective argue that the characteristics of managerial work just outlined are those traditionally associated with masculine behaviour. Women are greatly underrepresented in senior management positions in industry and commerce, and Al-Khalifa (1992) pointed out that since management training has become more widespread in education, the percentage of female head-teachers has fallen. This suggests a further assumption in traditional management theory, consistent with social attitudes in the early twentieth century when Taylor wrote: that management is a male task.

Much work has been done to remedy some of the deficiencies of this model. Mayo (1933) and Follett (in Metcalf and Urwick 1942) took a less pessimistic view of human motivation, stressing the importance of working conditions and suggesting that self-interest was not the only basis upon which people operated. Others have suggested that management should not be about control but about facilitating or enabling people to do their work. This has normally been presented in terms of managers setting up systems and procedures within which work could be carried out, intervening to repair or adjust them when they fail, and finding means of generating new ones to cope with new circumstances (Morris 1975; Cuthbert and Latcham 1979). Within the system, individuals get on with their work with a minimum of supervision or control.

Although these writers have moved this school of management writing away from the narrowly mechanistic metaphors which underpin Taylorism, two crucial dimensions link them together. First, managers are concerned with directing and controlling their workers, either directly through supervision or through the construction of self-regulating systems. Second, because the world is an orderly and rational place, it is possible to identify both unambiguous goals for an organization and a set of activities that will achieve those goals better than any other. This emphasis on rational planning and direction establishes it as the view expressed in the most recent Ofsted handbooks of guidance for school inspection (e.g. Ofsted 1995).

2 Non-rational management

An entirely different stance on the nature of management questions this assumption of rationality, and may also challenge the extent to which management is a control activity. Even within the Taylorist tradition, rationality was seen as necessarily limited by Simon (1948), who argued that managers could never know everything about a situation – a precondition of full rationality. The best that could be expected was what he called 'satisficing' actions. Some more recent writers have adopted a perspective which sees management as being about coping with chaos, and assumes that much of our behaviour may not be rational at all. For example, Mintzberg (1990a, first published 1975) dismisses our five managerial tasks as nothing more than vague objectives in the back of managers' minds, and argues that management is typically about coping with crises, and keeping the ship afloat amidst constantly threatening seas.

In Mintzberg's view, managers' responsibility for their units or sub-units within an organization gives them the *authority* to take decisions and set the direction of work, but they gain the *ability* and *knowledge* to do this from the informal network of information and understandings which they acquire from being there. Their decisions are not so much guided by the data in computerized information systems as by information from informal sources, such as colleagues' gossip or friendly chats at the golf club or health club. They learn how to judge which sorts of information can be relied upon and which can be discounted. They also 'know' which clients or colleagues are important and which ones are less significant. Thus managers bring to bear on any situation a range of organized but essentially personal and non-scientific information – an assumptive world – and act accordingly.

Mintzberg also suggests that the formal authority which managers possess over their units or sub-units within their organization provides them with an element of status. The combination of formal authority and status fashions particular kinds of social relationships, and within them managers play different roles at different times. Through their actions in playing out these roles they acquire information which enables them to take decisions on behalf of the unit. Mintzberg analyses ten roles, which he groups under three headings as follows:

Interpersonal roles:
Figurehead
Leader
Liaison

Informational roles:
Monitor
Disseminator
Spokesperson

Decision roles:
Entrepreneur
Disturbance handler
Resource allocator
Negotiator

The figurehead and leader roles are closely interrelated. 'Figurehead' is essentially a positional role. It incorporates key ceremonial and formal tasks which must be carried out by significant members of the organization for presentational or public relations purposes. The leadership role exerts both direct and indirect influence on the work of others. It involves, among other things, motivating others and reconciling individual and organizational desires and expectations. The liaison role is also important, involving the contacts managers make with colleagues outside their unit, and Mintzberg claims that research shows that managers spend more of their time working with others outside their unit than they do with their colleagues inside it. (They spend least time of all working with their superiors.) Through liaison they develop the informal network of contacts through which they gather the crucial 'soft' information which keeps them one step ahead of the opposition. By opposition, we do not only mean outside competition for markets: we may face opposition from within our organization, for example in our quest for resources.

In Mintzberg's view, this information places managers at the centre of their organizational units, typically more knowledgeable than their subordinates even if not omniscient. They are both spokespersons for their unit into the wider organization and disseminators of information into their units.

The interpersonal and informational roles are major sources of the means to carry out the four decisional roles Mintzberg identified. As entrepreneurs, managers act to initiate change and generate additional activities and resources, while as disturbance handlers they respond to problems which arise in their units, such as the sudden illness of a key member. The resource allocator role covers the distribution of tasks and responsibilities as well as money and materials, and is an absolutely crucial role. The last decisional role is that of negotiator, which covers anything from smoothing over minor disagreements between colleagues to negotiating new contracts of employment or with potential suppliers.

Instead of management as the rational sense of one best way to achieve a goal,

Table 5.1   Insightful and cerebral faces of management

Insightful	Cerebral
Stresses commitment	Stresses calculation
Sees the world as an integrated whole	Sees the world as the elements of a portfolio
Uses a language which emphasizes the personal values and integrity of the individual manager within the organization	Uses the words and numbers of rationality

Source: The Open University (1992: 18)

Mintzberg offers more intuitive *non-rationality*, when there is no one best way, but many possibilities. We decide how to act, not on the basis of the systematic evaluation of data, but on a combination of data, gossip, best-guessing and hunch. He therefore argues that we must identify the skills involved in coping with non-rational circumstances of chaos and uncertainty, which are necessary to discharge effectively each of the ten managerial roles he identified. He further emphasized that these ten roles formed an integrated whole, a *gestalt*, and could not be seen in isolation. However, in a commentary (Mintzberg 1990b) on a later reprint of his original article, he suggested that we should perhaps see the rational and non-rational models as complementary, and that his analysis identified an insightful dimension to set alongside the cerebral, analytical view of management. Elsewhere, I summarized the difference between the two views as shown in Table 5.1.

This alternative dimension moves thinking about management firmly away from management as an activity aimed at bringing about the organization's completion of its key tasks in the one best way towards one based on a much greater acknowledgement of the importance of taking risks and having to back judgement. Certain of the tasks of the rational model still have to be carried out: planning is necessary, and organizing. But instead of a language of control and demand, Mintzberg's later comments move us towards a set of meanings resting upon shared commitment, empowerment of the workforce, and delegation. Table 5.2 summarizes the difference between the meanings and assumptions of the traditional rational/cerebral model and those of the non-rational, insightful perspective just discussed.

Table 5.2   Rational/cerebral and non-rational/insightful models of management

	Rational/cerebral	Non-rational/insightful
Relationship between manager and managed	Control	Empowerment
View of organizational activity	Segmentation	Holism
View of the world	Totally rational: one best way	Limited rationality: multiple and perhaps competing rationalities

Source: Bennett *et al.* (1992: 8)

Good and bad management: a question of values and meanings?

It is clear from the preceding discussion that writers from the two broad schools identified there would be quite likely to come to different judgements about the quality of management activity they witnessed in any particular setting. We must also recognize that our own thinking about educational management is expressed through language which has particular meanings surrounding it, and involves us in making statements which derive from specific assumptions and starting points. For example, many teachers and academics resist the meanings implicit in the use of commercial and business language in relation to education. For them, saying that education exists in a marketplace, and using production metaphors to describe the process of learning and teaching, turns education into a commodity and imports an alien set of values into education. However, we suggested at the start of the chapter that part of our work of improving on our professional practice may involve questioning those very values which act as building blocks to our traditional understanding of right and wrong.

Moving to judgement: what do we need to examine?

We can consider this question by taking three specific foci:

- the particular organizational activities, or 'functions' for which managers are responsible;
- the criteria by which we assess how well those functions are discharged;
- the activities which managers undertake, and what they need to know and be able to do in order to do them.

In making these judgements we also relate the overall pattern of activities we observe to our overall concept of management.

Functions

Most management theory identifies four specific management functions. Marketing management involves ensuring that what is done in the organization is wanted by the people it is intended for. Financial management involves ensuring that the organization has sufficient resources to perform its key task, and that those resources are used to maximum effect. Personnel management is concerned with ensuring that the necessary people are available to do the tasks needed by the organization, and the final function, 'production' management, is used as the omnibus term to describe whatever the organization does as its primary activity. Schools and colleges 'produce' education.

Not all the meanings and assumptions in this apparent commodification of education need be hostile to the interests of the learners. One is the 'primacy of production': organizations exist for a purpose, and the management of demand, resources, and staff should be geared to providing the means to achieve that purpose. Thus, educational management is about facilitating teaching and learning, and managers who lose sight of this should not be deemed competent. Second, there is also an implicit expectation that the 'production' activity somehow increases the value of the resources employed, a concept which has now received official acceptance in the research for ways of assessing a school's 'value-added' for the DfEE 'league tables'. Thus, children leaving school should have benefited from their time there. Third, there is an assumption that the product is wanted: it is serving a perceived need. However, it might appear to assume that the organization's work involves taking inert raw materials and processing them in some way. This is a danger in much current official writing on schools, and within the school-effectiveness literature more generally.

The finance and staff functions have always been acknowledged in education. Curriculum management is the equivalent of production management, and the primacy of production implies clearly that curriculum and financial decisions should be interwoven, with curriculum issues and needs driving the financial decisions rather than the other way round. And the central government's policy of creating quasi-markets in the public services has placed a premium on effective marketing management.

Criteria of judgement

If management is purposive activity, then a key criterion of judgement is whether or not it is achieving its purposes: whether it is *effective*. This term needs to be distinguished from its two companions, *economy* and *efficiency*. The easiest way to distinguish them is to think of the relationship between inputs, intentions and outcomes. Economy is concerned purely with reducing the amount of resources being used – the input – without regard to the consequences. Using less photocopier paper would be an economy, but might affect the quality of the resources available to students.

Efficiency goes one step further, by relating the actual inputs to the actual outcomes. It requires some means of measuring both. Thus, if your measure of output was examination passes in a given subject, and if you could increase class size without affecting the examination results achieved by the students, then you would be more efficient. Similarly, if the results improved year on year while the class size stayed the same, that would also be more efficient.

Effectiveness compares your intentions with what you actually achieved. If you intended to achieve better examination results, then any action which achieved this would be effective against that goal, even if it was terribly expensive, such as one-to-one tuition. In practice, managers would seek to balance efficiency and effectiveness. In the examples in the previous paragraph, if your goal was improved examination perform-ance, then keeping class sizes constant would be effective as well as efficient, whereas increasing class size would not, since exam results did not improve.

Clearly these are very simple examples, and in practice there is always a trade-off between different goals, as well as between the issues of effectiveness and efficiency. Even with examination results to hand, measuring educational effectiveness is difficult. How do you judge the effectiveness of, say, a sex education programme? When we add in the staff function, assessing both efficiency and effectiveness can be even more problematic, since even when your intentions can be defined clearly it can be difficult to measure how far you are successful.

These three criteria are almost universally observed among management writers. A fourth 'e', which introduces a moral and ethical dimension into the goals managers seek to achieve as well as the means they employ to achieve them and the actions they require of others, is the issue of *equity*. This refers to the extent to which access to resources by actors in the organization can be defended on the grounds that it either does not disadvantage any individual in their work or compensates them for previous disadvan-tage. It is the basis, for example, of the equal opportunities policies in place in most institutions, and can have profound implications for assessing management practice in areas like staff development, student services and curriculum provision.

Activities

To discharge their managerial duties, managers must be able to understand and analyse a situation and act as they deem appropriate. Thus, a manager may decide that a meeting is necessary to resolve a problem. Once it is under way, it may be necessary to encourage a reticent member to speak, curb an overbearing colleague or even discipline those whose behaviour threatens others. Summarizing the discussion and keeping it from getting diverted may also be necessary. After the meeting, a summary of the results is needed, and it may be seen as appropriate to report to senior colleagues on what happened. Our manager needs therefore to be able to exercise discretion in order to decide what to do at any given moment, and to call upon a repertoire of specific actions that may be appropriate. This refers us back to the discussion of assumptive worlds and theories-in-use at the start of this chapter, as the manager calls upon their knowledge and experience of similar situations and their understanding of what it is proper to do.

The capacity to act appropriately in a particular setting has been analysed in a number of ways, for example as skills, competences and capabilites. In a sense these three concepts are nested within each other. Skills may be seen as highly specific technical activities which can be defined in detail and learned through drill and practice. Because such detailed specification is possible, we can also define different levels of skill relatively easily. For example, when assessing someone's ability as a clarinet player, we can examine their ability to read music, their manual dexterity (how fast can they play semiquavers), their breath control, and so on, and to compare two candidates in a reasonably consistent way.

Competences may be seen as clusters of skills. For example, 'can maintain sound discipline in a classroom' could be seen as a competence, in that it would rest upon the exercise of a range of discrete skills, each of which could be described independently of the others. It would also require the teacher to be able to identify which ones to use, and when. Running a meeting thus becomes a competence because of the number of separate skills involved. We will look shortly at two different approaches to analysing management as a set of competences.

Some writers have suggested that the concept of competences does not provide a sufficient basis for analysing management, or any other professional practice. The ability to recognize the need for a meeting can be seen as a higher-order competence than the cluster of skills to run it once it is set up, resting on a deeper understanding of the wider situation in which the manager functions. Thus knowledge and understanding link with knowledge of how to do something and with the ability to predict the likely outcomes of a course of action to form what have been called meta-competences (Fleming 1991) or capabilities (Cave and Wilkinson 1992; Eraut 1994).

Two competence-based models of management

The concept of capabilities has not yet been developed extensively within management education, whereas much training and development is carried out within the competence-based framework. It is therefore appropriate to conclude this chapter by examining briefly the two major models of management competences. The first was developed by the Management Charter Initiative (MCI 1991, 1995) within the UK's national vocational qualification (NVQ) framework; and the second, by the American company McBer (reported by Boyatzis 1982). We can compare them by posing three questions:

- Are we concerned with 'satisfactory' performance or 'superior' performance? The two may involve practitioners in doing different things.
- Are the competences we define in relation to our measure of performance (satisfactory or superior) to be regarded as specific to that job in that setting or as generic to all such jobs wherever they are to be found?
- Do we see the development of management competences as resulting on a hierarchical view of managerial work, with full competence being necessary at each level of seniority since the competence requirements at the next level will require *additional* competences rather than a *different* set?

The MCI model of competence

MCI claim to identify the basis of *satisfactory* management performance. Because they are working within the NVQ model, they engage in what is called 'minimum competence testing', in which the set of competences represents a baseline statement of performance. The result is a detailed statement of what are claimed to be all the competences required for satisfactory performance of a management post at a particular level of seniority (junior, middle or senior). Consequently, a candidate for an MCI award has to show ability in every element of the competence statements which MCI have prepared.

MCI competences are argued to be generic to *all jobs at that level of seniority*. They are related to characteristics of the job, not of the person doing it. The person has to be able to show competence in all the tasks required of them in the job. Further, the structure within which the competences are defined relates them to the *key purpose* of the organization, and to the *roles* which that level of management seniority must perform in order to achieve it. Thus, in order to establish which competences are required for a job, we have simply to identify the level of seniority that it occupies within the management structure.

An important point which arises here is that since the competences are job specific rather than person specific and represent a minimum standard of acceptable performance of the job, they cannot be 'partly' possessed or demonstrated. One is either 'competent' or 'not competent' in the MCI scheme.

Because the competences are defined in relation to the job, and jobs are differentiated by level of seniority, the MCI model assumes that management skills grow by accretion. The competences for 'management 1' performance are also required for 'management 2' performance, although the criteria by which satisfactory performance of them is judged may change as do the circumstances in which they are demonstrated. The additional competences required for the next level can be seen in most cases to develop from a sound grasp of others in the previous level.

Management development within the MCI model is therefore a steady process of developing a satisfactory standard of performance in a complete set of competences, and then carrying them forward to a more sophisticated standard as you move on to a more senior post. The McBer is more complex and difficult, because it rests on entirely different assumptions. It is worthwhile to mention that when the MCI moved from defining middle management competences to preparing the 'standards' for senior management assessment, their hierarchical model could not be sustained, and the pattern of development by accretion does not carry through from level 2 to level 3 as it did from level 1 to level 2.

The McBer model

McBer competences are defined as the basis for *superior* rather than satisfactory performance. They were defined by identifying managers who were generally agreed by colleagues to be superior, and differentiating what they did from the rest. So whereas the MCI model is an all-or-nothing view of competence, the McBer approach allows that superior managers may not possess all the competences identified for superior performance in that position, although the very best managers will, of course, possess them all.

Because they are concerned with superior rather than satisfactory performance, McBer competences are related to characteristics of the person in the job rather than the job itself, and are generic to a quality of performance at a given level of seniority. Consequently, whereas MCI competences relate to the role played by the post in discharging the key purpose of the organization, McBer competences relate to the clusters of actions which the individual performs in doing the job.

Within the McBer system competences are not just possessed or not possessed. Because they relate to personal characteristics, competences come in different forms, and can be possessed at different levels of consciousness. Some, such as stamina or self-control, may inform our actions unconsciously, while others may be consciously deployed, like a personal commitment to care for the feelings of others. These levels of competence are called, respectively, traits and motives, and social role and self-image. A third level of consciousness is the specific skills which the manager is able to demonstrate, such as what the model calls 'the diagnostic use of concepts' – in effect, the ability to call upon practical and theoretical knowledge and ideas to assist in understanding a problem and defining an appropriate course of action. Traits, motives, social roles and self-image are crucial to all managerial performance, not merely superior performance, since they are the means by which we link our assumptive worlds and theories-in-use to practice.

Second, some competences are what are called 'threshold' competences: necessary for superior performance but not in themselves a guarantee of it. It is argued that managers who possess them are able to develop those competences which do ensure superior performance, while those without them cannot.

In the McBer model, there is no hierarchical relationship between the competences. Some competences associated with superior performance at one level are not associated with it in a more senior position, and may even be associated with poor performance.

The differences between the MCI and McBer competency models are summarized in Table 5.3.

Conclusion

Competence-based models are not the only approach to management development, and these are not the only two. They are, however, increasingly influential. This chapter has

Table 5.3   Comparison of the MCI and McBer models of management competence

MCI competences	*McBer competences*
1 Competence defined as the basis of *satisfactory* performance	Competence defined as the basis of *superior* performance
2 Competences are either possessed or they are not possessed: they cannot be partly possessed	Competences can be possessed by a manager at several levels: they can inform behaviour unconsciously (as traits or motives) or consciously (as self-image or social role), or be demonstrated as skills
3 All competences identified at a given level have to be demonstrated for satisfactory performance to be agreed	Certain competences are necessary as 'threshold' competences for superior performance: i.e. needed for it to be achieved but not causally related to it
4 Competences are related to the characteristics of the *job*	Competences are related to the characteristics of the *person in the job*
5 Competences are related to the roles which make up the job	Competences are related to the clusters of action which make up the job
6 Each set of competences incorporates and extends those of the previous level of managerial seniority	The competences required for superior management performance at a given level of seniority do not automatically incorporate all those which were required for superior performance at a more junior level

Source: The Open University (1992: 29, amended)

concluded with this comparison of MCI and McBer not to advocate one or the other, but to demonstrate how careful consideration of the three questions posed at the outset can lead to a clear sense of what your personal management development needs may be.

References

Al-Khalifa, E. (1992) Management by halves: women teachers and school management, in N. Bennett, M. Crawford and C. Riches (eds) *Managing Change in Education: Individual and Organizational Perspectives*. London: Paul Chapman Publishing.

Argyris, C. and Schön, D. (1978) *Organizational Learning in Action: a Theory in Action Perspective*. Boston, MA: Addison-Wesley.

Bennett, N., Crawford, M. and Riches, C. (1992) Introduction: managing educational change: the centrality of values and meanings, in N. Bennett, M. Crawford and C. Riches (eds) *Managing Change in Education: Individual and Organizational Perspectives*. London: Paul Chapman Publishing.

Boyatzis, R. E. (1982) *The Competent Manager: a Model for Effective Performance*. New York: Wiley.

Cave, E. and Wilkinson, C. (1992) Developing managerial capabilities in education, in N. Bennett, M. Crawford and C. Riches (eds) *Managing Change in Education: Individual and Organizational Perspectives*. London: Paul Chapman Publishing.

Cuthbert, R. and Latcham, J. (1979) Analysing managerial activities, *Coombe Lodge Information Bank, no. 1410*. Blagdon: Further Education Staff College.

Deem, R., Brehony, K. and Heath, S. (1995) *Active Citizenship and the Governing of Schools.* Buckingham: Open University Press.

Eraut, M. (1994) *Developing Professional Knowledge and Competence.* Lewes: Falmer.

Fleming, D. (1991) The concept of meta-competence, *Competence and Assessment*, 16: 9–12.

Gulick, L. and Urwick, L. (eds) (1937) *Papers on the Science of Administration.* New York: Columbia University Press.

Management Charter Initiative [MCI] (1991) *Management Standards Implementation Pack.* London: MCI.

Management Charter Initiative (1995) *Standards for Managing Quality.* London: MCI.

Mayo, E. (1933) *The Human Problems of an Industrial Civilisation.* Boston, MA: Harvard Business School, Division of Research.

Metcalf, H. C. and Urwick, L. (eds) (1942) *Dynamic Administration: the Collected Papers of M. P. Follett.* London: Management Publications Trust.

Mintzberg, H. (1990a) The manager's job: folklore and fact, *Harvard Business Review*, March–April: 163–76 (orginally published 1975).

Mintzberg, H. (1990b) Retrospective commentary, *Harvard Business Review*, March–April: 170.

Morgan, G. (1986) *Images of Organization.* London: Sage.

Morris, J. (1975) Developing resourceful managers, in B. Taylor and G. L. Lippitt (eds) *Management and Development Training Handbook.* New York: McGraw-Hill.

Office for Standards in Education [Ofsted] (1995) *Handbook of Guidance for the Inspection of Nursery and Primary Schools.* London: Ofsted.

The Open University (1992) Making Sense of Management. Unit 1 of E629 *Managing Educational Change.* Milton Keynes: The Open University.

School Management Task Force [SMTF] (1990) *Developing School Management: the Way Forward.* London: HMSO.

Simon, H. (1948) *Administrative Behaviour: a Study of Decision-Making Processes in Administrative Organizations.* New York: Macmillan.

Taylor, F. W. (1911) *Principles of Scientific Management.* New York: Harper.

Young, K. (1981) Discretion as an implementation problem, in M. Adler and S. Asquith (eds) *Discretion and Welfare.* London: Heinemann.

6 | Competence in educational management*

JANET OUSTON

Introduction

This chapter draws on two areas of study: management competence and school effectiveness. These are both areas which have created considerable interest over the last few years in education management, but are rarely considered alongside each other. The two areas are reviewed, similarities between them are explored, and their contribution to education management is discussed.

Both areas appear to have the potential to contribute to better managed, more effective, schools. School effectiveness has been researched for nearly 20 years, across many countries and differing educational systems. The interest in managerial competence is, in the UK, a more recent development, although in the USA this work started in the late 1970s. Both are concerned with identifying good practice – very broadly school effectiveness research focuses first on what pupils achieve, and the management competence movement on what teachers do. This chapter will be more concerned with the competences approach, reflecting the current interest in management competence in education and the move nationally to competence-based accreditation (CNAA-BTEC 1990a, b, 1991; Jessup 1991; Fletcher 1991).

The competence approach

What is it that is attractive about the competence approach? Its initial appeal was that it might provide a structured description of management in education; it might offer a comprehensive overview of what good education managers do and, in the longer-term, help us to develop a coherent theory of education management. It might offer guidelines

*This is an edited version of the article 'Management competences, school effectiveness and educational management' that originally appeared in *Educational Management and Administration*, published in 1993.

to help us decide what a comprehensive management development programme ought to include.

First what is meant by competence? A basic definition is that given by the Training Agency (1988):

> A description of something which a person who works in a given occupational area should be able to do. It is a description of an action, behaviour or outcome which the person should be able to demonstrate.

More recently the School Management South (SMS) project (Earley 1992a, b and c) has developed the Management Charter Initiative (MCI) (1990) approach to managerial competences for schools. The MCI focused on developing a generic approach to management competences, which are intended to be applicable across a wide range of organisations. Earley extended this approach to schools, redefining and adding to MCI's scheme. The SMS analysis divides management in education into four 'key roles or functions': the management of policy, learning, people, and resources. These are then sub-divided in tasks with associated performance criteria.

In a recent research project (Ouston *et al.* 1993) teachers with management responsibilities were asked to describe the knowledge, skills and qualities they needed to be able to carry out their main responsibilities effectively. Their responsibilities were classified according the SMS scheme; senior managers in the sample reported that just under half were concerned with the management of people (42 per cent) while those with middle management roles reported management of people and of learning (37 per cent) as being of equal importance. Both Earley's work (1992a, b and c) and our smaller scale study suggested that the SMS approach did 'make sense' to teachers although they did not perceive their responsibilities as spread equally across all four areas.

Through the remainder of this chapter I will use two approaches to competence as examples: the School Management South (Earley 1992a, b and c) approach which is skills- and behaviour-focused, and the National Educational Assessment Centre Project (1991) approach which is concerned with qualities, such as judgement and values. These are currently the most widely used in education management and offer a contrasting approach. They are not, however, the only schemes of managerial competence. Esp (1993) has recently reviewed these, and other, approaches to competence.

Approaches to competence

Within the competence movement there has been considerable debate about the balance to be sought between skills, qualities, 'personal effectiveness', knowledge and understanding. The 'fundamentalist' wing focuses entirely on skills and performance, arguing that personal effectiveness, and knowledge and understanding, are evident in performance, and do not have to be considered separately. But even the fundamentalists acknowledge the problem of assessing the performance of senior managers because the complexity of these roles makes an entirely skills-based approach impractical even though it might be theoretically possible.

The 'liberal' wing argue that qualities are more important in senior management roles: e.g. creativity, problem solving skills, good judgement, and it is these that are the key to managing schools.

Earley (1992a) sets out very clearly the contribution that the management competence approach might make to the development of education managers but also expresses some reservations:

> Competence is a necessary but not sufficient criterion condition for good management. We could all imagine an individual fulfilling competences as described in a particular area and yet failing to be perceived as a good manager. It is the very bits that are explicitly not assessed in this approach, i.e. the personal qualities that so often attain or hinder the achievement of the 'Key Purpose'.
>
> (Earley 1992a: appendix 3)

There are several other aspects of some approaches to management competence that remain problematic. Questions of value and philosophy are not addressed in the MCI/SMS approach. We know how important it is for schools to have a clear philosophy to underpin their practice (Greenfield 1991). This is even more important at a time when schools are required to respond to the market-place. Yet there is little in the SMS competences to help us. The 'Key Purpose' of education management is said to be to 'Create, maintain, review and develop the conditions which enable teachers and pupils to achieve effective learning' (Earley 1992a). What is meant by effective (or competent), and is it the same for all? These questions also tend to undermine the apparent clarity of the school effectiveness research, and as I shall argue later, is one of several common issues that underlie both the competence-based approach and the study of school effectiveness. It should be pointed out that a lack of explicit focus on values is not an inevitable consequence of the competence approach. The National Educational Assessment Centre (NEAC 1991) approach includes educational values as one of its competences, and other occupational areas (such as those for outdoor education, training and recreation) have also made them explicit (Everard 1992).

The competency approach feels as if it may contribute to the de-professionalisation of teaching. There is little about being proactive in defining the role and activities of those working in schools. Or does this merely reflect a change which started elsewhere? Ribbins (1990: 92) argues that teachers are no longer 'independent professionals' due to the 'evolving reality of life and work in schools'.

The competency approach also seems to underestimate the complexity of education management. Does the attempt to break everything down into elements of performance actually destroy what we are studying? Everard summed up this reservation by saying that the competence approach 'is like using a quantity surveyor rather than an artist to capture the grandeur of St Paul's' (Everard 1990: 15). Barth (1986) and Vaill (1991) also express their unease with 'list logic'. Education managers have to be able to do many things at once, using different competences in different combinations according to context. It is quite possible to imagine a senior teacher who can perform all 'the competencies' but not in the everyday environment of a large school. It is also quite possible to imagine a teacher who manages excellently in one school culture and is completely incompetent in another. This raises the whole question of context which is only partly met by the addition of range statements to the list of competences.

The approach is very individualised. Effective leaders have to empower their colleagues to contribute to the management of the whole institution and ensure that all the management tasks are undertaken by someone. They do not have to do everything themselves. The management team as a whole has to have the required competences (Belbin 1981) rather than each individual. It is, of course, possible to use competences in this way although it was not the original intention of the MCI scheme.

Lists of competences are based on past practice and may become out of date very quickly. Cullen (1992) describes this as 'driving using the rear view mirror'. In a time of rapid change competences will reflect what good managers could do yesterday, rather than what they have to do today and tomorrow. They may also not include new tasks (for example, marketing and fund-raising) which very quickly become important for the effective management of the institution.

But is a skills-based model actually valuable, even in non-managerial work? If one is concerned with the competence of mechanics to change car wheels it is possible to assess whether they can do this. But skill is only one part of performance. We also need to know whether they will do it effectively every time – questions of motivation, of inter-personal relationships of physical and psychological state will intervene. Within the competence movement these psychological issues are grouped together under the heading of personal effectiveness (Grubb Institute 1988; Taylor and McKie 1989, 1990; MCI 1990) but in the SMS approach they are subsumed within 'managing people'.

Might a focus on qualities be more productive?

The argument for using qualities rather than skills seems to centre around three of the issues discussed above:

- that managers work in an integrated way – managing is not a sequential exercise of discrete competencies' (Burgoyne 1989: 57);
- the importance of values in underpinning education managers' decisions and actions (Barth 1986, 1990);
- the need to include aspects of individual and social psychology and what has become called 'personal effectiveness'.

The definition of a quality is not unproblematic: does a skill plus the relevant personal effectiveness become a quality?

Hay (1990) argues strongly that higher level 'managerial characteristics' are more appropriate than 'managerial competences' in complex organisations. One of the major difficulties in assessing qualities, however, is the problem of reliability. There appears to be a tension between reliably assessed skills that may not offer much validity, and possibly valid qualities that cannot be assessed reliably. [. . .] Examples of a qualities-based approach to competence are presented by Boyatzis (1982), Burgoyne (1989), Jenkins (1989), Pedler et al. (1991) and Southworth (1990).

The role of knowledge and understanding

None of the 'schools' of competence deny the importance of knowledge and understanding in managing organisations but it receives less emphasis than skills and qualities. For example:

Competent managerial standards, as specified by MCI Management Standards, are supported by a body of knowledge and understanding of facts, figures, theories, methods, procedures, possibilities, opportunities and threats. Without this knowledge and understanding effective action is not possible.

(Management Charter Initiative 1990: 1)

MCI divides knowledge and understanding into three groups: purpose and context; principles and methods; and data (MCI 1991). But this is factual knowledge rather than theoretical or conceptual knowledge.

In general the competence movement is not concerned with assessing knowledge and understanding for its own sake, seeing this as the traditional path in British education, i.e. assessing 'what you know' rather than 'what you can do'. But it is important even at the lower NCVQ levels. For example, a mechanic is faced with an engine that is misfiring. There may be many reasons for this and the problem may be best solved using knowledge and understanding of how engines work in addition to specific skills. For professionals, too, knowledge and understanding will underpin effective performance.

We now move on to look at some of the issues that arise in the study of school effectiveness and to draw out some similarities with those in the competence approach.

Studies of school effectiveness

The study of school effectiveness started with an interest in school differences. The question was 'do schools differ from one another in their outcomes once differences in intake are taken into account?' This was a black box model: the interesting questions concerned input and outcome; there was no attempt to explain the differences between schools. In the second stage researchers tried to relate what went on at school to outcomes adjusted for intake. This developed into the school improvement movement: the assumption here was 'if we make ourselves more like effective schools our outcomes will improve'.

The features of effective schools

Three or four years ago I could safely have presented a list of the features of effective schools. Now I cannot. As Reynolds (1992) argued, nearly all the old truths that we taught our students were the specific features of effective schools have been disproved. This may be due to four rather different reasons.

First, just as there are different definitions of managerial competence, there are different definitions of effectiveness. Here the main contrast is between relative effectiveness and absolute effectiveness. Second, the variables selected for study have varied. It does not seem surprising that if you ask different questions you come up with different answers. Third, the key features that are found to relate to school differences in outcome will depend on how similar, or different from each other the schools are. Fourth, it has been assumed that research findings could be transferred across different cultures and communities. Thinking back to our own study of London schools in the mid 1970s (Rutter et al. 1979) the features that emerged as typical of effective inner city comprehensive schools would not, I think, have been found in an identical study of surburban grammar schools in the same city at the same time. The process of moving from apparently simple and universal truths to an appreciation of the complexity of the issue, to the need to try to be aware of all the inter-relationships between culture, context, values, and behaviour may well become typical of the study of managerial competence. Is the competence movement now where the school effectiveness movement was 10 years ago?

Reynolds and Packer (1992) argued (although they do not use this language) that studies of school effectiveness in the 1990s will become studies of school management.

This is partly because schools are loosely coupled systems: even if one could prescribe exactly the features of an effective school one could not put them into effect without taking account of the special demands of management in a loosely coupled system with professional staff rather than in a more tightly line-managed structure. Leithwood and Montgomery (1986) and Leithwood *et al.* (1987) among others talk about the effective school leader being a 'problem solver' rather than a 'good administrator'. Similarly, effective schools are seen as 'learning schools' (Barth 1990).

The link that has not been made explicitly is that effective schools are well-managed schools, and well-managed schools have competent managers.

Common issues in effectiveness and competence

One of the central issues in school effectiveness research is disentangling causes from effects. I will give a simple example as an illustration: one of the findings reported in *Fifteen Thousand Hours* (Rutter *et al.* 1979) was that the more effective schools had pot plants in classrooms. But no-one would believe that buying five dozen pot plants will make a school more effective. We are confusing description with prescription, and further, we are confusing description of an indicator of school effectiveness with a prescription for school improvement. Of course one would hope that they are linked, but through complicated institutional and inter-personal processes rather than directly.

The competence approach has a similar problem: we attempt to describe competent managers and then teach other managers to be more like them. Vaill (1991) offers an example to illustrate the issue.

> If I see it raining, I can predict that I will see people with umbrellas. But if I see people with umbrellas, can I predict with equal probability that it will rain? No. . . . Probabilities are not symmetrical in many cause–effect situations, yet I see no one in the competence movement seriously considering this phenomenon in the study of managerial competencies.
>
> (Vaill 1991: 36–7)

A related issue is the question of validity. We can assess the tidiness of head's desk and we might be able to do this quite reliably. But would it be a valid way of assessing the effectiveness of the head? How do we distinguish between valid indicators and spurious ones?

A major problem that the school improvement movement has inherited from its intellectual grandparents is the question of what is meant by effectiveness; a consensus has sometimes been taken for granted. The grandparents – school differences researchers in the mid-1970s – made their own definitions which those reading the research could either accept or reject. This is a central issue in daily practice, in school improvement and in management competence programmes. Who is to define good practice and effective outcomes? Different groups of stakeholders will have different definitions. For any individual school these definitions are at the heart of its philosophy and values.

Why have so few links developed between these two areas of study?

It is surprising that there have been few links made between school effectiveness and management competence. It is self-evident that poor management will lead to a school being less effective than it might be. Reynolds (1992) makes all these points very cogently: he argues that school improvement in the 1990s must be more concerned with internal aspects of school life, and with those more challenging areas of values, philosophy, culture and management, but this has not been a general approach.

Both approaches are 'movements'

One of the first similarities to explore is the fact that 'effectiveness' and 'competence' are both often referred to as 'movements'. This suggests a commitment to using a particular framework to look at schools and their organisation and management.

Farrar and House (1986) in their report on the evaluation of Project Excel distinguish between 'programs' and 'movements'. They suggest that programmes are 'structured educational reforms with an implementation blueprint' (p. 163) while movements are about 'change by conversion' (p. 184). While this may be slightly overstating the case it does pick up the rather special quality of commitment which seeps through papers on both competency and school effectiveness in its later years. It is probably this commitment to what have become 'movements' which has kept the areas of study apart. They also had very different antecedents – the school effectiveness work grew from the study of institutions while work on competences grew out of the assessment of individuals. Vaill (1991), too, distinguishes between 'cults' and 'fields of enquiry'. A cult promotes 'a feeling from outside that one either buys the approach or one doesn't'. This is contrasted with 'fields of enquiry' where 'divergent views, debate and the expectation of further development are the norms' (p. 64). Perhaps cults and movements can't talk to each other.

Uses of competence models in education management

Earlier it was suggested that the managerial competence movement might help to provide a firmer conceptual base for our understanding of management in education. This is perhaps best approached through a review of how competences are used in education.

There seem to be four different broad uses, which are often treated as if they are indistinguishable, when in fact they are rather different. It is important to consider them separately as the competence model has different strengths and weaknesses in each area.

The four ways of using the competence model are:

- as a basis for appraisal and accreditation of a manager's current performance, and possibly using the outcomes as a basis for performance related pay;
- for selection and promotion;
- to define training needs;
- to plan management development programmes.

The first expectation of competence, set out at the start of this chapter, was that it might help us to understand what management in education is, that is to provide a comprehensive description of the role of a manager in education. This is only done in general terms and does not seem to be an area of concern for those working with competence-based models. Rather it feels as if it is taken for granted. The MCI/SMS approach sets out a key purpose, and key roles or functions. But the problems in this approach seem to be located in defining the performance criteria and range indicators rather than in these original definitions. But are the key roles (of managing policy, managing learning, managing people and managing resources), and the units, elements, performance criteria and range indicators totally comprehensive for all schools? Do they have to be, or are we in the same position as the school effectiveness researchers in arguing that certain measures are indicators of success, of competent management performance, rather than complete descriptions of the competent performance?

Appraisal and accreditation of current performance

If skills are clearly defined in behavioural terms, then they can be assessed directly. But there are several related issues here.

The competence approach focuses on assessment under conditions as near as possible to those in which they are normally displayed, ideally in the workplace. 'Performance must be demonstrated and assessed under conditions as close as possible to those under which it would normally be practised' (NCVQ 1989). Black and Wolf (1990) acknowledged the problem of assessing the performance of senior managers in competence terms:

> In general we find that performance evidence is not appropriate or feasible for assessing standards that deal with irregularities and other non-predictable events. However, the most pressing reason for using knowledge assessment concerns standards that imply or specify competence involving a wide range of variation. In such cases, it would be theoretically possible to continuously observe performance until the full range had been exhausted, but this is quite impractical. Such circumstances are most likely to occur in higher NCVQ levels.
>
> (Black and Wolf 1990: 17)

As they suggest, some of the most effective management actions may be almost invisible as they prevent problems occurring. An effective manager can be seen to deal effectively with a crisis; a more effective manager doesn't have crises to resolve.

Selection and promotion

Competency approaches to selection and promotion must be seen as merely one source of information to be taken into account in the selection process. There are, however, concerns that the information provided by competence-based assessment will be seen as being more important than other sources. It is expensive, and it looks 'scientific'. Will this lead governors and others to give the assessment more weight than it deserves?

Using the competence model for selection and promotion has all the problems related to the assessment of current performance, with three additional problems:

- If one is assessing someone for promotion it is not, by definition, possible to see them at work in that role. We have therefore to develop indicators of what will be good performance in the future. We have to develop psychometric measures, or simulations, to test out qualities and skills that predict future good performance.
- We also have to build into the selection model a view of what future demands might

be. If the model is very skills based, rather than qualities based, it is likely to reflect the present rather than the future.

- If the promotion is in a new school, the mesh between the new staff member and the institutional culture is very important, as is the mesh between the members of the new management team (Belbin 1981).

Identifying individual training needs

The competence model is often said (Jessup 1991, for example) to offer a direct link between assessment and training. But is it always entirely straightforward? Taking an example from the SMS standards, one of the performance criteria concerning disciplinary actions is 'staff are kept informed of the current procedures'. If this was not happening it could be identified as a 'training need' and the relevant action taken.

But if one is working in a qualities framework, this becomes more difficult. If, for example, a weakness is identified in an individual's problem analysis, decisiveness or sensitivity, the approach does not suggest how it might be remediated. This is not to say that one cannot help people to develop their sensitivity, but that the competence models do not offer any obvious process by which this might be achieved. We cannot move directly from a low score on a particular area of competence to individualised management development programmes. Taking another example, imagine a teacher who scores low on 'vision'. Can we send him/her on a one day 'vision course' to improve their performance? Ratings might well improve, but actually developing the ability to clarify and articulate a personal, and an organisation's, vision would take a long time and might require major conceptual changes and changes in management style.

Boak (1991) in his book on management learning contracts sees the move from assessment of performance to planning individual training programmes as quite unproblematic. But he focuses on skills rather than qualities, and on relatively junior managers. Other reported work includes using management development contracts between heads and deputies in primary schools. Mentoring, too, seems likely to offer a more productive approach to these important issues.

These questions have parallels in the potentially misleading links between 'school effectiveness' and 'school improvement'. Purchasing pot plants may make an ineffective school look more like an effective school for a while. But if the management processes of the school don't change, then nothing important will change in the longer-term – and the pot plants will probably die.

Planning management development programmes

Over the last 10 years management development programmes in education have moved from 'learning about' to 'learning how to'. Poster (1987) has explored this in more detail. Competence models will encourage this development even further.

Management learning must take account of process, on a model of how adults learn. Our own work (Gold 1993) is based on Kolb's (1984) learning cycle – usually on starting with the participants' experience, through structured reflection, conceptualisation, experimentation, and new experience. The new experience is reflected on and the learning cycle continues. What people take away from our programmes is, ideally, extended skills underpinned by new or expanded concepts and understanding. Using this model to develop sensitivity, for example, one has to plan a very careful mix of experiences, reflection, support for emerging new concepts and the opportunities to experiment. We find this model of adult learning very effective, but it has two features that do not fit the ethos of a competence-based programme. First, there is an emphasis on underpinning concepts, and second, being away from the workplace for a brief period is valued. It is difficult to become a 'reflective practitioner' (Schön 1990) in the hurly-burly of school life. This view was not supported by the Task Force on School Management (Department of Education and Science 1990) which argued for school-based management development. Alexander (1991) says that, using this model of professional development, 'the poor school ends up merely recycling and reinforcing its inadequacies' (p. 5). This is our concern too.

I have not been very positive so far about the contribution that a competence-based approach might make to professional development. It has one, but not in the way that those in the competence movement often suggest. It seems possible that a sensitive and effective assessment of an individual's competence, using either of the models discussed here, might provide valuable material for the reflective stage of the learning cycle. The profile which results from competence-based assessment may be an important piece of evidence which individuals can use to help them understand their own management performance and to develop new strategies.

Mentoring within the school is an interesting current development in many schools and LEAs: it certainly fits the competence model more comfortably, and is task and outcome focused – a requirement for the model (Jessup 1991). Perhaps the most helpful comparison is with clinical training in medicine, where students are closely supervised in their early clinical work. This is not done instead of a theory-based education, but alongside it.

The very individualised nature of the competence model (as usually implemented) is of little help in planning school-based organisation development programmes. Sometimes individual development needs become apparent, but often interpersonal skills and the culture of the staff and the school as a whole are the most powerful influences on its effectiveness. Even if the school does not take a collegiate approach, and is very 'managerial', the culture of the school and its effectiveness is not totally under the control of senior staff. Other teachers, parents, pupils and the wider community will all influence its development. An organisation development approach, which places these issues centre-stage may be more powerful and more effective than one based on either competence models or school effectiveness research.

Key issues

There are several key issues that have emerged in this chapter, and some are similar in both the school effectiveness and the competency approach.

In each there may be a confusion between description and prescription. In describing an aspect of good practice, what is described may be a consequence of actions elsewhere rather than the cause of positive outcomes. In both areas of study we need to distinguish between processes, indicators and outcomes.

A major problem for both approaches is finding a balance between general descriptions of good practice and the particular needs of specific schools at particular times in their history. General descriptions are needed, but individual schools need help to develop the right management style for themselves. Working within either of these approaches there has to be a compromise between the universal and the individual.

The level of variable under consideration is also a key issue in both areas. Relatively low level, behavioural, variables can be measured reliably but may have little validity. Higher order variables may have validity but be difficult to measure reliably. Integrating different types of variables into one explanatory model is a major challenge.

Research in competence and school effectiveness usually results in a list of features. What weighting should be given to each? Is 'managing people' more, or less important than 'managing policy'?

Finally, should we be concerned about the consequences of using either of these models? Has the school effectiveness movement improved the quality of education? Will the competence model improve how our schools are managed? Studies of school effectiveness 15 years ago can now be seen as leading to the pressure to publish exam league tables. What will be the consequences of the competency model in the year 2000?

References

Alexander, R. (1991) *Primary Education in Leeds: Briefing and Summary.* Leeds: University of Leeds School of Education.

Barth, R. (1986) On sheep and goats and educational reform, *Phi Delta Kappan*, 4: 293–6.

Barth, R. (1990) *Improving Schools from Within: Teachers, Parents and Principals can Make a Difference.* San Francisco: Jossey-Bass.

Belbin, R. M. (1981) *Management Teams: Why They Succeed or Fail.* London: Heinemann.

Black, H. and Wolf, A. (1990) *Knowledge and Competence: Current Issues in Training and Education.* Sheffield: Department of Employment COIC

Boak, G. (1991) *Developing Managerial Competencies: the Management Learning Contract Approach.* London: Pitman.

Boyatzis, R. E. (1982) *The Competent Manager: a Model for Effective Performance.* New York: John Wiley.

Burgoyne, J. (1989) Creating the managerial portfolio: building on competency approaches to management development, *Management Education and Development*, 20(1): 56–61.

CNAA-BTEC (1990a) *The Assessment of Management Competences: Project Report.* London: CNAA.

CNAA-BTEC (1990b) *The Assessment of Management Competences: Guidelines.* London: CNAA.

CNAA-BTEC (1991) *The Assessment of Management Competences: Opening up the Debate.* London: CNAA.

Cullen, E. (1992) A vital way to manage change, *Education*, 13, November 1992.

Department of Education and Science (1990) *Developing School Management: the Way Forward.* London: HMSO.

Earley, P. (1992a) *The School Management Competences Project: Final Report.* Crawley: School Management South.

Earley, P. (1992b) *The School Management Competences Project: a Guide to Evidence Collection and Assessment.* Crawley: School Management South.

Earley, P. (1992c) *The School Management Competences Project: Standards for School Management.* Crawley: School Management South.

Esp, D. (1993) *Competences for School Managers.* London: Kogan Page.

Everard, K. B. (1989) Competences in education and education management, *Management in Education*, 3(2): 14–20.

Everard, K. B. (1990) A critique of the MCI TA NCVQ competency approach as applied to education management, *Education Change and Development*, 11(1): 15–16.

Everard, K. B. (1992) Personal communication.

Farrar, E. and House, E. (1986) The evaluation of Push/Excel: a case study, in E. House (ed.) *New Directions in Educational Evaluation*. London: Falmer Press.

Fletcher, S. (1991) *NVQs, Standards and Competence*. London: Kogan Page.

Gold, A. (1993) Women-friendly management development programmes, in J. Ouston (ed.) *Women in Education Management*. London: Longman.

Greenfield, T. (1991) Re-forming and re-valuing educational administration: whence and when cometh the phoenix? *Educational Management and Administration*, 19: 200–17.

Grubb Institute (1988) *The Wider Implications of Personal Effectiveness*. London: The Grubb Institute.

Hay, J. (1990) Managerial competences or managerial characteristics? *Management Education and Development*, 21(5): 305–15.

Jenkins, H. O. (1989) Education managers – paradigms lost, *Studies in Educational Administration*, 51: 3–26.

Jessup, G. (1991) *Outcomes: NVQs and the Emerging Model of Education and Training*. Lewes: Falmer Press.

Kolb, D. A. (1984) *Experiential Learning: Experience as a Source of Learning and Development*. Prentice-Hall: Englewood Cliffs, NJ.

Leithwood, K. A. and Montgomery, D. J. (1986) *Improving Principal Effectiveness: the Principal Profile*. Toronto: OISE Press.

Leithwood, K. A., Rutherford, W. and van der Vegt, R. (eds) (1987) *Preparing School Leaders for Educational Improvement*. London: Croom Helm.

Management Charter Initiative [MCI] (1990) *Management Competences: the Standards Project*. London: MCI.

Management Charter Initiative (1991) *Management Knowledge and Understanding Specifications*. London: MCI.

National Council for Vocational Qualifications (1989) *National Vocational Qualifications: Criteria and Procedures*. London: NCVQ.

National Educational Assessment Centre Project (1991) *Headstart: Newsletters 1 and 2*. Oxford: NEAC.

Ouston, J., Gold, A. and Gosling, P. (1993) The development of managers in education, in J. Ouston (ed.) *Women in Education Management*. London: Longman.

Pedler, M., Burgoyne, J. and Boydell, T. (1991) *The Learning Company: a Strategy for Sustainable Development*. London: McGraw-Hill.

Poster, C. (1987) School management training in the United Kingdom, in K. A. Leithwood, W. Rutherford and R. van der Vegt (eds) *Preparing School Leaders for Education Improvement*. London: Croom Helm.

Reynolds, D. (1992) School effectiveness and school improvement: an updated review of the British literature, in D. Reynolds and P. Cuttance (eds) *School Effectiveness: Research, Policy and Practice*. London: Cassell.

Reynolds, D. and Packer, A. (1992) School effectiveness and school improvement in the 1990s, in D. Reynolds and P. Cuttance (eds) *School Effectiveness: Research, Policy and Practice*. London: Cassell.

Ribbins, P. (1990) Teachers as professionals: towards a redefinition, in R. Morris (ed.) *Central and Local Control of Education after ERA 1988*. London: Longman.

Rutter, M., Maughan, B., Mortimore, P., Ouston, J. and Smith, A. (1979) *Fifteen Thousand Hours: Secondary Schools and their Effects on Children*. London: Open Books.

Schön, D. A. (1990) *Educating the Reflective Practitioner*. San Francisco: Jossey-Bass.

School Management South (1991) *School Management Competences Project: Standards for School Managers*. Crawley: SMS.

Southworth, G. (1990) Leadership, headship and effective primary schools, *School Organisation*, 10(1): 3–16.

Taylor, T. and McKie, L. (1989) *Report on Desk Research for the Employment Department*

Training Agency: Project 7 Personal Effectiveness. Bridgewater, Somerset: Somerset Area Management Centre.

Taylor, T. and McKie, L. (1990) *Summary Report on Personal Competence: a Management Competence Standards Project.* Bridgewater, Somerset: Somerset Area Management Centre.

Training Agency (1988) *Guidance Note 3.* Sheffield: Training Agency.

Vaill, P. B. (1991) *Managing as a Performing Art: New Ideas for a World of Chaotic Change.* San Francisco: Jossey-Bass.

Note

This chapter is a revised version of my contribution to the BEMAS Workshop on Management Competences and Schools Effectiveness held at the James Gracie Centre, Birmingham in December 1991.

I would like to acknowledge the contribution of members of the BEMAS Competences Group to my understanding of management competences. Summaries of the earlier workshops are reported in Beck and French, 1990a and 1990b. Bertie Everard (1990a,b, 1991) started me thinking about competence and Peter Earley pointed me towards a great deal of useful published and not quite published material.

7 | Developing managerial capabilities*

ERNIE CAVE AND CYRIL WILKINSON

A two-phase research project undertaken by the Education Management Unit of the University of Ulster investigated two issues: What do education managers need to be good at? How can their capability be improved?

In the first phase the researchers sought to identify and distil essential capacities which the education manager requires in order to perform effectively in key areas of management. A management capability model emerged and is presented as a working tool which might be used in planning management development initiatives. The second phase explored how the model might be used to plan development programmes that are more specifically targeted in their intentions.

The background

A major concern in management literature has been the development of management competences. Since the purpose of the study of management is to improve performance, it is not surprising that attention should be focused on an analysis of what abilities managers need in order to be effective, and various categorizations have emerged. [. . .]

In the field of education the growing recognition of the crucial importance of good management practices in school was dramatically strengthened by the impact of 'local management of schools' imposed by the 1988 Education Reform Act. Central government clearly regards management development as a key element in its declared strategy for ensuring improvement in the quality of education to meet the needs of industry and the economy. Fortunately the years that followed the Act have coincided with the period when serious doubts are being expressed about the basic idea of

*This is an edited version of Ernie Cave and Cyril Wilkinson's chapter entitled 'Developing managerial capabilities in education' in *Teaching and Managing: Inseparable Activities in Schools*, published in 1987.

analysing a professional management task into itemized elements of competence. It is increasingly recognized that the overall ability to perform effectively is more than the sum of a set of subordinate abilities. Jacobs (1989) makes the point that while it is possible, by obtaining and carefully analysing performance data, to identify clusters of behaviour that can be reliably and logically classified as competences, what is obtained is only a partial and fragmented view of the complexity of management. Management performance involves other activity which is difficult to isolate and describe; it involves qualities and abilities which are not easy to observe or discover; it has outcomes which defy measurement.

The Management Task Force set up by the Secretary of State for Education to identify and explore some of the issues involved in management development in schools has largely rejected the prescription of training in an arbitrarily determined set of skills as the way forward. This has contributed to a growing conviction that those who manage are in the best position to identify what their needs may be. Thus the identification of need is a major concern among providers of management development and it is generally held that it is essential for schools to feel ownership of the programmes through being fully and directly involved in planning their content, style and procedures.

The idea that managers themselves are best able to determine their own development needs has a common sense appeal, and the needs of practitioners as they perceive them provide a reasonable starting point in attempting to determine what competences are required and how they might be developed. There are, however, a number of obvious difficulties. Even those strongly committed to full participation by schools in devising education management programmes admit that 'current concerns force an attitude of short-termism and coping with immediate practicalities rather than long-term planning' (Styan 1991). Thus it is not surprising that solutions to pressing problems are a need more strongly felt than the search for underlying generic capabilities. Also, it cannot be assumed that practitioners, however willing, will be able to engage in the diagnostic and analytical process necessary to identify competences associated with effectiveness. The methods required to probe beyond and beneath the easily identifiable daily concerns and practices of managing are likely to be based on rigorous analysis, reflection and debate by practitioners and are as yet largely underdeveloped.

The research methodology

In determining an appropriate method of enquiry the researchers were informed from three sources: The Peer Assisted Learning Project of the Far West Laboratory for Education Research and Development, San Francisco (The PAL Project), personal experience of peer group interaction, and focus groups as a form of qualitative research.

In effective peer group interaction, an integral part of the action research approach, groups are encouraged to engage in reflective enquiry which seeks to analyse and understand their own and others' practice leading to courses of action for sustained improvement. Creative thinking is also encouraged as a complementary activity. This means the ability to form novel associations from looking at the elements of managerial reality in an open and unconstrained way. Such an approach offers the possibility of uncovering, if they exist, elusive generic capabilities from complex realities.

The focus group as a form of qualitative research has many characteristics in common with features of the above approach: 'The hallmark of the focus group is the explicit use of the group interaction to produce data and insights that would be less accessible without the interaction found in a group' (Morgan 1988). The style of approach is exploratory rather than hypothesis testing and based on interview and interaction. Surprisingly focus groups have not been widely used in research in the social sciences or education, but the method clearly offers a valuable vehicle for group members experienced in rigorous reflective analysis.

For this research six headteachers were chosen from the primary, secondary and further education sectors. [. . .] The researchers acted as moderators, adopting a detached style which allowed members to raise and explore issues they felt were significant but maintaining proximity to the focus of enquiry. [. . .] In each of the tape-recorded sessions members were encouraged to identify situations/incidents in their practice, to reflect on the intentions and outcomes of the action taken, and to attempt to distil from their discussions what they perceived to be the capacities necessary for success.

PHASE 1

Group deliberations

The constraints of a relatively brief chapter prevent a detailed account of each of the sessions. As decision-making is the vital element in the managing task two contrasting decision issues are selected as examples. In the account which follows contributors are identified by sector (primary (PS), or secondary (SS), or further education (FE)); status (maintained (M), i.e. Catholic, or state (S)); and gender (male (m), or female (f)).

Example 1

During the opening session in Drumcree High School, whether or not to join Education for Mutual Understanding (EMU) was offered as an issue requiring a Yes/No decision within a short time-span. EMU is a major curriculum project in Northern Ireland and is heavily resourced and supported by the Department of Education and the present education minister. It seeks to encourage sympathetic and understanding relationships between Catholic and Protestant schools. However, it has been opposed by many local politicians, churches and community members who see it both as a first step towards integrated schooling and an imposed initiative from central government at Westminster. Everyone in the group regarded it as a critically important decision with clear political overtones as well as educational implications. In two schools in particular the political/community aspects dominated. One school is in a strongly nationalist area seeking to preserve its distinctive Irish culture and identity. Nevertheless the headteacher saw his task as persuading the governors to enter the project. The other school is in a staunch unionist area and the headteacher was well aware that her governors would oppose any political interference they perceived as emanating from Westminster. The EMU issue instigated a lengthy discussion about the tactics that might be used. There was some disagreement over the question of how much direction/information should be given to a board of governors. All concurred that they were able to influence their boards of governors and a vital tactic was the winning of support of key figures. All were able to recognize the key figures in their governing bodies and stressed the paramount importance of good relationships with the chairperson. They felt it was also important to know the interests, dispositions and beliefs of all members of the boards of governors.

It was also apparent in this opening session that many of the concepts and capacities identified and sharpened in later group meetings as constituting what managers need to be good at were freely used. Having recognized EMU as a potentially emotive political issue, they saw the capacity to read the situation as critically important: the board of governors, teacher attitudes, community perceptions, resource implications, reactions of the Department of Education and the area boards (LEAs) were consequential variables in the circumstances. Concepts like balanced judgement, political acumen, judicious caution, and skills like reconnaissance, persuading, negotiating and bargaining recurred in the discussion.

Example 2

Some of the literature on decision-making distinguishes between 'routine' decisions (structured, certain, simple, recurring, standardized) and 'non-routine' decisions (unstructured, uncertain, complex, non-recurring, novel). In one group session the danger of assuming that routine recurring decisions are necessarily simple and certain became apparent. The conclusion was reached that the capable manager is one who has the insight to recognize when apparently simple decisions may have complex undertones.

Discussion had centred on the broad issue of the expected consequence of the new legislation which has been introduced in Northern Ireland in parallel with the Education Reform Act 1988. One of the group, almost as an aside, posed the question: 'What do we do if a teacher asks for leave of absence not provided for by the regulations?' On the face of it this is a routine issue where agreed procedures and required information are readily available. In the case of further education this indeed appears to be so. The FE principal pointed out that his staff have clear contracts and 'it should just be played by the book'. He added, 'Of course, in FE the principal can distance himself from such decisions'. In the primary and secondary sectors the situation is less clear cut. Although regulations governing leave of absence exist, the primary and secondary headteachers felt that strict adherence to such a tight delineation could easily lead to staff also playing by the book. They argued that flexibility was needed but that such flexibility could create its own potential difficulties and that the exercise of judgement, tact and sensitivity was essential.

The conversation broadened into a fuller discussion of the kinds of relationships between headteacher and teaching staff that characterize effective schools and colleges. Marked differences in attitude and opinion became apparent which partly reflected differences in context but, more markedly, differences in personality and perceptions. In particular the female members emphasized the importance of close, supportive relationships. Once again the issue of relationships with staff seemed to hinge on balanced judgement.

[. . .]

When the attention of the group was directed to the focal issue of what the manager needs to be good at in establishing and maintaining co-operative relationships or, more broadly, in managing people, the usual interpersonal skills were offered – communicating, negotiating, bargaining, influencing, counselling. There were, however, many caveats expressed and there was a general consensus that more fundamental cerebral capacities distinguish the more effective manager from the less effective: thinking on your feet, balanced judgement, assessing the situation.

Summary and conclusions

What emerged from the conversations was a more complex picture than presented in much of the literature on management competence. In the end the group identified three elements that constitute capability:

1 Knowledge – relevant information relating to the school's context, functions and processes which the manager needs to possess or have ready access to.
2 Skills – techniques that can be acquired through training and that can be improved through practice.
3 Higher order capacities – generic cognitive abilities which determine appropriate action.

The proposition which emerges from the investigation is that while knowledge and skills are prerequisite tools in the process of managing a given situation the group strongly argues that it is the higher order capacities which are the vital elements in the process of using knowledge and skills in effective action.

There was common assent on the main areas of knowledge required by senior managers in schools: professional knowledge of educational principles and practices, knowledge of theories and models of management, and knowledge of the social, political and legal contexts. Equally the discrete skills required by managers were generally agreed: persuading, bargaining, explaining, listening, reporting, informing, counselling, appraising, chairing, interviewing, and team building are typical of a list which keeps being added to. Skills have been enumerated in key areas like curriculum, organization and resource management, and development programmes are often predicated on the assumption that these can be effectively managed through the acquisition of skills that are teachable, learnable and transferable. Few analyses have been made of the nature of the enabling capacities needed to apply skills appropriately in the complex situations in which managers in schools find themselves daily. Since these higher order capacities were deemed by the group to be those which characterized the above average performers, they naturally became the main focus of continuing discussion. The following key higher order capacities were finally identified from a distillation of complex interrelated concepts: reading the situation, balanced judgement, intuition and political acumen.

Reading the situation

This emerged as the overriding capacity and was voiced in a variety of ways: 'picking up the vibes around you'; 'keeping your antennae out'; 'being aware of other possibilities and options'; 'able to assess and weigh up all the factors in the situation'; 'being alert and receptive to what is going on'.

It was also seen to apply to a wide range of decision-making circumstances: long-term strategic planning, handling crisis situations and recurring, daily encounters. The FE principal in particular stressed that sensitive awareness and diagnosis are important in the light of the new legislation and the growing volume of boundary management. The views expressed seemed to recognize that 'reading the situation' involves more than mere diagnosis; it includes continuous response and deliberate action to influence evolving circumstances. The need for action was constantly stressed. Reconnaissance, identification of areas requiring attention, analysis, reflection, synthesis and evaluation were seen as contributory elements, many of which occur in the other cognitive activities which are identified.

Balanced judgement

The ability to exercise balanced judgement was also seen as critical. Group members saw it as related to problem-solving in that, once a situation has arisen or a problem has been recognized, analysis follows and key factors are identified and evaluated in the process of choosing a course of action. It was clear that as the group distilled their thinking over a number of sessions they did not see it as an exercise in mechanical logic. There was considerable agreement that the kind of judgement necessary is significantly different from judgement in the legal sense: 'You have to be prepared to base decisions on much softer evidence than would be accepted in a court of law. You very rarely have time to collect all the evidence you would like and you have to exercise judgement on a partial picture. Values also can't be left out of the picture.' (FE/S/m). The issue of values arose in a number of contexts but particularly in relation to the context created by the new legislation. [. . .]

It is interesting that while many writers speak about making sound judgements the recurring theme in the discussion was about balanced judgement. The group saw the examining and weighing of the advantages and disadvantages of factors in often ambiguous and conflicting circumstances as important as the testing of decisions against the priorities and values of the school.

Intuition

Intuition was seen as serving judgement, following a long debate about the relationships between experience, creative thinking, judgement and intuition. The group did not agree with a conception of intuition as devoid of thought. 'Intuition is more than mere hunch or guesswork. It may start as a gut feeling but is tested against the bank of your own experience.' (FE/S/m).

Two key elements recurred in the attempt to capture the essence of intuition: the part played by experience and the part played by a thinking process. The groups saw stored memory and ordered experience as important. It is interesting that they independently derived a conception close to that outlined by a number of recent writers (De Bono 1982; Ishenberg 1987; Mintzberg 1987), who suggest that the basis of intuition lies in the ability spontaneously to tap the mind's compressed store of experience, knowledge and understanding. [. . .] The group perceptions of the role of thinking in intuition are similar to aspects of the concept of creativity developed by a number of writers. Henry (1991) regards creativity as 'associated with imagination, insight, invention, motivation, ingenuity, inspiration and intuition'. The cerebral aspects of intuition were constantly stressed by the group.

Political acumen

While political skills have featured prominently in lists of what managers need to be good at, the group make an important distinction between possession of political skills, like bargaining, and political acumen: 'It's not enough to know how to bargain but when to bargain. Timing is all important.' (FE/M/m). Their notion of political acumen is closely tied in with thinking on one's feet, learning from experience, reading the situation and using intuition: 'It is about hearing what people are not saying. That's part of political awareness.' (PS/S/m). Thus political awareness has to do with sensitivity and with flexibility to take account of changing situations rather than relying simply on experience. [. . .]

Review

In an early session one group member captured the initial feelings about effective headteachers: 'You know who they are but you don't know why they are.' (PS/S/m). In the final review session the group claimed to have come to a clearer understanding of the 'why'. They felt that while they had greater conceptual clarity it was still difficult to put the essence into words. They seem to confirm the assertion in Pye (1988) that managerial behaviour is 'something about which we can know more than we can tell'.

[. . .]

PHASE 2

For the second phase of the investigation three headteachers from the original group were retained. Three new members were included. There was a deliberate widening of group background to include a broader spectrum from education and the health service. In the account which follows contributions are identified as before by sector: primary (P), secondary (S), further education (FE), higher education (HE), area board (equivalent to LEA) (AB), nurse education (NE), and by gender: male (m), or female (f).

Throughout the five sessions held, the three key elements of knowledge, skills and higher order capacities identified during the first phase were reconsidered and confirmed: that is, managerial capability is realized in effective action in which knowledge and skills are used appropriately through the exercise of higher order capacities.

The four higher order capacities of reading the situation, balanced judgement, intuition and political acumen were also confirmed throughout the sessions. Creativity was seen as making a vital contribution to the higher order capacities and managerial capability, particularly in times of complex, turbulent change in public and private sector management. Kindred terms like imagination, insight, originality and inventive thinking were seen as appropriate in such times. The group believed that effective management integrated the more systematic analysis, reflection and synthesis implied by classical, rational approaches with creative perspectives which look for new, unanticipated, unexpected ways of seeing, thinking and doing. In this the group are reflecting the view emerging in recent management literature that rational enquiry and non-rational insight should be complementary. Wisdom also appeared as a central concept in the group discussions and there was some debate about what constituted the wise manager. [. . .]

The central concern for the second phase was the question: what are the implications for planning management development programmes? The group felt that much of the thinking on management development failed to distinguish clearly enough between management processes, key management areas and managerial capability. Group members argued for a three-dimensional model which recognized that managerial capability is exercised in key management areas through generic managing processes.

There was agreement that in education, as in all organizations, generic management processes can be identified which include deciding, communicating, devising and influencing (Wilkinson and Cave 1987). The key areas identified in educational institutions were resources, curriculum, organization and administration. With the changing emphasis on competition and accountability external and boundary management were seen as crucial areas. The group argued that management development programmes need to identify the underlying capacities required to be good at these processes in these areas.

The single overriding message that the group stressed is that management development initiatives should develop managerial capability and need to be clearly targeted in their intentions. The three elements of knowledge, skills and higher order capacities clearly interrelate. [. . .]

The transmission of required knowledge is relatively straightforward and may be offered in oral, written and visual forms or in combination. Equally, well-established procedures for the acquisition of management skills exist through approaches like workshops, social skills training programmes and those employing more sophisticated technology like interactive video. Although not underestimating the importance of acquiring specific and appropriate knowledge and receiving training in management skills, the new group reaffirmed and strongly supported the belief that higher order capacities are the determining factor in effective management action. While they agreed that higher order capacities are needed at all stages in a teacher's career, they argued that they assume increasing importance with promotion.

Much group debate centred on how higher order capacities might be developed. They questioned the usefulness of 'second-hand' experience like simulation exercises in that 'solutions' are more easily arrived at freed from the constaints of a real context. They also felt that facile answers to simulated situations can be accepted when the problems presented are not owned by the participants and therefore concerns of accountability do not arise. They maintained that, while higher order capacities may develop *through experience* there are also ways in which *learning from experience* can be assisted: 'You probably have to learn it on the job but it's more than learning on the job. This is where the group is so important. The sense you make of your own experience results from the group. This has to be related back into your continuing experience.' (P/m).

Thus the value of sharing and utilizing the breadth of experience and expertise through peer group interaction as has taken place in the focus group was recognized and the group came down heavily in favour of this approach. It developed precisely the kinds of self-analysis, awareness and critical reflection through which the higher order capacities might be developed: the research method becomes the developmental medium. [. . .]

However, members emphasized that peer group conversation needs monitoring and guidance. They saw a real danger in sessions becoming anecdotal. The term 'mentor' was used to describe this advisory, guiding role and it was felt that this person should be outside the group. They regarded it as essential that the mentor should have high credibility as a practitioner, and the consultant in the medical world was offered as a pertinent example. The importance of identifying accurately the essential needs of managers was stressed and it was argued that the mentor had a crucial role to play in diagnosing the underlying causes rather than the symptoms, and in recognizing the importance of the lasting and the long-term rather than the immediate and short-term. [. . .] In the final session it was proposed that underpinning the thinking processes which are at the heart of effective management is the asking of right questions in an attempt to arrive at appropriate answers. Such questioning and ensuing reflection may be applied to past experience, to present circumstances and to anticipation of the future under the guidance of an experienced, skilled mentor.

[. . .]

References

De Bono, E. (1982) Letter as appendix, in B. Heirs and B. Pherson, *The Mind of the Organisation*. New York: Harper and Row.

Henry, J. (ed.) (1991) *Creative Management*. London: Sage.

Ishenberg, D. (1987) The tactics of strategic opportunism, *Harvard Business Review*, November/December.

Jacobs, R. (1989) Getting the measure of management competence, *Personnel Management*, June.

Mintzberg, H. (1987) Crafting strategy, *Harvard Business Review*, July/August.

Morgan, D. (1988) *Focus Groups as Quantitative Research*. London: Sage.

Pye, A. (1988) Management competence in the public sector, *Public Money and Management*, Winter.

Styan, D. (1991) Local management of schools: changing roles and relationships, in P. Holly (ed.) *Developing Managers in Education*. Cambridge: CRAC Publications, Hobson Publishing PCC.

Wilkinson, C. and Cave, E. (1987) *Teaching and Managing: Inseparable Activities in Schools*. London: Croom Helm.

Acknowledgements

The researchers record their indebtedness to the members of the focus groups for their vital contribution: Martin Bradley, Jim Billingsley, David Green, Raymond Harbinson, Jim Hunter, Sister Yvonne Jennings, Louis Knox, Penny McKeown, P. J. O'Grady and John Watson.

8 | Some moral dilemmas in educational management*

JORUNN MØLLER

Background

Major reforms on almost all levels in education are now taking place in Norway, as in most of the Western industrialized countries. In the public debate, a key word in these reforms is decentralization. But parts of the reforms can be identified as centralization (Karlsen 1993).

The policy statements on the Norwegian restructuring[1] of schools are outlined [. . .] in Parliamentary Report No. 37 (Ministry of Education 1990–1) 'On organization and guidance in the educational sector'. The Norwegian Ministry of Education is decentralizing the regulation of education by law and is giving the local authorities more autonomy. At the same time it is centralizing the control of goals by means of a new national curriculum where the goals are more clearly articulated, and tied to a national evaluation programme. The principal or headteacher is being given increased formal power and a key role in implementing the curriculum and evaluation programme. The new role demands more active participation in issues concerning classroom practices, more supervisory activities, and emphasizes the employer role.

[. . .]

In this context, I chose to undertake research in collaboration with people in leadership positions at different levels in the school system. Although leadership is not necessarily connected with formal position, I wanted to examine how principals and superintendents experienced and conceptualized their leadership role in a specific political and cultural context. [. . .] An action research approach (Kalleberg 1990) was chosen, although the choice was also inspired by Schön's (1984) advocacy of an alternative approach to research on educational administration.

*This is an edited version of a chapter by Jorunn Møller's (1996) entitled 'Reframing educational leadership in the perspective of dilemmas' originally written for *School Administration: Persistent Dilemmas in Preparation and Practice* edited by Stephen L. Jacobson, Edw. S. Hickcox and Robert B. Stevenson (Praeger Publishers, an imprint of Greenwood Publishing Group, Inc., Westport, CT, USA, November 1996). Reprinted with permission, all rights reserved.

The action research approach also offered the possibility of contributing to the practical concerns of principals and superintendents in a situation where new role prescripts demanded more active participation in issues concerning classroom practices. These administrators saw action research as a means both to develop their own competence and to improve practice (Carr and Kemmis 1986; Elliott 1991). At the same time the action research approach could contribute to a better understanding of educational leadership: how principals and superintendents described educational leadership, how they explained their actions in specific situations, and how these descriptions could be related to the historical and cultural context.

The study

In preparing the study, I cooperated with the School Director of the County of Oslo and Akershus, and constructed a three-stage negotiation with municipalities and schools to ensure clear agreement that the participants were willing to commit themselves to a collaborative project over a two-year period.
[. . .]
Their decision to participate was a combination of an interest in exploring promising new ideas, expectations of professional growth, and getting a chance to work closely with peers from other schools. [. . .]
We negotiated what was of practical concern to the principals and the superintendents and tried to sort out our sharing and separate interests, as far as it was possible to say in advance. [. . .]
The negotiation procedure was important to prevent misunderstanding that otherwise could emerge later. Throughout the project I learned this was not just a question of establishing the right technical procedures (Jenkins 1978). It also became a moral issue (Møller 1994).

Observation, peer review and journal writing

The main features of the project were connected to observation, counselling, peer review, journal writing and reflection among colleagues and facilitators. In the project we emphasized observing everyday situations. [. . .] We wished to investigate what kind of learning opportunities arose in daily activity when one made use of systematic observation and reflection. We agreed upon eight observation days at each school and each superintendent's office. In addition seminars and group meetings were organized, where the participants reflected on their experiences with observation, journal writing and peer review.
The criteria for observation emerged out of a shared discussion of theory and practice. The principals and superintendents were asked to explicate the 'theory' of leadership implicit in their own practices. [. . .] The discussion often centred around the questions: What does it mean to exercise good leadership practice? What did you do in practice that serves as an example of your 'theory' of leadership? How can you explain it? Argyris and Schön's (1978) distinction between 'espoused theory' and 'theory-in-use' functioned as an analytical framework. We also tried to combine experiences with theory by providing analytical concepts which could be helpful in analysing the practice.
[. . .]

Reframing educational leadership

When we started our collaborative research project, each principal and superintendent was asked to register management/leadership actions and reflect on their own leadership on four different days during a week. An alternative was to describe a critical incident where they didn't know how to handle a situation, or where they felt uneasy with the solution they had taken. The purpose of journal writing was to become aware of the kinds of situations one pays attention to and the thinking attached to it.

The principals' journal writings show a day with constant interruptions where they continually have to respond to emergencies. Housekeeping and maintaining order are given significant weight, and all problems are seen as important. The superintendent, staff and parents must be satisfied, the school must be supplied with adequate materials and, in addition, they have to take care of teaching duties as part of their job. They are strongly action-orientated and have very little time for reflection on actions taken. Time pressure was mentioned as a frustrating aspect of their job.

The superintendents' journal writings show a similar pattern. This pattern is consistent with findings reported in Fullan's (1991) summary of research on principals and district administrators, and in research on leadership conducted in Sweden (Stålhammar 1985; Lundgren 1986).

Among those who focused on critical incidents, the journal writings were dominated by the managing of conflict on an *ad hoc* basis. The ambiguity in the nature of demands is a significant element in the job of being a principal or a superintendent. In a way they are squeezed between the intentions of the state and policymakers, what parents require, what teachers expect, and what students need. Their journals show how the principals or superintendents complain about teachers not doing their jobs, how depressed they feel about managing conflicts among staff and parents, and illustrate the difficulties attached to implementing a national curriculum which they believe in.

The combination of being a teacher and a principal was stated as particularly difficult at the school level. It resulted in an even more fragmented day where one often had to leave activities unfinished. [. . .]

Towards a dilemma language of educational leadership

Administrators are to some degree caught in a constant struggle, 'pulled at the same time upwards toward state mandates and downwards toward collegial/parental expectations' (Crowson and Hannaway 1988: 3). The contradictory expectations toward principals and superintendents result in predicaments requiring choices where competing values cannot be fully satisfied. Which expectations are most important? To whom does one owe loyalty in a conflict? Sometimes one has time to reflect on what is desirable, and it is possible to consider both moral values and practical consequences. But often the decisions are taken spontaneously and intuitively. Decisions can only in retrospect be analysed, understood and given meaning.

The action research project offered an opportunity to reflect systematically on action with colleagues and an external facilitator. Together we were engaged in developing an analytical framework which could help us analyse, understand and give meaning to what had happened in specific situations which called for leadership. Often leaders described their actions in everyday practice as a choice between different sets of dilemmas. The notion of a dilemma captured the contradictory demands they experienced, where there were no right answers. Each course of action carried its own cost and benefit. The challenge was to find adequate compromises (Berlak and Berlak 1981; Cuban 1992). By organizing and stimulating reflection on action among peers, it became possible to discover how different factors were interrelated. This gave leaders an opportunity to become aware of internal and external forces affecting their own solutions, and to clarify alternative courses of action.

[. . .] Two general areas of dilemmas emerged: dilemmas related to loyalty and dilemmas related to control and steering issues. Although overlapping and complex, they can, nevertheless, be divided this way for analytical purposes. One will find moral and ethical dimensions interwoven, particularly within dilemmas related to loyalty.

[. . .]

The *dilemmas of loyalty* were expressed in actions where the principals found it difficult to decide with whom their loyalty should lie in times of conflict. Which groups were most important? Was it possible to discover a pattern of decisions? Should they owe loyalty to students and parents, teachers, superiors, to a common curriculum, to personal pedagogical values?

The *dilemmas of steering* were expressed in actions where there was a tension between:

administrative control *versus* professional autonomy
challenge   *versus* support
change   *versus* stability

[. . .]

What I have chosen to describe as dilemmas of loyalty are related to significant moral and ethical issues. At the heart of educational practice is the making of moral decisions (Cuban 1992: 7). My choice not to use the concept of moral or ethical dilemmas in this context relates to the way these dilemmas were perceived by the practitioners. Moral imperatives are not necessarily part of the leaders' pattern of dilemma resolution, even though the same dilemmas can be reframed in a moral perspective. The data from the project show several situations where principals and superintendents discuss and have to decide to whom and to what they owe loyalty. [. . .]

The dilemmas of steering have become even more problematic owing to the paradox of decentralization and centralization. The Ministry of Education and politicians expect principals to be the most important change agents for school development in a culture where individual autonomy has been a central value for a long time. The 'zones of influence' (Berg 1990: 83; Shedd and Bacharach 1991: 59) are being disturbed by mandates from the state. But it will still be a question of how much it is possible for the principal to influence classroom practice, and whether the principal has anything to offer in order to improve practice. Without a common language for analysing teaching and limited traditions for reflecting on teaching, both teachers and principals must now learn very quickly to communicate (Little 1988).

Dilemmas of loyalty and steering can both be analysed in the perspective of *legality and legitimacy* (Berg 1990: 28–9, 1993: 170–1). These key concepts relate to the tension between formal and informal steering of schools:

Generally speaking the term state legality pertains to the formal steering of schools codified and manifested in the form of curricula, rule systems, and so on. Social

> legitimacy for its part stands for those informal control mechanisms that are rooted in such things as traditions, rituals, school code/culture, trends in public opinion and/or other unwritten rules.
>
> (Berg 1993: 1)

These concepts highlight a perspective of leadership as relational and dialectic (Ljunggren 1991; Wadel 1992) and encourage identification of power relations and conflicts of interests in schools. A basis of a relational conception of power can be found in Giddens's (1984: 93) definition:

> Power within social systems can thus be treated as involving reproduced relations of autonomy and dependence in social interaction. Power relations therefore are always two-way, even if the power of one actor or party in a social relation is minimal compared to another.

To see power as a relationship means that both the actions of subordinates and the actions of superordinates influence the structures of domination. And all actors both constitute and are constituted by the structures in which they find themselves. A similar approach to understanding leadership has been offered by Foster (1989), Bates (1989) and Smyth (1989). The legitimacy of leadership cannot be commanded, it can only be granted. In the same way that teachers may limit a principal's actions, the principals may limit a superintendent's actions, and vice versa (Cuban 1988: 194–5). Micropolitical actions will be mobilized when there is a threat of losing obtained autonomy (Hoyle 1986; Blase 1988; Ljunggren 1991). This is an important phenomenon that traditional theories of leadership based on a structural or human-resource perspective (Bolman and Deal 1991) neglect.

The dilemma orientation and everyday experiences

When applied to specific situations of leadership, 'dilemma language' shows how interwoven different dilemmas are. Everyday practice is complex, and the same situation can comprise several dilemmas. As you unravel the patterns of dilemma resolutions, a different kind of dilemma often turns out to be involved as well (Groundwater-Smith 1993). Understanding educational leadership in the perspective of dilemmas should therefore include considering the same situations through the perspective of different dilemmas. In the following examples of some dilemmas I highlight a specific dilemma by referring to specific leadership actions. To some degree, however, I try to show how the different dilemmas are connected to each other and can be analysed from the perspective of state legality versus social legitimacy.

Administrative control versus professional autonomy

Teacher autonomy is often seen as the symbol of professional status and positively regarded; it is also taken for granted that it will limit the power of the principal. I will, however, distinguish between individual autonomy concerning the autonomy each teacher has in his or her classroom, and collective autonomy, concerning the school as a whole (Hoyle 1986: 120; Berg 1993: 58). As I show later, collective autonomy is synonymous with professional autonomy, not individual autonomy. In the Norwegian context neither external nor internal accountability issues have emerged on the agenda until recently. There has been a strong norm of non-interference in the teacher's classroom activities.

Social and economic change have, however, accentuated the opposition between control and autonomy in schools. In the media there are complaints about the quality of education, and the lack of necessary academic and social qualifications obtained by students by the time they enter university or employment. Teachers are depicted as antagonistic to change. The Ministry of Education responds by placing the principal in a key role in change efforts and school improvement. Their increased formal power may also mobilize the micropolitics between principals and superintendents.

The following situation[2] highlights the dilemma of *administrative control versus professional autonomy*.

The staff at Hillside, a primary school, has painstakingly developed a shared vision and formulated a shared policy. Glasser's 'school without failure' has inspired teachers to organize their relationships with students in specific ways, involving students in curriculum planning and problem solving. They are trying to break down the boundaries between the different classes and share responsibility for all students at the school. When new teachers are employed, both the principal and the teachers are engaged in sharing their vision and motivating for commitment.

When Hansen got tenure at this school, he received a lot of information about how the school was working, what goals they had set, and how they tried to accomplish them. In conversations with the principal, Hansen says he will be committed to the school's vision. There is, however, often a gap between espoused theories and theories-in-use. The principal very soon understands that Hansen is not able to differentiate the curriculum in class. He is also unwilling to accept shared responsibility for all the students. His concern is his own classroom and his own students. He doesn't care about other students.

The principal decides that he has to do something, and initiates several conversations with Hansen. He gives him pedagogical literature to read, and he ensures that experienced teachers are willing to share their knowledge with Hansen. However, nothing seems to have any effect. Now Hansen insists on teaching in his own way. To the principal a dilemma emerges, and he frames the dilemma by the following questions: Can I accept that a teacher refuses to follow the school policy? For how long shall I accept this when this teacher has declared that he will be loyal to the school's vision when he started working at the school? When is the time for support, and when is the time for confrontation and demands? When do you use sanctions? What kind of sanctions do I have? The principal fears that non-interference will have a negative effect on the rest of the staff. Is it a good idea to try to persuade this teacher to move on to another school where individual autonomy is still accepted?

The dilemma concerns what it means to be a professional, and when the principal has the right to intervene. It can be analysed through the lens of *legality versus legitimacy*. No doubt, seen from the perspective of legality, the principal has the right to intervene with classroom activities in this situation. But the question is if this will be of any help to the students. The principal can to a very small degree influence employment policy.[3] Hiring is done by the school board at the municipal level where the teacher unions also have an important voice. The opportunity to influence firing is even less. Thus, in reality the principal lacks sanctions. He is left to rely on argumentative authority. The many conversations with the teacher, referred to in this example, have the purpose of convincing the teacher that changing practice is to the benefit of the students. But we do not know if this teacher is a bad teacher for the students. We only have the principal's perception and description of the situation.

[. . .]

As the situation at Hillside school illustrates, building a shared vision doesn't solve the dilemma of steering. The stability of staff members may change. New people come in without the same ownership of and commitment to the vision. The principal and the teachers are left with the challenge of including new members of staff in the established culture without disempowering them. How can one create a balance between mandates and menus? And maybe the established culture needs critical voices?

The situation also highlights what it means to be a professional teacher, and who is going to define standards for good teaching. This can explain why the dilemma is difficult to manage. Neither the principal nor anyone else can prescribe what is going to happen in classrooms. One needs to maintain a balance between individuality and collaboration and recognize that there must be room for individual ways of teaching. However, teachers have a lot more collective tasks now compared to earlier days. Thus, the need for developing a collective knowledge base and to reflect on teaching among peers has increased. The system is in addition only partially independent. As a profession, teachers have freedom of movement within the limits defined by what society expects of its schools. However, these boundaries for action are abstract, indistinct, and often contradictory. But it is not correct to interpret the autonomy given by society as an individual freedom. The autonomy is given to the profession. It means that the teaching profession has the right to construct and uphold standards of good teaching. However, teacher autonomy has long been interpreted as the right of each individual teacher to make independent judgements about classroom practice (Little 1988).

The standards of good teaching are to a great extent implicit, and critical reflection – which could serve as a protection against arbitrariness in teaching and also guard against the power of the profession – is not taken care of. Both principals and teachers need to examine closely their own and others' professional judgements (Handal 1989).

From the arguments above, it should follow that individual autonomy is difficult to accept. But the principal's dilemma doesn't disappear with that. To change a culture of 'privacy' in teaching requires a long-term strategy where in-service training is combined with support, challenge and patience.

Dilemmas related to issues of loyalty were also evident in the situation at Hillside school. As a middle manager, the principal has the responsibility to implement the common curriculum. In this case, the principal found that the teacher did not differentiate his teaching in proper ways, although having a mixed ability group in the class. Consequently, one could say that the principal should intervene. He will find support in the school law, but, nevertheless, the possibility of action seems a lot more limited. At the same time, as an employer, the principal has a caring responsibility for his staff. What is the best way of caring in this situation?

Similar steering dilemmas (as described at the school level in this case) can be found in the relationship between the principal and the superintendent. In this relationship the principal is the subordinate, and the superintendent is subordinate in the relationship to the regional authority. They are at the same time bosses and subordinates. They are expected to lead and direct others while obeying orders. In fact, teachers, principals and superintendents have a lot in common. Even though the settings vary, they perform the same instructional, managerial and political roles, share the same commitment to a common purpose anchored in student growth, and work within bureaucratic organiz-ations where members are simultaneously subordinates and superiors. But how they define their limit of what can or cannot be done, will differ and affect a whole range of practices (Cuban 1988: 179).

Change versus stability

The debate about restructuring in Norway is focused on the principal as a change agent. But both at the school level and at the district level, leaders experience the internal pressure of stability rather than change. Even though we have a state education policy embodied in legislation, curricula and regulations, it is passed through various kinds of filters, from the central government to the regional, the municipal, and the school levels. Furthermore, state directives, often being highly contradictory, are interpreted by different people at different levels. Sometimes it is considered, at school level, as good leadership to create resistance to state reforms because significant values are at risk in the context of budget cutting.

[. . .]

My study reveals that principals' approach to change is very cautious, even when they have strong pressure from superordinates to act as change agents. It seems best to be on the safe side, not disturbing everyday practice too much. Yet there is an acknowledgement of the need for changes in schools. One situation which happened at Village school illuminates the dilemma of *change versus stability*.[4]

The principal and vice-principal at Village school asked a peer for consultation and observation concerning a staff meeting they were planning. The topic was new role expectations towards teachers. The leaders found some teachers' attitude towards caring problematic. By putting this topic on the agenda of a staff meeting, and following up later with in-service training, they hoped for less complaints about students. According to the principal, the teachers were complaining too much instead of asking what is the best way of helping children in need of caring. Empathy and priorities could be a better solution. But at the same time the principal knew he could very easily be perceived as increasing the teachers' workload, stress and guilt instead of giving necessary support. He wanted to initiate change in the staff culture without increasing stress.

In the staff meeting they chose to focus on what they should do with students who were impolite and did not show respect for teachers, causing so much trouble and stress. The teachers wanted to focus on this because they felt insecure. They did not know how to manage them. In the meeting teachers shared their own experiences, and gave each other advice concerning classroom management. If anybody started to complain, the principal or the vice-principal tried to turn the perspective to focus on positive aspects of the same situation. The leaders expressed satisfaction with the meeting.

Will processes like this result in changes in the relationship between teachers and students? Are the leaders too cautious in their approach to change? Shifting perspective, this situation can also give an example of the dilemma of *challenge versus support*. The teachers at this school have worked here for many years. The principal identifies the school as traditional, and there is low motivation for experimenting with new approaches to teaching. They don't have pressure from parents either, and according to the principal, most parents are satisfied with the work done by the teachers. Experimenting with new approaches will increase teachers' insecurity at work. Teaching is already perceived as difficult and overloaded. Seen from a cultural perspective, it is probably a good idea to take very small steps towards change at this specific school. The principal believes that support is the most important leadership strategy to use, even though he tries to be loyal to the superintendent's expectations of stimulating a more collaborative culture in the school.

[. . .]

Loyalty to students/parents versus loyalty to teachers

Most leaders say they will place emphasis on the interests of students if there is a conflict between students and teachers. But in everyday practice, it is far more difficult. The principal is responsible for the care of employees, and the teachers expect their boss to support them in conflicts. Sometimes it is also difficult to judge what is to the benefit of students. Often the principal chooses to compromise between different interests. A situation from Village school illustrates a perceived need for compromise:[5]

Two students in grade six have, according to a teacher, been very impolite. The teacher insists on their making a formal apology in front of their classmates. The students, understanding what happened differently, refuse. This makes the conflict even worse. The teacher complains to the principal, and so do the students and their parents. After listening to both parties, the principal and the vice-principal think that the teacher in this situation has behaved unwisely. Nevertheless, they have to find a compromise, and even though the teacher can be criticized, so can the students. They have also behaved badly. The principal and the vice-principal are afraid what will happen to the teacher's reputation in the neighbourhood if they don't give her support. As employers they feel an obligation to be supportive both to teachers and students. While the students will leave for another school next year, the teacher will go on teaching at this school, and they have to take care of a good relationship. The challenge is to get both the students and the teacher to understand that the same incident can be understood from different perspectives. But will they succeed?

In one way this example shows that long-term consequences are important when choosing what to do. Even though both the principal and the vice-principal agree with the students, they choose not to show it. They fear a deep conflict with the teacher. This observation gives support to Campbell's (1993) conclusion concerning the way principals cope with ethical conflicts in schools. According to her study, principals are reported to justify administrative decisions based on consequentialist arguments. By doing this they reflect a decision-making framework within which moral/ethical values are largely suspended. [. . .]

However, when talking to the principal and the vice-principal about this incident, it becomes clear that their decision isn't only based on a desire to avoid conflicts with the teacher. It is felt as an ethical dilemma concerning right or wrong. An ethic of caring was visible in their reflection, and they wanted to be a caring person both to students and to teachers. [. . .]

What happened at Village school can also be understood as a dilemma between *challenge versus support*. Which strategy will be perceived by whom as a caring strategy? The teacher has a problematic relation with these students, and she expects the principal to support her when she is getting into difficulties. That is part of the school culture. What kind of leadership is needed in the long run? As both Huberman (1989) and Sikes *et al.* (1985) have pointed out in their research on career cycles of teachers, human development is a far more discontinuous and sometimes random business when one begins to look at individual lives. Having formal responsibility for teachers' development, it may be difficult for a principal to know when support is the right strategy for growth, and when challenge is a better alternative. But to confront this teacher can probably be very unpleasant to the principal.
  [. . .]

Conclusion

In this chapter I have looked at educational leadership from a perspective of dilemmas. The dilemmas experienced by principals and superintendents constitute an analytic 'language' for looking at leadership in action. Examples of dilemmas of *loyalty and steering* were analysed in the perspective of *state legality and social legitimacy*. This offered an opportunity to relate what was happening within a local context to more general political, social and cultural issues, and to examine how the hierarchical structure and the micropolitical activities within schools both steer and restrict our activities and perceptions.

To understand dilemmas as reflections of the contradictions in society doesn't remove the individual's responsibility to act. Individuals will interpret the dilemmas differently and have different capacities for managing the dilemma. Nevertheless, contradictions in society are an integral part of the explanation of the situations explored. Individuals both shape and are shaped by structure and culture.

The immediate interpretation of a situation in terms of dilemmas is seldom the only way of understanding what is happening. The participants in the project discover that by clarifying one dilemma, another one may be unravelled. Sometimes the process of clarifying and reflecting on what is going on causes more frustrations than emancipatory feelings for the participants. Apparently, this may have a connection to leaders' aspirations to be considered as professionals in a job where they feel they continually have to respond to daily emergencies.

The initiation of change in schools probably presupposes a combination of change in structural frames, and a practical and theoretical education for principals and superintendents, as well as for teachers. This education should include an understanding of the type of control that state and society exercise on the school, as well as an understanding of the micropolitics of schools.

Notes

1 Restructuring is used as a term which embraces major changes to the organization of teaching and learning, to decision-making structures, to the conditions of teaching, to the patterns of roles and power relationships in schools, and to the content of education (Hargreaves 1991).
2 The description from Hillside is based on the principal's presentation of a case which was discussed with peers at a meeting. The principal at Hillside school needed advice about what to do in this specific situation. Hillside school is a primary school with 220 students and 19 teachers.
3 This is an issue that is currently under debate in Norway. Many politicians have called for a change in the law so that principals can appoint teachers, but so far the teacher unions have succeeded in fighting against any alteration.
4 The description from Village school is based on field notes from peer consultation, observation in a staff meeting and peer review. Village school is a primary school with 200 students and 18 teachers.
5 The description is based on separate interviews with the principal and the vice-principal. They both mentioned the same conflict when interviewed, probably because they were trying to find a compromise during the week when the interviews took place.

References

Argyris, C. and Schön, D. (1978) *Organizational Learning: a Theory of Action Perspective*. Boston, MA: Addison-Wesley.

Bates, R. (1989) Leadership and the rationalization of society, in J. Smyth (ed.) *Critical Perspectives on Educational Leadership*. London: The Falmer Press.

Berg, G. (1990) Skoleledning och professionellt skolledarskap. Pedagogiska institutionen, Uppsala universitet, januar 1990.

Berg, G. (1993) Curriculum and State Schools as Organizations. Department of Education, University of Uppsala, January 1993.

Berlak, A. and Berlak, H. (1981) *Dilemmas of Schooling: Teaching and Social Change*. New York: Methuen.

Blase, J. (1988) Teachers' political orientation vis-à-vis the principal: the micropolitics of the school, in J. Hannaway and R. Crowson (eds) *The Politics of Reforming School Administration*. London: The Falmer Press.

Bolman, L. G. and Deal, T. E. (1991) *Nytt perspektiv på organisasjon og ledeise*. Oslo: Ad Notam.

Campbell, E. (1993) Strategic leadership or suspended morality? How principals cope with ethical conflicts in schools. Paper presented at the XXI Annual Conference of The Canadian Society for the Study of Education, Ottawa, 10 June 1993.

Carr, W. and Kemmis, S. (1986) *Becoming Critical: Education, Knowledge and Action Research*. London: The Falmer Press.

Crowson, R. and Hannaway, J. (1988) The politics of reforming school administration, *The Journal of Education*, 3(5): i–xii and 1–218.

Cuban, L. (1988) *The Managerial Imperative and the Practice of Leadership in Schools*. Albany: State University of New York Press.

Cuban, L. (1992) Managing dilemmas while building professional communities, *Educational Researcher*, 21(1): 4–11.

Elliott, J. (1991) *Action Research for Educational Change*. Milton Keynes: Open University Press.

Foster, W. (1989) Toward a critical practice of leadership in J. Smyth (ed.) *Critical Perspectives on Educational Leadership*. London: The Falmer Press.

Fullan, M. G. (1991) *The New Meaning of Educational Change*. London: Cassell Educational.

Giddens, A. (1984) *The Constitution of Society*. Berkeley and Los Angeles: University of California Press.

Greenfield, T. B. and Ribbins, P. (1993) *Greenfield on Educational Administration, Towards a Human Science*. London: Routledge.

Groundwater-Smith, S. (1993) Introducing dilemmas into the practicum curriculum. Paper presented to the 5th National Practicum Conference. February 1993, Macquari University, Sydney.

Handal, G. (1989) Lærerne og 'den andre profesjonaliteten', in K. O. Jordell and P. O. Aamodt (eds) *Læreren – fra kall til lønnskamp*. Oslo: Tano.

Hargreaves, A. (1991) Restructuring restructuring. Postmodernity and the prospect for educational change. Paper presented at AERA, Chicago.

Hargreaves, A. (1994) *Changing Teacher, Changing Times*. London: The Falmer Press.

Hoyle, E. (1986) *The Politics of School Management*. London: Hodder and Stoughton.

Huberman, H. (1989) The professional life cycle of teachers, *Teachers College Records*, 91(1): 31–58.

Jenkins, D. (1978) An adversary's account of SAFARI's ethics of case-study, in C. Richards (ed.) *Power and the Curriculum: Issues in Curriculum Studies*. Nafferton Driffield, England: Nafferton Books, Studies in Education.

Kalleberg, R. (1990) A Constructive Turn in Sociology. Working paper, April 1990. Institute for Social Research. University of Oslo.

Karlsen, G. (1993) *Desentralisering – løsning eller oppiøsning?* Oslo: Ad Notam.

Little, J. W. (1988) Assessing the prospects for teacher leadership, in A. Liebermann (ed.) *Building a Professional Culture in Schools*. New York and London: Teachers College Press.

Ljunggren, C. (1991) Skolledning och mikropolitisk handling. Pedagogiska Institutionen, Uppsala universitet, November 1991.

Lundgren, U. (1986) Att organisera skolan. Stockholm: Liber Utbildningsförlaget.

Ministry of Education (1990–1) Parliamentary Report No. 37: On Organization and Guidance in the Educational Sector. The Ministry of Education, Research and Church Affairs, Oslo, Norway.

Møller, J. (1994) Dilemmas in action research. Paper presented at Nordic Society Educational Research meeting in Vasa, 10–13 March.

Nodding, N. (1984) *Caring: a Feminine Approach to Ethics and Moral Education*. Berkeley and Los Angeles: University of California Press.

Schön, D. (1984) Leadership as reflection-in-action, in T. J. Sergiovanni and J. E. Corbally (eds) *Leadership and Organizational Culture*. Urbana and Chicago: University of Illinois Press.

Schön, D. (1987) *Educating the Reflective Practitioner*. San Francisco, Oxford: Jossey-Bass.

Shedd, J. B. and Bacharach, S. B. (1991) *Tangled Hierarchies: Teachers as Professionals and the Management of Schools*. San Francisco, Oxford: Jossey-Bass.

Sikes, P. J., Measor, L. and Woods, P. (1985) *Teacher Careers: Crises and Continuities*. London: The Falmer Press.

Simons, H. (1987) *Getting to Know Schools in a Democracy: the Politics and Process of Evaluation*. London, New York and Philadelphia: The Falmer Press.

Smyth, J. (ed.) (1989) *Critical Perspectives on Educational Leadership*. London: The Falmer Press.

Stålhammar, B. (1985) *Skolledning i förändring*. Stockholm: Liber.

Wadel, C. (1992) Endring av organisasjonskultur. Tidvise Skrifter nr. 7. Høgskolesenteret i Rogaland, Stavanger.

Watkins, P. (1989) Leadership, power and symbols in educational administration, in J. Smyth (ed.) *Critical Perspectives on Educational Leadership*. London: The Falmer Press.

PART 2

The organization and professional development

9 | Teacher professionalism and managerialism

LESLEY KYDD

Introduction

This chapter considers teaching as a profession and the ways in which teachers consider themselves to be both professionals and managers. From the perspective of educational managers, professionalism is important since managing professionals within educational institutions raises complex issues such as those associated with professional autonomy and practices which are not always easily resolved. The chapter explores the ways in which notions of teacher professionalism are changing and the factors, particularly an increasing emphasis on management, which are contributing to these changes. Professionalism is an important concept for teachers since it shapes how we do our jobs; it also raises certain expectations on the part of the community and society in general about how we will behave and what kind of standards we are expected to meet.

Teacher professionalism

Traditionally teacher professionalism has been explained on a comparative model – researchers have compared teaching to both the traditional professions of the law, medicine and the church as well as to the newer professions. They have sought to define criteria common to particular occupational groups which would lead them to be able to say that a group is a profession. In other words achieving professional status meant that occupational groups would go through a series of processes and changes which would allow them to meet more and more of the criteria which define a profession. They would then arrive at some kind of end state – the profession – which was seen as the superior occupational structure: professional status is desirable and confers upon those professionals certain privileges. Thus claims to professional status have derived from the exercise of professional judgement, professional autonomy, the right to self-regulation, expertise in a body of knowledge highly valued by society and a relationship with the 'client' based on common understandings of 'mutual' good (Humes 1986). Although this represents the ideal profession, it contains enough of the reality to sustain the powerful ideology of profession and professional behaviour in society. Often the criteria form a sort of cloak or 'contrived' professionalism, since when the traditional professions are under pressure, their restrictive practices, which are often a trade union kind, come to the fore.

However, if we were to rely wholly on the comparative model to explain teachers' professionalism we would be failing to take account of the differences between professions, the contexts in which the professions practise and the internal structures which maintain, or in some cases mitigate against, the achievement of professional status for occupational groups. In addition, notions of the ideal profession do not explain the complex ways in which the professions are acted upon by the broader political, social and economic context (Siegrist 1994). Indeed there are those researchers who would claim that teaching is not a profession and that the role of teachers in society has been devalued by a number of factors which will be considered later. Whether we consider teaching to be a profession or not is not the real issue here. The purpose of this chapter is to provide some frameworks within which you can consider your own professionalism and management role and the factors which shape those areas of your working life.

Changes in teacher professionalism

A number of developments in recent years have led to changes in the ways in which teachers do their jobs and the relationships the profession has both within educational institutions and with the wider community. It is often held that during the 1960s and 1970s some kind of political consensus existed whereby education was accepted as being part of the 'national good'. The governance of the education system was based on notions of a tripartite relationship between central and local government and the teaching profession. The strength of this model was partly based on the belief of the teaching profession that their authority as the 'experts' (particularly in matters of the curriculum) in the relationship was seen to be 'equivalent to authority derived from the political process' (McPherson and Raab 1988). However, the 1970s saw the breakdown of the postwar social democratic consensus in education against a background of economic recession. The recession added to the difficulties inherent in a period of what was and still is economic restructuring in world markets.

At this time the education system was singled out for criticism as failing in its contribution to the creation of economic wealth. Schools were said to be remote from the world of work and the culture of industry, and politicians of both the right and the left added their voices to criticism of teachers and teaching methods. Much of this criticism was drawn together in the speech made at Ruskin College in 1976 by the then Prime Minister James Callaghan. This speech not only cast doubts upon the achievements of the education system, it also signalled that traditional forms of teacher professionalism, particularly curriculum autonomy, had failed to produce the country's wealth creators. In other words, the role and efficacy of teachers as the experts in the tripartite was called into question.

From the perspective of the teaching profession one of the most influential outcomes of this criticism was the direct linking of the activities of schools to economic benefits. The general acceptance of such causation meant that for teachers there would, in the future, be an expectation that their professional activities would have to be more efficiently and effectively managed to produce economically tangible outcomes. Thus the 1970s provided a particular mind-set for the restructuring of teachers' professionalism and the management of educational institutions in the 1980s. Teachers could no longer be considered the experts in the policy-making partnership since government held that investment in the education system had failed to produce sufficient economic growth. More importantly, the activities of teachers and teaching were to take greater account of the economic outcomes of schooling.

The election of a Conservative government in 1979, and its lengthy and continuous period in office, was to have a profound effect on the teaching profession. The 1980s saw an enhancement of the role of the politicians in the management of schools generally and in particular, in prescribing the content and management of the curriculum. Perhaps, the most important aspect of Conservative Party policy has been the introduction of the ideology and practices of the marketplace to the organization and management of public services, including the education system.

A succession of education Acts have been passed to facilitate the marketplace in education. In summary they have led to the incorporation of colleges; the encouragement of schools to opt out of local authority control; the introduction of the Parents' Charter allowing parents to select their children's school; the delegation of budgets to individual educational establishments; and in 1988 the setting up of the National Curriculum. All of these changes have been accompanied by a formalization of systems of accountability both within schools (through for example systems of appraisal) and externally (through for example Ofsted and the publication of examination results).

If we consider some of the criteria by which teachers have generally defined themselves as a profession, then these changes have made a marked impact on traditional notions of teacher professionalism. For example, can claims to professional autonomy be sustained in a situation where the curriculum is centrally managed and defined? Do teachers possess a body of knowledge highly valued by society? Does the increased role for parents and governors in school choice and governance, respectively, detract from the role of teachers as knowledgeable professionals?

At the same time as these changes were taking place, the 1980s also saw the movement to vocationalize the culture of schools. A whole set of reforms and changes were introduced to make education more relevant to the workplace. In 1982 the Technical and Vocational Education Initiative (TVEI) was introduced. It represented a major change not only in the emphasis and content of the school curriculum but also in the ways in which schools should be managed. It was intended to foster what was called the 'new vocationalism' through, for example, encouraging young people to take vocationally relevant qualifications, preparing young people for work and stimulating closer collaboration between education and industry (TVEI 1984). It was also important from the perspective of educational policy making. The TVEI was implemented through the Manpower Services Commission (MSC), which was part of the Department of Employment (DoE), and not through the Department of Education and Science (DES). The scheme was also well funded at a time when educational expenditure was being held down. TVEI, therefore, marked a change in the traditional academic curriculum of schools, meant that schools and budgets had to be managed according to the targets set by the MSC and illustrated the enhanced role for politicians in changing curriculum, management and the balance of power away from local government and the teaching profession in the governance of the education system.

Alongside the TVEI, the 1980s also marked the growth of a national system of competence-based qualifications under the auspices of the National Council for Vocational Qualifications (NCVQ) in England, and Scottish Vocational Education Council (SCOTVEC) north of the border. The NCVQ framework describes occupations in terms of competence and where appropriate, equivalence to the more traditional academic qualifications, and schools now offer mixed menus of the two types of qualifications. For teachers this has led to the outcomes of their training being described in terms of competence. Some researchers see competence as a reductionist policy which values the outcomes of learning within a restricted range of behaviours but does not value the knowledge and qualities which underpin that learning.

From the vocational agenda has come an increased emphasis on management, particularly on forms of industrial management stressing inputs, outputs and efficiency, which can be described as neo-Taylorist (Pollit 1990). The introduction of such schemes as the TVEI coupled with a great many government reforms have led to changes in the perceptions and practices of those involved in managing schools, with changed roles and new tasks for those in managerial positions. Centrally prescribed curricular changes similarly affect teachers' self-perceptions as traditional professionals and their role in the governance of the education system.

Managerialism in education

These factors have contributed to the emergence of managerialism both as a political philosophy and as a set of systems and practices designed for the management of public services. As a 'movement' it is concerned with the promotion of markets as an organizational tool for the running of public services, and its rhetoric is much concerned with effectiveness and efficiency, particularly in terms of resource management. It is not simply a set of broad assumptions about the unique potentials and rights of management. It is also a much more specific set of models of efficient organizational functioning and of techniques through which such smooth functioning can be achieved (Pollit 1990).

Managerialism relies on a generic model of management drawn from the private sector. This does not easily take into account differences between the private and public sectors or between the different kinds of services carried out in the latter. For example, there are different professional and managerial relationships in the health service and the education service. The health service is managed by professional managers whereas the education service is managed by teachers. In addition, an emphasis on management and systems of management can conflict with the traditional role of professional teachers and notions of providing a service.

An increased emphasis on management can also change the relationships between the state and professional groups. If managers and managing are given increased importance and responsibilities then this may be done at the expense of the professionals who formerly managed the organization. It then becomes a way in which the power of professional groups can be relocated by the state. Thus changes in organizational practice are linked with the redistribution of power between the state and the institutions/systems through which it delivers welfare services. Hence 'there has been a widespread transformation of bureau-professionals themselves into managers in the context of devolved or decentralised management systems' (Fairley and Paterson 1995).

One of the characteristics of managerialism has been its adoption of the discourse of some idealized notion of business; education is considered as some kind of commodity which consumers purchase. In this case education is purchased by parents choosing which schools to send their children to. Schools then thrive or decline on the basis of pupil numbers; parental choice effectively mediates between good and bad schools in the educational marketplace. In the language of industrial discourse the curriculum is the input, pupils are the throughput and success is designated by limited measurable outcomes.

The curriculum now tends to arrive in schools in neatly packaged portions each complete with aims, objectives, tasks, worksheets, homework and assessment. In other words, as the content of the curriculum has become more standardized so the number of curriculum packages has increased. 'The pre-packaged curriculum compensates teachers for lack of preparation time but in the long term . . . they limit the intellectual and emotional scope of teachers' work' (Apple 1993). For teachers this means that where once they were able to exercise considerable professional autonomy over the selection of knowledge and the ways it would be taught, their activities in the classroom are now more tightly controlled. This leaves teachers with less room for exercising both professional autonomy and professional authority. Standardization of the curriculum and increased measurement of its outcomes 'ensure[s] that teachers deliver the curriculum effectively and efficiently' (Aronowitz and Giroux 1991).

Managerialism also raises questions of control, since it hinges on the introduction of systems through which activities within institutions cannot only be managed but can also be monitored often on a 'line-management' basis. From the perspective of education it can be argued that teaching and assessment are now more systematized through the use of curriculum packages and various forms of national testing. In addition, local management of schools means the introduction of financial management systems which often have to be managed by teachers who are not necessarily skilled or trained in this field. Staff development too is now often managed through appraisal systems. These systems are often paper driven and time consuming; they clearly shift the focus of the debate from one of teaching to one of managing systems and accounting for the outcomes of this activity. In everyday terms teachers often have to spend more time on paperwork than they do on lesson preparation. What seems to have happened is that policymakers have invested heavily in managerial systems rather than in enhancing the preparation, professional development and motivation of teachers (Darling-Hammond 1988).

The use of markets as a mechanism for delivering and regulating services, and an enhanced role for the managers of those markets, can conflict with the traditional values and activities of teachers as professionals. There are, for example, tensions between education and the workings of the market; questions of survival for the institution may clash with the activities needed to ensure that survival and maintain the notions of service to others central to teachers' professional culture (Bowe *et al.* 1992). Managerialism then raises a whole set of issues which conflict with traditional notions of teacher professionalism.

An interesting feature of the current debate is the apparent inability of the teaching profession itself to withstand the changes which are being made (Callahan 1962). One of the traditional criteria of a profession is that its members are given a high status by society and are rewarded commensurately. However, there are as Lawton (1990) has said 'simply too many teachers'. Nearly everyone has experience of the education system (and an increasing number at a level equal to the education of teachers), therefore the mystique of teaching no longer exists (if it ever did). Teachers often consider themselves to be poorly paid in comparison with other professions and often do not feel sufficiently valued by both politicians and society generally.

There are also other structural issues which tend to make the teaching profession vulnerable to central control. The majority of promoted posts are still filled by males whereas the majority of teachers are female. For a large proportion of teachers the job provides a second income. Both of these factors point to structural conservatism – in other words, gender and economic imbalances in the structure of the profession make it susceptible to intervention by the politicians. In addition, a promoted post in education generally means a move away from teaching. One of the real difficulties which the teaching profession faces is that by accepting the management orientation of the promotion structure they devalue the job of teaching. On the other hand, the route to being a manager is still via teaching.

Finally, the profession's participation in the governance of the system in which it works has been reallocated to other groups. For example, teacher training in England and Wales has been reallocated to the Teacher Training Agency; the role of parents in the management of schools has been enhanced through school governing bodies in England and Wales and to a lesser extent in Scotland through school boards; and the curriculum is now prescribed in the National Curriculum (though this does not apply to Scotland where there is no legislated national curriculum).

Conservative reforms of the school system and the rise of managerialism raise a number of interesting issues for the teaching profession in general and for those who manage schools in particular. In the past it has been widely held that those in management positions and particularly headteachers were 'the leading professionals, i.e. the leading teachers in their field'. It was felt essential that schools were managed by those who were good teachers. In this sense, then, notions of good teaching and good management were conflated.

In a managerialist environment this duality is more difficult to sustain. The intensification and increasing specialism of the management task changes the paradigm of school managers. Where headteachers were responsible primarily for the construction and teaching of the curriculum, their role is now more clearly built around such tasks as managing budgets, marketing the school, devising, implementing and monitoring development plans and so on. 'For heads and teachers their respective roles in meeting National Curriculum requirements are transformed from being those of professionals, more bound by their common professional membership, than divided by their rank, to those of manager and managed' (Ferguson 1994). There has been a shift in the role of the head from senior colleague to institutional manager. In other words, headteachers now primarily manage and retain only a small part of their former 'leading professional' role.

Not only are traditional notions of teacher professionalism being reframed, the role of teachers in managing educational institutions is being moved away from managing the curriculum towards managing tasks and systems. 'As responsibility for designing one's own curricula and one's own teaching decreased, responsibility over technical tasks and management concerns came to the fore' (Apple 1990). All of this pushes the teaching profession away from its traditional concerns and activities towards a new direction. The intensification of management controls is replacing the wisdom, experience and self-monitoring of the practitioner, and leading to the devaluing of capacities which are difficult to define but which make a difference between experienced and novice teachers. What is clear is that the rise of managerialism calls into question the role of the autonomous professional and the rights of teachers to make decisions about what is taught and how it is taught. The debate is framed not in intellectual terms about what it means to be an educated person but in the economic language of industrial management. Signs of this are an enhanced role for government in controlling the governance, management and activities of the education system, the use of the discourses of industrial management to describe educational activities and a changing role for those who manage the education service. The profession's response to the management and operation of tightly regulated government systems is one of the major challenges facing teachers as we move towards the next century.

References

Apple, M. (1990) Is there a curriculum voice to reclaim? *Phi Delta Kappan*, 71(7): 526–30.

Apple, M. (1993) *Official Knowledge: Democratic Education in a Conservative Age*. London: Routledge.

Aronowitz, S. and Giroux, H. A. (1991) *Post Modern Education*. Minneapolis, MN: University of Minnesota Press.

Bowe, R., Ball, S. and Gold, A. (1992) *Reforming Education and Changing Schools: Case Studies in Policy Sociology*. London: Routledge.

Callahan, R. (1962) *Education and the Cult of Efficiency*. Chicago: University of Chicago Press.

Darling-Hammond, L. (1988) The futures of teaching, *Educational Leadership*, 46(3): 4–10.

Fairley, J. and Paterson, L. (1995) Scottish education and the new managerialism, *Scottish Educational Review*, 27(1): 13–36.

Ferguson, R. (1994) Managerialism in education, in L. Clarke, A. Cochrane and E. McLaughlin (eds) *Managing Social Policy*. London: Sage.

Humes, W. (1986) *The Leadership Class in Scottish Education*. Edinburgh: John Donald.

Lawton, D. (1990) The future of teacher education, in N. J. Graves (ed.) *Initial Teacher Education: Policies and Progress*. London: Kogan Page.

McPherson, A. and Raab, C. (1988) *Governing Education. A Sociology of Policy since 1945*. Edinburgh: Edinburgh University Press.

Pollit, C. (1990) *Managerialism and the Public Services: the Anglo American Experience*. Oxford: Basil Blackwell.

Siegrist, H. (1994) The professions, state and government, in T. Becher (ed.) *Governments and Professional Education*. Buckingham: Society for Research in Higher Education and Open University Press.

Technical and Vocational Education Initiative [TVEI] (1984) *Operating Manual*, Annex 2. London: MSC.

10 Selection: predicting effective performance

COLIN MORGAN

A lady on the West Derbyshire Conservative candidate selection committee said: 'There must be something in this young man if he rescued a dog. Let's have a look at him.'

(Profile of Matthew Parris, *Observer*, 7 September 1986)

'Two weeks ago I saw him in shorts and banjo doing a music-hall act. This is why I'm pushing him [for a head's post] now' – LEA member. This candidate got the job.

(Morgan *et al*. 1983: 91)

'Don't judge the personalities but their performance . . .'

(Kionsuka Matsushita, Chairman, National Panasonic, quoted in Pascale and Athos 1981: 54)

This chapter addresses the oddities and defects of much of traditional selection practice in educational institutions in Britain, and the improvements and additions which can be made to selection practice to enhance significantly its effectiveness; it also discusses what should count as management effectiveness in job selection both for the hirer and the candidate. The standpoint of this chapter is that from a management perspective, job selection should be about evidence tied to occupational performance, past and expected, rather than qualities approved of for wider reasons.

In Britain selection practices are very much 'taken for granted'; it is rare that we question their predictive value. Reference will be made below to what the research evidence has to say about the predictive validity of the common selection tools we use, as well as discussing those selection methods which recent researches suggest improve the likelihood of more effective appointments. Two dimensions of the whole issue of making selection more effective will be considered: the *technical management* aspects where concepts of prediction, reliability, validity, effectiveness, efficiency, developed abilities and latent ability are invoked; and the *micropolitical management* aspects. Technocratic ends are not pursued in a vacuum but often have to take account of a complex web of human and power relationships. This micropolitical dimension can be particularly challenging to the technical requirements of good selection practice in educational settings. Hence this chapter will endeavour to illustrate how a 'best technical' approach can be applied in schools in the face of difficulties that can arise from the existence of different groups of selectors and their micropolitics.

How does education generally measure up in practice to a rational view of the nature of selection and the principles that arise from it? What in any case is a rational view of selection? Selection is, or should be, an act of prediction and not a blind gamble. That is, it should have the intention of predicting as accurately as possible that a person can perform a certain job. The whole purpose of using a deliberate and systematic selection process, rather than a random method of, for example, sticking a pin in a list of applicants while blindfolded, is to eliminate the elements of chance or 'hunch' by the progressive accumulation of evidence tied to job performance. In educational appointments and in many other employment contexts a focus on job performance figures lowly in selectors' concerns, and is very often wholly subsidiary to the pursuit of social acceptability criteria. However, the literature and research validation studies in selection make clear that in rational selection procedures the linkage to job performance is achieved by carrying out four key steps. These are:

1 The job to be filled is clearly defined and understood by the selectors, i.e. there is a good and clear job description.
2 The competencies to perform the job successfully are explicit, i.e. the job criteria or person specification have been prepared and are known by the selectors.
3 There is a planned provision for the assessment of all the required competencies, i.e. the technical assessment stages have been clearly conceived and scheduled.
4 There is a clear policy on how the final decision is to be arrived at and the final stage procedure ensures that all of the evidence of earlier stages is accumulated and considered before making a judgement.

The first two steps are all about job analysis so that 'what you as a selector are looking for' is unambiguously defined as common criteria for all, selectors and candidates alike. There are various schemata proffered in the literature to assist job analysis, but all in essence call for a rigorous description of what tasks or duties are to be carried out in the post in question.

Traditional selection in the educational world can fall far short of this approach, for frequently the published further particulars can hardly be called a job description. They are more dominated by information describing school organization as a whole, the ethos felt to be important, or the locality and the housing prospects, at the expense of specifics about the job itself in terms of the tasks expected to be carried out by the appointee and the abilities required to support those tasks. A most useful categorization for assembling a description of the competencies or abilities required in a job is the following categorization: knowledge bases; specific skills; and attitudes (KSAs). The basis of this list is very straightforward: to be functionally competent, job incumbents will need to know about certain things, so the knowledge component of a job needs analysis. Also, certain skills will be involved. A skill always involves doing and can be verified by eye or ear. If it cannot be heard or seen then the ability being considered is not a skill! An example of a skill often required might be leadership, which can be defined as the ability to influence and structure the activities of others in: (a) the formulation and determination of policy; (b) the solving of problems; and (c) carrying out decisions for the most productive outcome. Each of these elements of leadership can be directly observed (rather than inferred) by the adoption of the appropriate assessment methods in step 3 of the four key steps to a rational selection procedure which were outlined above.

The category of attitudes presents the greatest challenge in defining competency for a job, as it is very easy to interpret this requirement in terms of some social or other attitude value unconnected with the job itself. In fact, it is very easy to slip into defining attitude as personality in its colloquial sense, and to assume a link between observed personality and effectiveness even though, on reflection, we need only look at effective leaders – whether prime ministers, military leaders, or headteachers – to see that they are markedly different in their external personalities. What should be considered under the heading of attitudes is whether there are certain dispositions or attitudes relevant and essential to the carrying out of the job in question. For example, to be an effective journalist one should be disposed to be happy working under pressure and to deadlines; in creative teamwork of any kind, to accept compromise and collective responsibility; and in top management, to be at ease with the loneliness of the role.

Deriving the KSAs constitutes some very challenging preparation in a selection procedure. Rigorous studies have indicated how the KSAa are to be derived. The recommended approach is to use experienced and expert job incumbents in order to generate in the first place a comprehensive list of task statements in relation to the particular job. The same people are then asked to indicate what KSAs are required to perform each task category. The ultimate aim will be the creation of a tasks and KSAs matrix which is agreed as accurately representing the job by the experienced and expert reference group as suggested by the template indicated in Table 10.1.

KEY TASK CATEGORY	Knowledge	Skills	Attitudes

Table 10.1

When these knowledge, skill and relevant attitude requirements are clearly revealed, tests can then be designed to measure them. Also, any interview arrangements can be structured to allow for real job situations, as *critical incident* information will have been collected at the same time as the KSAs, and these critical incidents can be used as the basis for questions which challenge candidates to say how they would behave in given circumstances.

Analysis of knowledge, skill, and attitude requirements, then, produces a specification of the kind of person required to perform the job. The advent of published guidelines for equal opportunities in recruitment and selection has brought about more explicit person specifications than was the case in the past, and it has become practice to indicate in the specification which are the essential competencies from those which are desirable. The person specification (based rigorously as it should be on the determination of the key tasks and explication of the KSAs necessary to enact them) must then become the common denominator for all selectors and candidates, and should inform all interviewing and testing activity.

The requirements of the fourth of our key steps – clear policy on how the final selection decision is to be reached – are particularly challenging to the world of educational appointments, where we are so wedded to the tradition of making the final appointment decision either by, in the main, going round the table and talking matters through to a consensus or, less often, going straight to a formal vote after the last candidate's interview. In this context it is important that you are aware of the distinction between the intuitive, the actuarial, and the professional modes of coming to a decision on the selection evidence which has been accumulated, whether this has been from interview alone or a combination of tests and interviews. Coming to the final decision on the candidate to be selected poses the complex issue of how to compare evidence between candidate and candidate, and candidate and criteria. The problem is how to choose from comparisons of evidence across a range of criteria and between candidates who reveal different mixes of strengths and weaknesses – what Jauch (1976) has characterized as the problem of asymmetrical choice. There are three responses to this problem:

- *overall impression* – the 'gut feeling', 'intuition' or 'hunch', are terms used for this approach in the literature; this is the method traditionally used at the final stage of most school appointments throughout Britain;
- the *actuarial* or *mechanical* method – the aim of this approach is in some way to combine scores from selection instruments that have been validated so that intuition or individual judgement is wholly eliminated;
- the *clinical* or *professional* method – this can be summed up as the use of measurements or systematic assessments on job-related criteria plus the application of judgement or overall weighting.

The latter and to be preferred two approaches depend, of course, on all selectors using the same agreed assessment criteria and rating instruments. Therefore instead of each selector deciding individually what for a particular question constitutes an 'excellent', 'good', 'average' or 'poor' answer, the rating instrument should define these in behavioural terms.

Key defects in traditional selection practice

In educational appointments a number of selectors from different backgrounds, some professional, others lay, are usually involved. The problem with multiple selectors is that they can lead to multiple objectives being pursued independently unless systematic steps are taken to control the situation. The presence of different selector groups is much less conducive to the following of the four key steps unless these are made quite explicit and planned for in advance, instead of the whole appointment procedure being largely 'played by ear'. Though person specifications are nowadays more evident in educational circles, it can still be the case that most selectors go about their duties without agreeing in the first place the nature of the job to be filled; the specific competencies for which evidence is to be sought in the selection process; the range of assessment methods to be deployed to obtain the evidence of required competency; or how a final decision is to be arrived at when the evidence has been obtained on all the candidates. Consider this short extract from a major study of secondary headteacher selection:

the basis of the choice, as revealed in the discussions between selectors which followed the interviews, was invariably a shaky one; conjecture, hypothesis and uncertainty ruled the day in an uneasy combination with the alignments and power blocks among selectors. Rarely were issues of perceived technical competence made explicit and a candidate's suitability was judged through the different coloured filters of selector perceptions. The only filtering process shared by many lay selectors was that derived from recollections of their own experiences of headteachers. The fixed mental impression which many demonstrated appeared to be influenced by their own schooldays, acquaintance with other headteachers or reports from the neighbourhood. They look for candidates who match up to these images in terms of physical features, personality and other characteristics. Additionally they appear to be influenced by perceptions of the previous head of the appointed school and the ability of a candidate to fit the local peer group of heads. The following are statements made to commend (or otherwise) a particular candidate, by selectors in actual headteacher appointments [. . .]

'We need a character, someone like the heads of the other two schools, someone who can compete.'

'I did prefer candidate A . . . he just seemed to me to be a headteacher – I don't know what it was, he just had presence.'

'It all boils down to personality.'

(Morgan *et al.* 1983: 90–1)

This extract is intended to convey what a decisive role non-job related factors can play in the appointment of secondary headteachers.

More generally of course, and under the influence of guidelines from such bodies as the Equal Opportunities Commission, the use of questions on such non-job-related matters as marital status, religious affiliation, birthplace, etc. have diminished. Nevertheless, in traditional selection practice in Britain the selectors, whether 'professional' or lay, may not be exercising a concern to obtain the best person technically for the job. Other factors may be influencing them, such as to reward for past achievement in a different job, or, as is not unknown with the lay members from all political backgrounds, to reward achievement in some political or social sphere outside that of the school. In the absence of explicit guidance on suitable criteria, these non-job-related criteria can be used either by selectors who genuinely believe that such factors are in some way job-related or by selectors who were never even looking for job-related factors in the first place, but were preoccupied with tests of social acceptability. Hence, criteria embodying some idiosyncratic social value – such as silver hair, rescuing a dog, or the ability to socialize with the general community (banjo act on stage) – are seriously proffered and become influential among those by whom the candidate is selected. In 'play it by ear' selection the appointment activity becomes not about getting the best person *technically* but about the most *socially acceptable* candidate on the day.

The above extract demonstrates that there cannot not be effectiveness in the management of job selection activity in education if the selection criteria are not precisely connected with the key tasks of the job and their KSAs. Some of the world's leading experts in selection studies would argue that this connection needs to be very precise indeed – what they describe as 'point to point correspondence between predictor and criterion'. The general criticism being made in this chapter about the lack of such correspondence also applies of course in traditional procedures to the 'long' and 'short listing' activities as well as to the decisive interview stage.

There are three broad categories of defect to traditional practice which we now need to consider from the perspective of eliminating the defective elements and applying the appropriate remedy. They are:

- the problematic predictive nature of the interview as a selection method;
- the need to assess latent as well as developed abilities; and
- the problem of role differentiation between categories of selector, i.e. the professional/ lay problem in education.

For each of these topics there are important issues affecting the rationality of the selection process.

The interview as a selection method

Earlier staff selection was categorized as a problem of prediction: how to predict that a person will do a job effectively, or how to predict that one person will do it more effectively than another. What aspects of job performance the interview can predict is therefore a key question, because in education, the interview is traditionally the sole selection method used when candidates are present in person. The evidence on this question, and there really is substantial research evidence, is clear: the interview has the illusion of validity! It has a very poor predictive record indeed. It just does not generate much job-related evidence, nor ease of agreement between selectors where there are panels. Take this example from Lyons (1976) for instance:

> Sixteen university graduates were interviewed by two boards of 4 or 5 eminent persons, including two professors, a chief inspector and a headmaster of a public school. Each interview lasted 15–30 minutes. The board had to assess: alertness; intelligence; intellectual outlook *re* 'value of personality for a Civil Service job'. Members of each board gave a mark to each candidate. He was then discussed and an average mark agreed on. The marks of the two boards for each candidate were then compared and for two of the candidates the ratings were:

> | Candidate | Board A Rating | Board B Rating |
> | --- | --- | --- |
> | A | 1 | 13 |
> | B | 11 | 1 |

> If there had been 6 vacancies to fill, 5 of the six recommended by Board A would have been different from those chosen by Board B.
>
> (Lyons 1976: 174–5)

There are even more stark examples than this one in the literature. Ghiselli and Brown (1955: 166) cite the rankings given to 57 applicants interviewed by 12 sales managers. There was virtually no correspondence at all between the lists of the 12 selectors. For several candidates some selectors had ranked them first while others had ranked them last. The interview as a selection method therefore has very poor reliability, and many studies made to compare subsequent performance with interview success have shown that there is a very low correlation, so that the interview also has low validity. In the 1950s the world saw some major researches on the interview – the McGill and Minnesota studies (see Morgan 1973) – which for many serious students of selection destroyed for ever any faith in the interview. Practically every couple of years since then, some academic has written an 'interview revisited' chapter to summarize and review the

Table 10.2   What the interview as a selection tool can achieve

Can	confirm biographical factors and assess their significance, if any; assess technical knowledge and experience (though other methods can be better); assess verbal communication skill (to some extent); throw light on intellectual ability (to some extent).
Cannot	assess many job-related skills which need to be observed in situation analogies or measured by validated tests.
May	cast light on candidate attitudes, personal energy, and range of interests which may have some possible relevance to the job.
Can mislead and falsify	because the whole interaction visual and impression factors and hence decisions tend to mirror the values of selectors.

very latest research on the subject. I have not been able to find one of these that alters significantly the judgement of the major landmark researches – that the panel interview has a predictive validity little better than chance! Drawing on the findings of the many researches on the interview, Table 10.2 is intended to summarize the utility of the interview as a selection method.

Prime questions for students of selection are, why is the interview so popular if it has demonstrated such low validity? Why if it only has the illusion of validity do interviewers maintain great faith and confidence in their judgements? Part of the answer to these questions could be to do with feedback. The feedback loops to interviewers are so tenuous that they can hardly connect selection failures with their own actions. Moreover it may well be that though the interview is not generally valid as a predictor of on-the-job performance, it does other things very well, such as selling the candidates the job, enacting good public relations, or maintaining political consent, as well as providing valuable evidence on sociability and verbal fluency, for example. We need to note though that there are claims to clear validity for what is called the *situational interview*:

> The situational interview is a structured interview in which applicants respond to a series of job-related incidents . . . we began with the collection of critical incidents. Job incumbents were asked to identify and describe incidents in which particularly good or poor job behaviour had been exhibited . . . after editing . . . the incidents were translated into relevant interview questions in which job applicants were asked to indicate how they would behave in a particular situation. Since applicants were unlikely to have had the experience necessary to deal with the critical incidents, all critical incidents were translated into questions which job candidates would have some knowledge of and/or experience with.
>
> (Latham *et al.* 1980)

Overall though, the continuing research evidence shows that even where interviews are conducted on a well-structured, in-depth and tied-to-the job basis, their predictive ability is only marginally rather than substantially improved. For example,

> the interview despite various innovations over the years, has never been consist-
> ently shown to improve selection. At best it introduces randomness into the

selection process; at worst, it colours selection decisions with conscious or unconscious biases. As such the interview presents a poor alternative to testing.

(Tenopyr 1981)

Often, selectors ignore the job and concentrate on social or other extrinsic factors because jobs are mostly about workplace skills, *doing* rather than knowledge or attitude. By and large skills cannot be evaluated in interviews. I say by and large because clearly there are a very few general skills such as oral communication ability that can be demonstrated, though even then their use is not being demonstrated *in situ*. Small wonder then that the interview as practised pre-eminently concerns itself with overall impressions – feel, image and 'personality' as the headteacher research showed.

In summary then, the clear message from interview research is that the interview must be structured to mitigate the effects of image and cultural embodiment factors (i.e. values favoured in the subculture of the particular selector group). Also, the interview should only be used in combination with other selection tools so as to focus on measurable observable aspects of performance rather than nebulous psychological traits, appearance, or social attitudes. This position therefore recognizes the interview for what it largely is – a tool mainly concerned with assessing kinds of social acceptability rather than technical assessment of job-related abilities, and looks to other types of assessment to assemble good job-related evidence.

The assessment of developed and latent abilities

A widely held axiom is that the best predictor of future performance is past performance, or what in horse racing circles is often called 'form'. Hence, form applied to job selection would mean: assess the applicant's *developed* abilities, and if these are the abilities required in the job in the future, there exists a match from which success or acceptability in the job can be predicted with some confidence. Unfortunately, there are two problems raised by this proposition, one potential, the other (for many jobs) actual. Both problems imply that the assessment of developed ability or form alone is too narrow a base for prediction and that a consideration of *latent* ability must be added to the predictive base.

The first of these problems concerning 'form' is a potential one connected with the accuracy of the information on developed ability in references, or how accurate/truthful/relevant they are. Research on the content of references in education shows that they are short on job-related evidence and long on an image of 'the good person' – often called boy scout or motherhood virtues – in the recommendations they make. Secure statements of previous performance would need to depend on developed systems of appraisal, i.e. a reliable 'form book', but these may not be reliably established in the institution where the candidate works. The question of the dating of references is an important one; some institutions have stock references for their staff that they keep on using without taking care to see that they are accurately updated.

The second difficulty about total reliance on form or developed ability, even when that can be established with accuracy, is that many jobs require tasks for which the candidate's ability is yet to be demonstrated, tasks for which she or he has no previous experience or form. The question therefore arises of how, in a rational approach to selection, some estimation of latent abilities or future form can be made. This requirement is particularly relevant within teaching, where upward mobility in the UK is characterized by what Andrews (1978) has called the generic professional model. That is, where appointment to the senior positions is based to a great extent on developed abilities as a teacher, and not on separate training qualifications for job roles different to the previous one. Traditional practice does not take account of the fact that in movement up the career path there are 'thresholds', the crossing of which imposes quite new sets of tasks to those previously experienced, e.g. movement to head of department, deputy headship and, *par excellence*, headship. The assessment of latent ability is therefore crucial in much educational selection.

The appointment to many posts requires consideration of what task categories and their associated KSAs represent new challenges to candidates, and the correct response to this issue of *latent ability* is to create tests that would enable the candidates to demonstrate their ability and behaviour in any future situation. Job simulation exercises, or *analogous tests* as they are often known, seek to produce the demands of real work situations by requiring candidates to carry out set tasks orally or in writing on an individual or group basis, or a combination of these. In terms of validity the key point about job simulation activities or analogous tests is that they have been consistently demonstrated to produce correlation measures of future performance substantially greater than has ever been shown for the interview. For staff leadership a test of latent ability could be a written and oral task involving a member of staff seen to be defective in terms of some duties. The candidate could be given a written résumé of the complaints involving the person concerned and then be asked to write down how they would set up a meeting with the offending staff member. Also, the format, objectives and notes of preparation for the meeting could be requested in written form. After completing this, the candidate could be asked to conduct a meeting with a staff member on a role-play basis while being assessed on the demonstration of leadership and counselling skills.

Systematically assessed simulations, role plays, oral and written exercises embedded in the key tasks of the post to which the appointment is being made, are therefore the means by which evidence of competence in the KSAs of the job can be demonstrated by those with no or little experience in that type of role previously. These are the instruments for measuring latent ability in regard to competencies for which the candidate has no form. Such analogous tests have been found in very many studies to be both reliable and valid. Some occupational spheres have seen the development of 'assessment centres' that run a concentrated battery of analogous tests over several days as a means of identifying latent senior managers. They are, of course, expensive and have been criticized on the grounds of their cost, that is, they have been caught up in an effectiveness/efficiency argument, with an ultra cost-conscious management approach seeking a given level of effectiveness at least cost. Job simulations or analogous tests as part of the selection process are gradually being more and more applied in schools by some heads. Tests can be carried out on a preliminary assessment day when in-depth 'professional' interviews are also held with all those shortlisted. Candidates' performances both in the interviews and on the tests can be scored on a five-point scale and the results entered in a matrix. After each candidate has been seen at final interview the matrix of scores can be distributed before any discussion of candidates has taken place so that the reaching of a decision is based on data from multiple assessment sources and not the interview alone. There is no doubt that the research evidence from Britain and North America clearly demonstrates the greater validity to personnel selection contributed by such tests. They are the means by which candidates can demonstrate competence in the key job tasks for which they have little previous experience, and by which selectors can assess whether candidates have the latent KSAs for the key job tasks in the next best context to the real situation.

Professional and lay role relations in educational selection

Professional identity within this whole terrain is problematic for teachers on two grounds. First, because there are no formal or explicit rules on role relations in educational appointments – the tacit assumption held by some lay selectors is that you as a professional are there to advise if asked, and not tell them which candidate in your view is technically best equipped to do the job. Second, because it is not usually apparent in what ways the 'professionals' are exercising (or indeed have acquired by training) professional selection skills different from those that the lay selectors (who anyway think they are the true professionals when it comes to the interview) are using, unless there is visible evidence to the contrary of a differentiated expertise.

A management approach would respond to this dilemma of selector's role relations and identities by deliberately creating for the teacher (or adviser) participants a truly professional selector role that is visibly differentiated from that played by the lay people. Where such an approach is adopted there is then a differentiated role on the part of the professionals. This is an essential part of a rational model of selection which both recognizes the four essential steps presented earlier and the need to place the role relations of the participants on a complementary rather than competitive basis. In contexts where 'lay controllers' participate in the selection of staff, complementary roles would mean that heads or other 'professionals' would lead the systematic determination of the job criteria; deploy multiple means of deriving evidence on the key competency requirements; and assemble and accumulate the evidence of candidates' strengths and weaknesses in the form of complete profiles which would be used by the lay members for their final decision (Figure 10.1).

In this complementary model it is therefore the role of the professional to assemble the evidence with as much selection expertise as possible, and the role of the lay members to decide upon it in similar manner to the role of a jury. Where lay selectors are not present, teacher selectors would still need to bring the same selection skills to bear, prior to making the decision on the basis of candidate profiles.

Selection of staff – a summary

Selection means prediction of satisfactory performance . . . the job specification disciplines the selectors to decide in detail for what it is that they are looking: the criteria must be clear so that the predictor, that is the measures used to predict the qualities to satisfy the criteria will be clear.

Lawrey (1990: 30)

The goal of any selection instrument is to adequately predict future job performance . . . the goal is the creation of point to point correspondence between predictor and criterion . . . that selection procedures that are behaviourally consistent with job or task requirements are desirable.

Schmitt and Ostroff (1986)

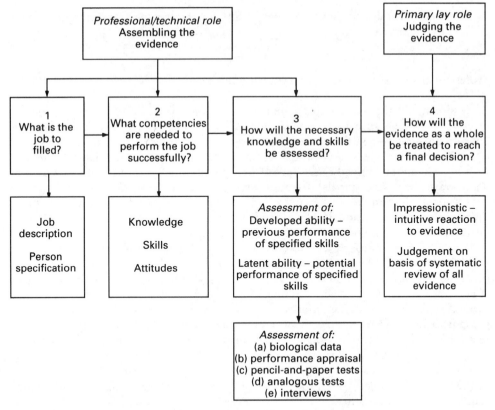

Figure 10.1   The complementary roles of professional and lay selectors

The quotations convey the perspective of this chapter – that from a management perspective there should be some causal relationship between the selection process and ultimate effectiveness in the job – that selection must be seen as an exercise in prediction if the objective is to achieve management effectiveness by securing the best, i.e. the most competent, person to carry out specific job requirements. Regarding selection therefore, good prediction needs to be seen as a key test of managerial effectiveness, and good prediction will be revealed by the absence of 'failures' in performance subsequent to appointment. It is rare indeed in Britain for managers to evaluate subsequent performance in terms of their earlier selection criteria, but this is a desideratum if selection procedures and instruments are to be improved.

This chapter has also aimed to convey that prediction requires a sufficient amount of job-related evidence, and that conventional procedures, which are almost wholly reliant on the interview, are inadequate in generating sufficient relevant evidence. In fact, the predictive record of the interview alone is dismal. It has been argued that the research evidence clearly shows that where tests are used, and especially where these are analogous to the job to be filled, the selection process and the odds in favour of more effective appointments are significantly improved. Moreover, they help screen out bias. Tests of job skills do not discriminate against certain groups – people do! Overall, the chapter has aimed to demonstrate that within the micropolitical constraints and conventional personnel practice of educational appointments, a management approach such as that set out in the four-step model will secure an enhanced role for the education professional, a differentiated role for the lay selectors, and allow for the assessment of latent abilities.

While maximization of the prediction of competence in the defined tasks of the specific job is the crucial management aim for selection, it should perhaps not be seen as the only one, however, as there is perhaps another interesting test of management effectiveness. Do the successful candidates, even though they may subsequently be performing excellently in the jobs to which they were appointed, feel fully happy about the job they are doing? That is, did they actually arrive in the job they expected, or was it significantly different in some way from that which they had understood from the published specification and discussion during interview etc.? Follow-up discussion about the scope of the job, its key tasks and KSAs with successful or less-than-successful performers alike, is a rarity in much British educational management, but clearly offers potential benefits for enhanced effectiveness in general as well as constituting a feedback loop to selection practice.

References

Andrews, J. H. M. (1978) *International Perspectives in the Preparation of Educational Administrators*, chapter presented at the fourth International Intervisitation Programme in Educational Administration (IIP), Vancouver.

Arvey, R. D. and Campion, J. E. (1982) The employment interview: a summary and review of recent research, *Personnel Psychology*, 35: 281–322.

Asher, J. J. and Sciarrino, J. A. (1974) Realistic work sample tests: a review, *Personnel Psychology*, 27: 519–33.

Ghiselli, E. E. and Brown, C. W. (1955) *Personnel and Industrial Psychology*. New York: McGraw-Hill.

Gilmore, D. C., Beehr, T. A. and Love, K. G. (1986) Effects of applicant physical attractiveness, type of rater and type of job on interview decisions, *Journal of Occupational Psychology*, 59: 103–9.

Jauch, L. R. (1976) Systematizing the selection decision, *Personnel Journal*, 555(11): 56–7.

Latham, G. P., Saari, L. M., Purcell, E. D. and Campion, M. A. (1980) The situational interview, *Journal of Applied Psychology*, 65: 422–7.

Lawrey, K. (1990) The selection of teaching staff, *Education Today*, 40(4): 30–4.

Levine, E. L. (1983) *Everything you Always Wanted to Know about Job Analysis*. Tampa, FL: Mariner Publishing.

Lyons, G. (1976) *Heads' Tasks: a Handbook of Secondary School Administration*. Windsor: NFER.

Morgan, C., Hall, V. and Mackay, H. (1983) *The Selection of Secondary School Heads*. Milton Keynes: Open University Press.

Morgan, C., Hall, V. and Mackay, H. (1984) *A Handbook on Selecting Senior Staff for Schools*. Milton Keynes: Open University Press.

Morgan, T. (1973) Recent insights into the selection interview, *Personnel Review*, 1: 4–13.

Pascale, R. T. and Athos, A. G. (1981) *The Art of Japanese Management*. London: Sidgwick and Jackson.

Schmitt, N. and Ostroff, C. (1986) Operationalizing the 'behavioural consistency' approach: selection test development based on a content-oriented strategy, *Personnel Psychology*, 39(1): 91–108.

Scottish Education Department [SED] (1984) *Learning and Teaching in Scottish Secondary Schools: School Management*, a report by HM Inspectors of Schools. Edinburgh: HMSO.

Tenopyr, M. L. (1981) The realities of employment testing, *American Psychologist*, 36(10): 1120–7.

11 | Identifying needs and priorities in professional development*

DAVID OLDROYD AND VALERIE HALL

Introduction

[. . .] Needs identification and prioritisation are the foundation stones of an effective staff development programme. Needs identification is a process that should be handled sensitively, efficiently but not mechanically. It should be democratic and not imposed. It has to take account of the needs of individuals, groups, the whole school, as well as those arising from LEA and national policies. It would be very easy for those charged with managing schools to focus attention solely on school development needs to the exclusion of the personal and professional development needs of individual teaching and non-teaching staff. The expectation that every school should draw up a school development plan promotes this switch in focus. As Hargreaves *et al.* (1989) point out, once the school development plans have been drawn up, many of the priorities will require active support for teachers in the form of INSET and professional development. In other words, their needs will be identified in relation to the requirements of the plan. Schools now have as a central concern the effectiveness of how the money is spent in relation to the school's development priorities. Any personally expressed professional development need of an individual teacher will, in future, be judged alongside the needs of the school as a whole.

This then is the framework for effective needs identification. In this chapter we focus first on the roles and responsibilites of those involved: individual and groups of teaching and non-teaching staff and those responsible for managing staff development in the school. Whose needs have to be taken into account and how can they best be involved in the process? Then we turn to the process itself and the range of methods available for identifying needs, whether of individuals, groups or the school as a whole. Finally, we

---

*This is an edited and abridged version of Chapter 4 entitled 'Identifying needs and priorities' in *Managing Staff Development* published in 1991.

consider how the information collected can be analysed and priorities identified to form the basis of the next stage in the INSET management cycle: planning the programme and designing activities.

Some principles for effective needs identification

We have already touched on some of the principles that are at the heart of an effective approach to needs identification. First, it is important not to lose sight of the intimate link between staff development and school improvement. School improvement depends on a staff-development policy and programme that balances the needs of individual teachers and heads with the school's own development needs. This means that schools face the challenge of finding ways of dealing with the tensions between the needs of individuals, teams, whole school and the LEA in planning staff development. Each group with an interest in the school's success will perceive its needs differently – governors, advisers, officers, parents, senior staff, individual teachers and, most importantly, pupils. This concentration on the needs of the school as a whole does not mean, however, losing sight of the importance of recognising teachers' career and life-cycle experiences. As Fullan (1990) points out, staff development must view holistically the personal and professional lives of teachers as individuals. Thus it becomes the sum total of formal and informal learning experiences accumulated across individual careers. The agenda then is to work continuously on the spirit and practice of life-long learning for all teachers.

The second principle is the need for staff to be fully involved in the process. The more they are encouraged to contribute to the identification of needs, the more staff development can play a key role in an overall strategy for professional and institutional reform. It is important that needs identification happens sensitively and systematically. It is a valuable INSET activity in its own right. Properly handled, it can promote professional reflection, particularly when it is linked to and raises awareness about school and curriculum review and development plans.

The third principle arises from its potentially threatening nature since, whatever means is chosen, it involves revealing a 'gap' between present and required or desired performance. This is equally true whether we are focusing on career development needs or those arising from the school's development plan. For example, a teacher may be seeking promotion but be unwilling to admit the absence of essential leadership skills. It is important, therefore, that it is handled sensitively, with an emphasis on development not remediation. Then it can support innovation, ensure a match between needs and provision and provide a basis for deciding priorities.

Fourth, needs identification must be followed by needs analysis from which emerge decisions about priorities for action. Nothing is more frustrating for staff than to go through a complex needs-identification process only to hear nothing further of its outcomes. It is a demanding task for everyone involved and the technical and human challenge of aiming at balanced priorities for INSET to meet individual, group and institutional needs cannot be underestimated. There are many potential pitfalls, including omitting some individuals or groups, gathering irrelevant information and offending sensitivities. The ultimate sin is to carry out a needs-identification exercise and produce a programme that fails to reflect what it revealed.

Roles and responsibilities

Identifying needs is a shared task between those responsible for managing staff development in the school and those who will benefit from the staff-development programme that results. Increasingly schools are involving more groups in their daily lives, each with claims to development if they are to fulfil their roles effectively. For example, the expectations of governor contributions are changing radically. Currently LEAs and the governor associations are taking a main responsibility for identifying and meeting their development needs. Yet in a truly collaborative 'Self-Developing School', they would be trained alongside their 'colleagues' in managing the school, since their needs too must derive from an analysis of where the school is now and where it wants to be. The role of administrative support staff, too, in the school is undergoing a rapid transformation, as LMS requires skills that have been hitherto underutilised or underdeveloped. Then, there are groups in the school, teaching or non-teaching staff whose needs may require separate identification since they derive neither from individual career nor school development plans. For example, it has been argued that the inequitable treatment of women and ethnic minorities in society may influence how they perform and are expected to perform in their job (e.g. Al-Khalifa 1988; Ranger 1988). Both women teachers and teachers from ethnic minorities have development needs arising from their ascribed status, in the same way as the staff as a whole group may have unrecognised development needs in relation to equal opportunities. In this chapter we focus predominantly on identifying the needs of teaching staff, without losing sight of the importance of including other groups in the process.

If responsibility for identifying needs is shared, it can be argued that it is neither a top-down nor bottom-up process. Figure 11.1 shows the range of approaches currently used. It schematises what should be an ongoing process of reflection on practice leading to needs being identified collaboratively. In reality different people are likely to play a more or less formal role in the process, using a variety of approaches and methods. [. . .]

In some schools, heads see identifying development needs as their responsibility or one to be shared with their senior management team. Others see it as an important part of the departmental or pastoral head's role. Whatever approach is adopted it is essential to have one person officially designated to coordinate the process so that the outcomes of needs identification at each level can be analysed and priorities identified. Example 11.1 shows how one LEA advises its school-based coordinators on their role in identifying needs. The tone of the guidelines is strongly developmental. It also advocates widespread staff

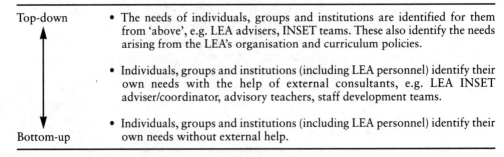

Figure 11.1   Responsibility for identifying INSET needs

Example 11.1   Extract from an LEA handbook for institution-based coordinators

How will needs be identified?
In any school there are three levels at which staff development will be desirable. It will be necessary to identify needs at each of these levels:
1 The whole school
2 A functional group
3 Individual teachers:
   (a) professional needs
   (b) career needs

1 The needs of the whole school
On completion of the school's curriculum review, staff development needs for the whole school will emerge. These needs will frequently arise from some major innovation such as 'Science from 5–16' or the introduction of GCSE.

2 The needs of a functional group
In any school, especially the larger ones, there will be groups of staff who have aims and objectives peculiar to the group. Such groups will include, for example, the reception teachers within a primary school or a number of primary schools, and an academic department or pastoral team within a secondary school. These groups will have their own special needs. In many cases a teacher will belong to more than one group, for example, both an academic department and a pastoral team. Such groups may not be confined to individual schools.

3 The needs of individual teachers
(a) Professional needs
Needs will arise from the desire of individuals to build on their strengths and to improve their performance both in the classroom and in all other aspects of their work; these needs will range across such things as reading skills, 'A' Level Physics, management, and pastoral care. Newly trained teachers and those new to their posts will need structured support and guidance.
(b) Career needs
Teachers will have aspirations about their future career development for which they require training in areas not of immediate relevance to their current post. It is important that this fact be recognised when considering priorities for training.

What methods can be used to identify needs?
Each school will find methods of identifying needs which are most appropriate to its own situation. The following suggestions are offered as examples which schools may wish to consider:
• diagnostic documents such as DION, GRIDS, and various adaptations of these;
• school of department audit;
• questionnaires specially designed by an individual school or group of schools;
• personal interviews.

What are our priorities?
The process of identifying need will lead to a variety of demands, not all of which can be met immediately. Thus it will be necessary for the school, or the group of schools, to decide on an order of priorities for training which will be acceptable to all staff. A school may concentrate on one aspect of its curriculum. Larger schools may wish to work on a number of aspects at the same time. These decisions will need to be made and incorporated into a staff plan for the school or group of schools.

	KNOW/CAN DO	DON'T KNOW/CAN T DO
KNOW	i.e. what I know I know/can do	i.e. what I know I don't know/can't do
DON'T KNOW	i.e. what I don't know I know/can do	i.e. what I don't know that I don't know/can't do

Figure 11.2   Using the Johari window to identify needs

participation and attention to teachers' individual career needs as well as those needs that relate directly to improving professional performance.

The challenge for the person responsible for identifying needs in the school is to help individuals sort out where they currently are in relation to specified knowledge/skills areas and where they would like to be. There are some heads who know what they can do but don't know what they cannot do until they do it. A head recently informed a senior member of staff of the desirability of her departure if the school was to save money. The resulting hostility in response to the head's behaviour suggests that s/he knew about budgets but did not know about communication and sensitivity. A French teacher called upon to include relevant work experience in her curriculum recalls only dimly some business French covered at university ('doesn't know what she knows') and recognises the need to update herself on modern commercial vocabulary ('knows what she doesn't know'). This 'Johari' window approach to helping people recognise their needs is summed up in Figure 11.2.

Both staff and managers of staff development share responsibilities in identifying needs. The responsibilities of individual and groups of teachers are twofold: to participate in any needs identification activities and to recognise the extent and nature of needs that are identified as a result. [. . .] The individual teacher, then, has a responsibility for identifying and acknowledging his or her own needs. The responsibility of the staff-development manager is to draw together the information into an overall profile for the school. Figure 11.3 shows the different stages of the process that need to be coordinated in order to arrive at a staff-development programme that properly recognises the multiplicity of needs at all levels.

To be effective, the process needs to be systematic, without losing its responsiveness to the context and the individuals that it is designed to serve. An individual teacher may express a strong personal 'need' to learn Mandarin Chinese, in anticipation of taking a school party to China. Professionally s/he has also admitted to having problems teaching slow learners. A deputy colleague is considering applying for a deputy headship in the next two years, having spent fifteen years as a head of department. Already, the

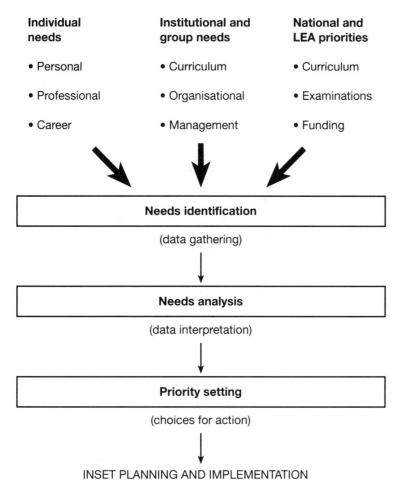

Individual needs	Institutional and group needs	National and LEA priorities
• Personal	• Curriculum	• Curriculum
• Professional	• Organisational	• Examinations
• Career	• Management	• Funding

Needs identification

(data gathering)

Needs analysis

(data interpretation)

Priority setting

(choices for action)

INSET PLANNING AND IMPLEMENTATION

Figure 11.3   Identifying needs: the manager's role

staff-development coordinator is faced with a range of individual substantial claims on the INSET funds available. The school has more. It is undertaking a whole-school curriculum review to see how far it 'fits' the demands of the national curriculum. It is clear that there are many disjunctures. The school is moving over to a faculty structure for which the departmental heads have received little preparation. Although the head and deputy in the school are regularly away on management courses, few of the school's middle managers have had similar development opportunities. These institutional and group needs have to be balanced with the individual claims on limited INSET funds. The position is still more complicated by the LEA's identification of teachers needing training in implementing the national curriculum, in using Standard Attainment Targets and in meeting needs arising in relation to the dozen or more priorities. The complex management task this implies is somewhat belied by the DES's simply stated requirement that LEAs 'ensure that appropriate action is taken of the expressed needs and views of

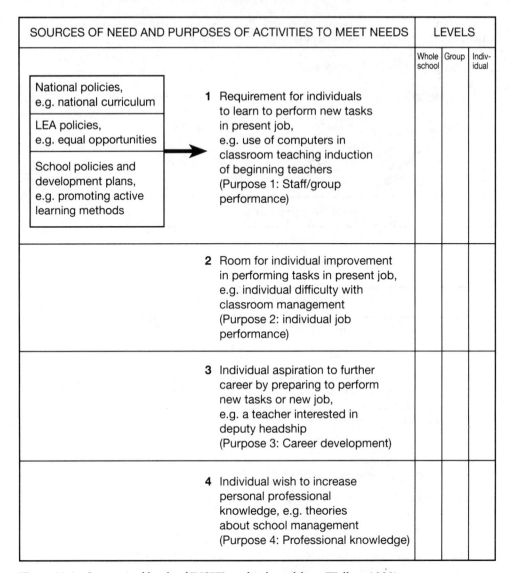

Figure 11.4   Sources and levels of INSET need (adapted from Wallace 1990)

teachers, schools and colleges' (Circular 6/86). The coordinator's responsibility is to arrive at a balance between these competing claims. [. . .]

Wallace (1990) has extended Bolam's (1982b) diagram to show how each purpose gives rise to a different type of INSET need, i.e.: the need to learn new skills in response to new situations, such as those created by current educational reforms; the need to respond to new policy requirements such as those relating to equal opportunities; and the need for continuing improvement in a present job or development for promotion. Figure 11.4 describes the sources of need and purposes of activities to meet needs at each of three levels: whole school, group and individual. It can be used as a proforma by INSET managers to build up an overall profile of levels of needs arising from different sources both within and external to the school.

So far we have highlighted the complexities of the needs-identification process. First, there is the tension between the needs of individual teachers and heads and the school's own development needs. This is further complicated by needs arising from LEA and national policies. Second, there are the different definitions of what is 'needed', emanating from the wide range of 'stakeholders' in the school. Then, identifying and recognising needs is a highly sensitive process of which teachers and others need to have ownership. Further, an uncoordinated process can be time-consuming and generate too many needs. As schools become increasingly collaborative enterprises, the development needs of a range of individuals and groups have to be taken into account. Agreement on the overall needs profile that emerges will depend on all partners in the process.

Choosing a method

Ways of identifying needs are as various as the needs themselves. Many needs-identification instruments are unwieldy or amass a plethora of irrelevant information that will confuse rather than enhance the INSET planning process. A survey of lessons from TRIST (Hall and Oldroyd 1988: 29) revealed that needs identification is best performed when:

- there are clear and concise LEA and institution guidelines for the curriculum and staff development, so that teachers/advisers know what they are supposed to do;
- there is a positive climate where teachers and advisers believe that it is possible to influence school and LEA policy;
- there is a clear strategy for consulting schools;
- there is some element of personal, face-to-face contact;
- all teachers can be involved in the process of consultation and negotiation at some level of the service;
- there is a system of evaluation and feedback that is known and acceptable to participants;
- the underlying message is that 'needs' are to assist development not solely or mainly to remedy deficiency;
- resources of time, space and people to be available and their probable limits are clarified; and
- school and LEA INSET priorities and programmes are demonstrably based on the needs identified.

Deciding which methods to use will depend on:

- how much information is wanted;
- what type of information is wanted (quantitative or qualitative); and
- how quickly the results are needed.

For example, using a questionnaire will generate a lot of fairly superficial quantitative information quickly, although analysing the results can be time-consuming. It is relatively impersonal, allows little room for personal expression and is inevitably top-down, since the categories are pre-defined. In contrast, staff-development interviews can provide a more narrow but deeper range of information about fewer people. They

---

At individual level
1 Self-review using a prepared check-list
2 Job analysis
3 Informal discussion with head of department/year
4 Observation as a teacher/manager
5 Individual appraisal interview
6 Questionnaire about priority INSET needs

At group/team level
Departmental review
Structured group discussion (including quality circles, brainstorming)
Team self-review using prepared check-list

At whole-school level
School development plan/annual curriculum review
Full staff meeting
Use of a commercial review instrument

Figure 11.5   Methods for identifying staff-development needs

take considerably more time and will be perceived as top-down or bottom-up depending on who conducts them and the relative emphases on development or accountability.

Figure 11.5 lists the range of needs-identification methods available, according to their appropriateness for identifying individual, group/team or whole-school needs. Figure 11.5 considers, with examples, each of the methods in turn.

Identifying individual needs

A starting point for helping teachers identify their individual needs is some kind of *self-rating form* to aid reflection, such as the one shown in Example 11.2. It would most probably be used in conjunction with either formal or informal follow-up discussion with a colleague. Initially it provides a teacher with a framework for reflecting on their job and how they are doing. The follow-up discussion can then focus on the ways in which the needs identified might most appropriately be met.

Example 11.2   A self-review check-list

1 List in order of importance the key activities you perform in the school.
2 Do you anticipate any significant changes in any of these activities during the coming year? If so, what are they?
3 Which aspects of your work give you most difficulties at the moment?
4 What development and training activities would help you to:
   (a) respond to the changes you have listed in (2);
   (b) deal with the difficulties listed in (3);
   (c) develop as an individual; and
   (d) contribute more effectively to the teams/groups of which you are a member?
5 Outline a specific proposal to meet your development needs, indicating your objectives, preferred method of learning and resources required.

This kind of self-rating form can be used in conjunction with analysing the *job description* to discover areas presenting particular difficulties or demanding hitherto undeveloped abilities. Increasingly with the advent of appraisal and school development plans, schools are ensuring that every member of staff has a comprehensive job description. They provide a framework for appraising someone's current job and a basis for considering the school's future needs when a vacancy arises. [. . .]

Individual teachers are asked to rate each of the tasks in which they are involved in terms of difficulty, importance and frequency. A reading across each task suggests the priority and standard of training required for that task.

As with all individual needs-identification methods, the results can be collated to provide a profile of needs across the whole school staff. They can also form the basis of informal discussions with a teacher's head of department or year or, as will be increasingly the case in the future, of individual staff-development or appraisal interviews.

Appraisals are a key means of identifying needs as long as they follow a development rather than accountability model, i.e. if they are about rewards in the form of provision of development opportunities to meet identified needs rather than sanctions in response to 'weaknesses'. Appraisals constitute one of the most personal means of needs identification, since they focus on individual teachers and their experience of the job. At the same time they take place against a background of what both the individual teacher and his or her appraiser know about the school's needs. [. . .]

By implication, the development needs of those responsible for managing appraisal, as well as those being appraised, are considerable. Appraisal thus becomes a way of identifying needs as well as generating developmental needs itself.

In preparation for the initial review meeting, both appraiser and appraisee will need copies of the appraisee's job description and the school department's development plan. Additionally many schools are asking teachers to complete the kind of staff development review form shown in Example 11.3.

The questionnaire puts considerable emphasis on achievements as well as any difficulties. Self-appraisal is not easy and teachers are often highly self-critical and find it hard to elaborate their achievements.

As well as self-review information, another source for identifying individual teacher needs is *observation* of their performance either in the classroom or in their capacity as a manager. Classroom observation as a means of identifying needs is a highly sensitive process. It is best conducted between 'critical friends' where a pre-condition for effectiveness is a degree of trust and openness. Figure 11.6 sets out the four steps in lesson observation, which can yield information on individual development needs that is 'owned' by the teacher concerned.

Information from the self-rating forms and classroom observation exercises can be fed into the *appraisal interview* itself. The interview serves several purposes, including that of identifying development needs, setting targets and exploring ways of achieving them. It should include:

- a review of the appraisee's job description;
- a review of work done, successes, areas for development since previous appraisal;
- discussion about future development and expectations in certain target areas; and
- professional and career development issues to be included in the report.

Any developmental targets will need to be agreed in the context of the school's

Example 11.3   Staff-development review

Pre-interview preparation
The purpose of preparation is to gather background information for a review interview. It is worth spending time answering the questions fully and carefully bearing in mind the *aims* of the interview, which are to consider:

1 your progress over the past year;
2 the context within which you have been working, especially ways in which it has influenced your performance;
3 your career aspirations; and
4 any other matters you wish to raise.

A confidential written report, agreed by both parties, will be drawn up afterwards to suggest ways to improve your effectiveness.

Points for you to consider
1 List your responsibilities.
2 Comment on your responsibilities in terms of areas in which you are generally satisfied. Explain why you are satisfied.
3 Consider areas in which you have experienced difficulty and would like to see improvements. Can you identify the reasons for these difficulties?
4 Give examples of where your job is
  (a) not satisfying;
  (b) satisfying; or
  (c) stressful.
5 Consider your relationships with
  (a) your pupils;
  (b) your colleagues; and
  (c) those to whom you are responsible.
6 What do you consider to be your main contributions to the development of the school in the last year?
7 If your job requires management skills, how would you describe your style and how effective it is?
8 Can you identify areas where you need further training or refreshment?
9 Are you engaged in any form of education or training at present?
10 How would you hope to see your career develop in the next three to five years?
11 What would you wish to have included among your key tasks next year?

N.B. It is essential that you give a copy of any questions to the interviewer(s) to assist their preparation a week before the date of the interview itself.

---

development plan and organisational goals, as well as in the light of available resources. As we described earlier, part of the appraiser's (or staff-development coordinator's) responsibility is to ensure that any support required to achieve the targets is provided. This means that the staff-development coordinator will need to be informed of the INSET implications of the appraisal interviews. At its best, the appraisal interview will further both individual and school development, giving teachers a formal opportunity to hear how well they are doing as well as receive help in identifying problems and working towards solutions.

Perhaps more than any other needs-identification method, staff-development or appraisal interviews walk a difficult tightrope between career and institutional development needs. [. . .] The career-stage chart in Example 11.4 shows how one school

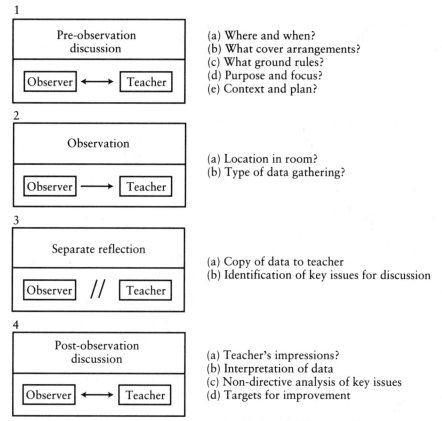

Figure 11.6   Four steps in lesson observation (Hall and Oldroyd 1990)

has conceptualised the kinds of needs that might arise at each career stage and ways in which they might be met.

For many people, undertaking a review of their development needs raises questions about their career as a whole. It is important that anyone responsible for supporting others in their development understands what is involved in careers counselling and careers planning.

'Progression' in the teaching profession largely means doing less and less teaching. The School Management Task Force (1990) emphasises the need to see all teachers as managers, working with other adults to support children's learning. This means that additional attention is necessary, when identifying management development needs, to those arising: first, from short-term issues such as local management of schools, national curriculum and assessment, appraisal and staff development, working with governors, strategic planning and monitoring and evaluation; and, second, from the management development objectives for the service as a whole.

Finally, individual teachers might be asked to complete a *questionnaire* about their priority INSET needs, the results of which will be collated in order to inform decision-making at school or LEA level. A questionnaire enables individuals to record

Example 11.4 A career-stage chart

Stage	Induction	Consolidation	Reflection/re-orientation	Advanced studies	Re-equipment	Top management prep./refreshment
Time in teaching	1–3 years	4–6 years	5–8 years	8–12 years	12–15 years	20+ years
Possible training	Induction courses	Short courses of full-time study, specific in content and application with more extended periods of part-time study	1-term secondments	Part-time specific specialist courses	Advanced studies 1-term/1-year secondments	Series of 1-day courses/20-day/1-term courses
Purpose of training	Supplement specific needs	Adding to knowledge and developing skills	Initiate a career change or confirm and enhance the direction to which already committed	Develop specialist expertise and knowledge	Extension of specialist expertise and knowledge. Re-equip for new substantial responsibilities requiring leadership and management	Top management or refreshment needs. Replenishing intellectual and cultural resources.

Compiled from some concepts in Bolam (1982a)

their perceived priority needs and preferred ways in which these needs might be met. [. . .]

Identifying group or team needs

Schools contain a variety of groups that form suitable units in which a more detailed review of needs as well as consequent INSET activities can be conducted. These include:

- senior staff team;
- management team (senior and middle managers);
- faculty/department heads' team;
- pastoral heads' team;
- interdisciplinary course team; and
- new staff induction group.

At its simplest, a group needs-identification process can be a *structured group discussion* based, for example, on the following questions:

- What are our current strengths?
- What are our current weaknesses?
- What INSET needs do these strengths and/or weaknesses suggest?
- What priorities arise from these needs?
- What type of programme and follow-through support might meet these priorities?
- How would we implement and evaluate such activities?

A variant of the group self-review discussion is illustrated in Example 11.5. It is suitable for one of the five staff days used for INSET. This group self-review was done by a humanities faculty with ten staff. It was conducted off the school site at the local teachers' centre.

The activity and 'developmental' outcomes are summarised in the example. The sequencing of the three sessions was arranged by the head of faculty to get the negative conclusions out of the way quickly, follow them with a mutual admiration session and then conclude with a very tangible 'what are we going to do?' session, which left the team feeling both encouraged and much clearer about where their developmental effort must be focused. The pattern of individual writing of reflections, followed by 'buzz groups' before the whole group aired views together, ensured maximum participation. [. . .]

Other ways of structuring this kind of group discussion might have included using a 'quality circle' approach or brainstorming. In the 'quality circle' approach a group of teachers sharing common problems meet to work out the group's INSET needs. Williams and England (1986) suggest the quality circle has three essential prerequisites for its success:

- an established tradition of teachers talking openly to one another about their teaching difficulties and problems;
- an experienced and sympathetic facilitator who is sensitive to educational changes and who is in a position to identify those teachers who would be most likely to benefit from membership of a quality circle;
- a link person who can contact potential providers in HE and elsewhere who are able to assist teachers in meeting their needs.

Example 11.5   Group self-review to identify needs (programme for faculty INSET day at local teachers' centre)

   9.15 Introduction to the day by head of faculty
   9.30 *Session 1: Retrospective*
          'What I like least about our faculty'
          (a) Individual recording of views on one side of A4.
          (b) Discussion of (a) in groups of three.
          (c) Report back from each individual on the discussion. Head of faculty compiles a summary.
 10.15 Coffee
 11.10 *Session 2: Introspective*
          'What I am happy about in our faculty'
          (a) Individual recording of views on one side of A4.
          (b) Discussion of (a) in groups of three.
          (c) Report back from each individual on the discussion. Head of faculty compiles a summary.
 12.30 Lunch (local hostelry – buffet meal)
   2.00 *Session 3: Prospective*
          'What we would like to achieve in the next year'
          (a) Whole-group discussion of targets for the faculty;
          (b) Individuals write down personal targets under three headings:
                1 Classroom teaching.
                2 Resource production.
                3 Relationships.

(Oldroyd *et al.* 1984)

Brainstorming is yet another method for identifying needs in a group. A flipchart and pens and marker board is required and the ground rules for brainstorming will need to be agreed. They are as follows:

1 First, members of the group suggest as many needs as they can, however absurd they may appear.
2 Each idea is recorded on the flipchart for everyone to see with no evaluation at this stage.
3 Members review the list and, if possible, group the needs, e.g. all those relating to introducing technology across the curriculum.
4 At this stage questions of clarification and discussion are allowed, as a result of which a decision may be taken to eliminate some of the alternatives.
5 The group goes through the remaining issues and says whether an issue is important (give two ticks) or unimportant (give one tick).
6 The areas of need with the highest number of ticks then became the basis for planning.

[. . .]

Identifying whole-school needs

Throughout, we have emphasised the need to match the needs of the school with the professional development of individual teachers. INSET opportunities can then be allocated fairly among the staff over time and the knowledge and skills acquired through INSET disseminated throughout the school. Increasingly LEAs are encouraging a 'bottom-up' approach, which makes individual staff and schools responsible for identifying their own INSET needs and feeding them into the LEA's total picture. Both the LEA and the school have a responsibility for creating a climate in which the whole process of needs identification is public, its relationship with priorities is defined and it is seen as ongoing – not a 'one-off' exercise. The approach aims to strike a balance between participation and ownership on the one hand and, on the other hand, the desirability of the LEA having an overall view of staff-development needs. In this way it can more effectively 'enable' the school's 'self-development'.

[. . .]

A range of techniques have emerged from the school-based review movement over the last decade for identifying whole-school needs. These range from sophisticated interventions involving external consultants over considerable lengths of time to single staff meetings. One LEA suggests the following sources to be tapped for evidence of a school's current strengths and areas of possible growth:

- the school's documentation (e.g. policy aims and guidelines, job descriptions, teachers' work plans);
- statistical information (e.g. capitation allocation, contract ratios);
- staff and others' views and opinions (e.g. about the range and quantity of teaching resources, provision for staff development).

From the range of information collected from these sources, a review document can be prepared that provides:

- the school's overall aims;
- statements of national and LEA priorities;
- a summary of recommendations for possible areas of development; and
- staff INSET needs: individuals and teams.

[. . .]

Using this kind of systematic approach means that staff-development needs are identified only when a recognised school need has been thoroughly explored and agreement reached about the direction of development to be taken.

[. . .]

Analysing needs and establishing priorities

Once needs have been identified the information collected has to be analysed so that INSET priorities can be established. How this is done will depend in part on whether the information is qualitative or quantitative. Quantitative information is more quickly analysed but runs the danger of losing the individuality of teachers' needs through aggregation. Qualitative information may have more face validity but be harder to reduce to manageable proportions to aid decision-making. There is a range of sources from which criteria for analysing and prioritising INSET needs can be derived. These include the following:

- school staff-development policy, e.g. extension of middle-manager training;
- school curriculum development plan, e.g. introduction of resource-based learning;

- school organisation development plan, e.g. rationalisation of departments into faculties;
- school equal-opportunities policy, e.g. review of sexist/racist language in text books;
- funding-agency requirements;
- availability of resources, e.g. increase in amount of INSET budget devolved to the school.

Plus – the overriding priority – better teaching and learning for pupils!

It is important that the criteria for analysing and establishing priorities have been agreed and made public so that staff feel that the resulting INSET programme is a fair reflection of their expressed needs. [. . .] It is at this stage that INSET managers are faced with a real challenge in achieving a balance between individual group and institutional priorities. Their decisions will depend on the outcomes of consultation with staff, financial constraints and any requirements from the LEA on how INSET monies should be spent.

Whatever priorities are finally agreed, they provide the basis for the next round of decision-making about:

- what activities to retain and in what form;
- what gaps need to be filled and how;
- how the programme can reflect LEA and school policies as well as individual needs;
- what resources, including supply teachers, are required and available to implement the programme;
- whether existing talent among staff members can be used to meet certain needs;
- the balance between individual, group, institutional and LEA priorities;
- the emphasis on innovation as opposed to the improvement of existing practice;
- the time required for negotiation with LEA and HE providers on INSET;
- the capacity of staff to cope with additional pressures arising from the proposals; and
- the impact on pupils of the absence of their teachers on INSET activities.

The next step is for the INSET coordinator to communicate the results of the needs analysis to all relevant individuals and groups within the school and to the LEA so that negotiation of appropriate training and development activities can be set in motion. Decisions can then be taken about how identified needs are best met and by whom, costs and timetable.

References

Al-Khalifa, E. (1988) Pin money professionals? Women in teaching, in A. Coyle and J. Skinner (eds) *Women and Work*. Basingstoke: Macmillan.

Bolam, R. (1982a) *School-Focused In-Service Training*. London: Heinemann.

Bolam, R. (1982b) *Strategies for School Improvement*. Paris: OECD.

Fullan, M. (1990) Staff development, innovation and institutional development, in B. Joyce (ed.) *Changing School Culture through Staff Development* (1990 yearbook of the ASCD). Alexandria, VA: ASCD.

Hall, V. and Oldroyd, D. (1988) *Managing INSET in Local Education Authorities*. NDCSMT. Bristol University School of Education.

Hall, V. and Oldroyd, D. (1990) *Management Self-Development in Secondary Schools: a Distance Learning Programme* (units 1–4). NDCEMP, Bristol University School of Education.

Hargreaves, D., Hopkins, D., Leask, M., Connolly, J. and Robinson, P. (1989) *Planning for School Development: Advice to Governors, Headteachers and Teachers*. London: HMSO/DES.

Oldroyd, D., Smith, K. and Lee, J. (1984) *School-Based Staff Development Activities: a Handbook for Secondary Schools*. York: Longman.

Ranger, C. (1988) *Ethnic Minority School Teachers* – a Survey in Eight Local Education Authorities. London: Commission for Racial Equality.

School Management Task Force (1990) *Developing School Management: the Way Forward*. London: HMSO.

Wallace, M. (1990) *Managing In-Service Training in Primary Schools*, NDCEMP, Bristol University School of Education.

Williams, M. and England, J. (1986) *Alternatives to Courses*, North West TRIST. London: MSC.

12 | The nature of appraisal*

CYRIL POSTER AND DOREEN POSTER

All organisations, whether they are factories, businesses, hospitals or schools, exist to provide a product or service to the satisfaction of their clients or customers. Appraisal is a means of promoting, through the use of certain techniques and procedures, the organisation's ability to accomplish its mission of maintaining or improving what it provides while at the same time seeking to maintain or enhance staff satisfaction and development. For employees in any concern to perform effectively, they must be well motivated, have a sound understanding of what is expected of them, have a sense of ownership and possess the abilities and skills to fulfil the responsibilities they are charged with.

In most organisations there takes place at regular intervals, usually annually, a formal review of some kind between staff members and their immediate managers. There is little conformity over what this review is called: performance review, performance appraisal, staff development review, staff appraisal are among the terms most commonly in use. There are two distinct trends in appraisal: the one focuses on performance, the other on development.

Performance review (or appraisal) focuses on the setting of achievable, often relatively short-term goals. The review gives feedback: on task clarification through a consideration of the employees' understanding of their objectives set against those of the organisation; and on training needs as indicated either by shortcomings in performance or by the demonstration of potential for higher levels of performance.

Staff development review (or appraisal) focuses on improving the ability of employees to perform their present or prospective roles, through the identification of personal development needs and the provision of subsequent training or self-development opportunities.

In sum, the former is concerned with the task, the latter with the individual. This

*This is an edited version of Chapter 1 entitled 'What is appraisal?' in *Teacher Appraisal: Training and Implementation*, 2nd edn, published in 1993.

distinction is, of course, an over-simplification, since the performance of any organisation depends on both the delivery system and those who deliver it. There are many
variations in the linking of these two views of the purpose of appraisal, and it is difficult
to conceive of any appraisal system that can wholly ignore the one or the other.

For simplicity and brevity we intend to use the word *appraisal*, glossing it only when it
is necessary to make our intention and meaning absolutely clear. Readers will be aware
that there has been antagonism to the use of this word. There are LEAs which employ the
term *staff development review*. Others have sought to establish the use of *staff
development and appraisal*. In general, however, the single word *appraisal* now has
widespread currency.

Individual and organisational needs

Appraisal is one of a number of techniques designed to promote the integration of the
individual into the organisation. Each individual comes into the organisation with a
unique set of needs and objectives, preferences for ways of performing and expectations
of a wide range of personal satisfactions. One is ambitious, keen to achieve well in a short
time and move rapidly up the career ladder, another may wish to do no more than
perform competently, gaining personal satisfactions elsewhere, in activities unconnected
with the workplace. The problem for individuals is to make a contribution within
organisations set up by others, in such a way as also to satisfy their personal needs. The
problem for organisations is to harness the unique talents of individuals and coordinate
their activities towards the achievement, by effective and efficient means, of organisational objectives. This process of matching the needs of individuals to the objectives of
the organisation can best be described as 'integrating the individual and the organisation'. That bland phrase may serve to hide the pressures that an organisation may put on
individuals to subordinate their own interests to those of the organisation, or,
alternatively, the devious ways whereby the individual may seek to subvert the
organisational objectives.

Organisations have at their disposal many interactive procedures whereby they may
monitor and control the integration of their employees. These include:

- recruitment selection, placement, induction
- training, coaching, delegation, mentoring
- promotion, pay and reward systems, including bonuses
- performance review and appraisal
- counselling, grievance and disciplinary procedures
- exit interviews.

Since it is unlikely that there will be a perfect match between the interests of the
individual and the organisation, there will always arise the need to find ways of
reconciling the differences. The strategies for handling these differences will vary from
one organisation to another: in one, the differences will be papered over; in another, they
will be fully explored and every attempt will be made to negotiate a mutually satisfactory
solution; in a third, the organisation will impose its solution. The approach to the
resolution of differences will also colour the organisation's choice of, or specific
approach to the use of, any of these integrating processes.

All organisations have become aware that the accomplishment of a task is not solely a matter of individual ability or motivation, but is often also dependent on the support of co-workers. A small team of cooperating colleagues working on a common task will usually handle higher levels of stress and better maintain confidence and morale in the face of problems than an individual working in isolation. Similarly, as was first discovered in the automotive industry in the USA many decades ago, teams work better if they have knowledge and understanding of the objectives and performance of other teams. Both for the satisfaction of the social needs of individuals and for the achievement of institutional objectives a supportive climate, with a high level of collaboration and communication, is desirable.

The needs of individuals have been extensively analysed by sociologists and occupational psychologists. Not surprisingly, it has been found that, while there are differences based on age, culture, personality and social class, there exists a fairly common set of wants and needs. For middle managers and professionals these include a need for responsibility, relative autonomy, a sense of achievement, interesting and challenging work, opportunity for personal growth and development and the occasion to use specific skills (Vroom 1964; Herzberg 1966).

Additionally, individuals need to be provided with essential information if they are to achieve the organisational objectives. They feel they have a right to know:

- what is expected of them, what objectives they should be trying to achieve, whether they have a right to share in the shaping of these objectives
- what are their areas of responsibility, authority and discretion
- the extent to which they are achieving their objectives and meeting performance requirements
- how they may correct any shortfall between their objectives and their performance.

These requirements suggest certain desiderata for any effective integrating process, including appraisal.

Organisational management styles

McGregor (1960) posited two polarised sets of assumptions about the way organisations regarded their employees: the well known Theory X and Theory Y. A bureaucratic, hierarchical organisation will act on the assumption that its employees:

> dislike work, have little ambition, want security and require to be coerced, controlled or threatened with punishment. In contrast, theory Y holds that staff will seek responsibility if the conditions are appropriate, exercise self-direction and control if they become committed to organisational objectives, and respond to rewards associated with goal attainment.
>
> (Dennison and Shenton 1987)

In real life organisations rarely conform wholly to either polarity. It is now widely accepted that organisational behaviour, while to some extent predetermined by the organisation's self-image, will swing on a sector arc between these two polarities according to the demands of the situation and the response of management to those demands. Burns and Stalker (1968) produced such a model in which the terms *mechanistic* and *organic* represent those polarities. The mechanistic type of organisation is defined as one:

> suitable to stable conditions, to a hierarchical management structure in which there is a clear definition of assigned roles, formal and mainly vertical communication, and a built-in system of checks and supervision. The organic type of organisation, on the other hand, is designed to adapt to a rapid rate of change, to situations in which new and unfamiliar problems continually arise which cannot be broken down and distributed among the existing specialist roles. Relationships are therefore lateral rather than vertical, and form and reform according to the demands of the particular problem.
>
> (Poster 1976)

While there has been an observable swing in the management of schools towards the more participative organic style of management the rate of change currently imposed on all educational institutions impedes them from developing a holistic style. Managers are forced to make situational responses to a welter of demands which appear to be in conflicting and contradictory styles but which may merely be a reflection of the pressure put upon them and the institution they manage. Appraisal, properly implemented, both helps to make staff more understanding of the cause of these variations in style while encouraging management to make more tempered judgements about the style required by a particular set of demands and to be less inclined to bend to whatever wind blows hardest.

Organisational climate and appraisal

Organisational climate is a concept that refers to the different cultures or qualities possessed by organisations regardless of whether the structure is hierarchical and bureaucratic or informal and dynamic, or whether risk-taking and the use of individual initiative is encouraged or frowned upon. Every school:

> has a particular culture, determined by the individual values and experiences which each person brings to it, the ways in which people act and interact and the footprints they leave behind them.
>
> (Beare *et al.* 1989)

The differences in organisational climate and culture will both determine and be determined by the processes used to integrate the individual into the organisation. The hierarchical institution is likely to regard the induction process, for example, as one in which the newcomer is given a thorough grounding into the organisation's operational system. The dynamic institution will use induction as an opportunity to demonstrate the breadth of discretion and responsibility available to the newcomer. It follows, therefore, that appraisal in the one organisation will be concerned with assessing the extent of the individual's conformity to the organisational ethos and with meeting targets; in the other, with the development of initiative, self-development and goal achievement.

There may well be some variation between the wants of the individual and the climate of the organisation. This variation becomes highlighted on each occasion when the individual makes formal contact with any of the organisation's procedures, appraisal above all. The dynamic organisation may seek to accommodate the individual's wants within the climate of the institution. It will not alter its culture to suit the individual; in doing so it might well disturb the equilibrium of other members of staff. It will, however, be prepared to study suggestions and criticisms, make them available, if helpful, to wider discussion, and absorb them into its culture if this can be done with profit. The organisation which is rigid in its unwillingness to explore any mismatch between the individual and the institution will create a climate of intense frustration, demotivation, low effectiveness and adaptability, poor morale, low job satisfaction, high staff turnover and the rest of the ills that beset a sick organisation.

We have postulated that appraisal is one of a number of procedures for integrating the individual into the organisation, and that the desired outcome is achieved in part by meeting the individual's social and psychological needs. Failure to meet those needs will result in organisational ill-health. However, an organisation which bases its appraisal processes solely on the meeting of these needs will not necessarily produce the intended or desired result. Appraisal must be to the benefit of *both* the individual *and* the organisation. The appraisal system, in addition to promoting the wellbeing of the organisation's members, must contain the hard characteristics of clear goalsetting, sound appraisal data and purposeful review.

The range of the appraisal process

Appraisal may have, provided its procedures are geared to recognising this, a range of purposes, some centred on the needs of the organisation, some on those of the individual, some on both. While unquestionably concerned with personal professional development, appraisal will also include procedures for assessing the individual's performance in discharging specific and agreed responsibilities. These will derive from the job specification and the goals set at the previous appraisal interview or on a new teacher's arrival at the school.

Thus appraisal, as we view it, brings together both staff development and performance review. If it does not, we can see no merit in it: it will be merely a cosmetic exercise. To review performance is not to be judgemental. Indeed, if performance is not reviewed there is only hearsay evidence on which to base staff development needs. How can teachers be helped to become better teachers if nobody in the school knows how they are performing? How can the school become a better school unless there is an awareness, not of the statistics of its academic achievement and truancy rate, but of what the school's teachers are doing to maintain and improve their performance in the interests of the students?

Performance appraisal must not be confused with merit rating. Appraisal, properly used, will provide the organisation with far greater benefits than any mechanical procedure for assessing eligibility for merit payments. Those who may find the case for performance-related pay attractive should study the arguments mustered in the wide-ranging contributions to the book edited by Tomlinson (1992). If it were to be introduced, then those tempted to find in the appraisal process a ready mechanism for their decision-making would do well to heed the many expert researchers from the USA, who are unanimous in stating categorically that appraisal should not be used for this purpose.

The potentialities of appraisal

It is widely claimed that a well-run appraisal system will benefit . . .

. . . individual members of staff by:

- giving them a greater sense of purpose through the provision of clear objectives
- encouraging self-development and personal initiative
- enhancing their self-esteem and self-confidence
- reducing alienation and resentment, by providing the opportunity for free discussion
- providing opportunity for the dissemination of career advice

. . . the organisation by:

- enhancing the communication of organisational aims to all staff and facilitating the coordination of effort
- channelling individual effort into organisational goals
- providing the opportunity to initiate problem-solving and counselling interviews
- contributing to the institutional audit or review
- giving managers greater control through the setting of objectives within a school development plan

. . . both individual members of staff and the organisation by:

- helping to build morale
- encouraging better communication, both vertical and lateral, and the creation of a more open style of management
- providing the means whereby the individual can influence the organisation
- facilitating the identification of talent
- providing a mechanism whereby individual effort may be recognised even when no financial reward can be given
- integrating the individual and the organisation.

No single system will ever achieve all these potential benefits of an appraisal system: the climate and circumstances of the organisation will determine which of the potential benefits might realistically be achieved and which could not be accommodated. In one organisation, the climate might be favourable primarily to the support and encouragement of the individual; in another, to entrepreneurialism and self-development; in a third, the required focus might be more narrowly conceived, on achieving specific objectives within tight resource constraints.

Again, the nature of appraisal as seen by one organisation may be developmental: to review and plan those steps which will best contribute to the personal and professional development of individual members of staff. Another organisation may see the purpose of appraisal as mainly concerned with maximising staff performance: to involve and develop each member of the institution in such a way as to create the maximum benefit for the organisation.

Any single system which sought to be so comprehensive that it combined all the possible benefits of appraisal would almost certainly create such a confused multi-targeted approach that it would fail. It is necessary to remind oneself that appraisal has to be resourced in terms of time and expertise; and the more conflicting its objectives the greater the resource needs are likely to be. The designers or adapters of any appraisal system – and it must be recognised that, even within a national system, there will be adaptation to the particular needs and circumstances of the school – must be clear about their priorities.

Models of staff appraisal

There are four ideal types of appraisal interview. The implication of *ideal*, we hasten to add, is that you are unlikely to meet any appraisal process that wholeheartedly and exclusively has the characteristics shown for any single type. What one can say is that one of these types, broadly speaking, represents the appraisal style that is being adopted by a particular organisation, although it may borrow from any of the other types some aspect that it finds suited to its conditions or requirements.

In Figure 12.1 the horizontal axis denotes whether the emphasis is on individual or organisation goals: that is, whether the main concern is for the growth of the individual as a means to organisational development or whether the interests of the organisation predominate. The vertical axis indicates the extent to which management sees itself as having a proactive role: that is whether its main concern is with the setting of objectives or performance targets, with the identification of training needs, with reaching agreement on developmental tasks, or with taking or sharing of responsibility for developmental growth and the achievement of objectives. The salient features of the four basic types are indicated in Figure 12.2.

There are clear strengths and weaknesses in all four systems. The left-hand polarity of the horizontal axis of Figure 12.1 emphasises individual responsibility but may place excessive reliance on the ability of all individuals to make sound judgements at all times. It also gives too little recognition to those occasions when the needs of the organisation may override those of the individual. The right-hand polarity may be highly effective in

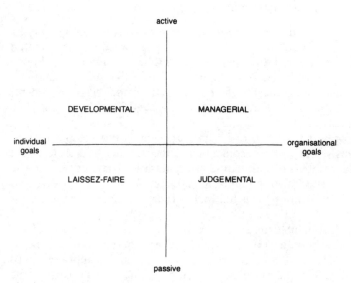

Figure 12.1   Types of appraisal interview

Developmental	Managerial
Assumes professional, collegial and collective authority to lie within the profession	Assumes right to manage: hierarchical position confirms authority
Has as its main concerns truth, accuracy, the maintenance of moral, ethical and professional values	Is concerned with doing and achieving, with efficiency and effectiveness
Works through peer appraisal of colleagues	Appraises through line management
Has a bipartite approach towards enabling self-improvement	Makes strong use of incentives and praise and reproach from superior
Seeks to produce agreed programme with shared responsibility for the achievement of objectives	Sets targets in order to maximise organisational objectives
Is concerned with longer-term, professional development	Is concerned with shorter-term assessment of performance

Laissez-faire	Judgemental
Recognises the importance of self-development	Uses appraisal to maintain social control
Allows managerial abdication from responsibility	Assumes managerial authority to make judgements
Encourages subordinates to raise issues	Collects data for the assessment of the subordinate
Demonstrates a lack ot focus, direction and purpose	Rates individuals against one another
Has a belief in the importance of self-motivation	Assumes the necessity of extrinsic motivation
Allows appraisee to decide on the need for follow-up	Uses system for merit rating and performance-related pay

Figure 12.2   Key features of the four basic types

setting institutional goals and making objective judgements, but may fail to capitalise on the knowledge and inner strengths that the individual has to offer.

The emphasis on objectives and yardsticks characteristic of the managerial type of appraisal has been criticised on several grounds: the rapidity of the rate of change may well invalidate or modify the goals that the managers have set; lower echelon staff have little control over the factors that affect goal achievement and, therefore, little motivation to take responsibility; and, particularly true of education, despite the present emphasis on the identification of performance criteria, there are large areas of activity in which specific targets cannot be identified and which may be undervalued in any review of this kind.

The growing influence from the 1970s onwards of humanistic psychology on management theory and practice has promoted the recognition of the value of individuals within organisations, and of their autonomy and self-actualising potential. Today individuals take and are willingly given far more responsibility for managing their own career progression, for determining their own goals within the broad limits of the organisational aims and objectives, and for assessing their own capabilities and developmental needs.

Nevertheless, while recognising and commending this, it must be accepted that few people are wholly capable of judging their own capacities, strengths and weaknesses without some form of catalyst. In some organisations, and increasingly in schools, that catalyst may be a *critical friend*, a peer or superior who acts as a sounding board for a colleague's assessment of their own abilities, progress and worth. In some few schools this provision may be built into the management system, sometimes by making it part of the role of the line manager, sometimes by the appointment of a senior manager as staff development officer, usually with a strong element of counselling and even troubleshooting in the role.

Yet the movement towards formalising and universalising a system of personal and professional staff development, rather then relying on hit and miss procedures has led to the institution of compulsory teacher appraisal in England and Wales. Teachers have accepted appraisal for staff development, recognising that any increase in personal skills and self-understanding leads also to the improvement of the effectiveness of the institution as a place of learning. [. . .]

References

Beare, H., Millikan, R. and Caldwell, B. (1989) *Creating an Excellent School*. London: Routledge.
Burns, T. and Stalker, G. M. (1968) *The Management of Innovation*. London: Tavistock.
Dennison, W. F. and Shenton, K. (1987) *Challenges in Educational Management*. London: Routledge.
Herzberg, F. W. (1966) *Work and the Nature of Man*. London: Staples Press.
McGregor, D. G. (1960) *The Human Side of Enterprise*. London: McGraw-Hill.
Poster, C. D. (1976) *School Decision Making*. London: Heinemann.
Tomlinson, H. (ed.) (1992) *Performance-Related Pay in Education*. London: Routledge.
Vroom, V. H. (1964) *Work and Motivation*. New York: Wiley.

13 | Appraising appraisal: some tensions and some possibilities*

BARRY HUTCHINSON

Introduction

Now that the steam and mists generated in the public debate about appraisal have evaporated, and staff appraisal is becoming a part of the fabric of university procedures, it is opportune to begin to reflect on the extent to which the claimed benefits (DES 1987) and the expressed worries and concerns (Dockrell *et al.* 1986) about appraisal are being borne out in practice. Appraisal was of course only one of a number of structural changes introduced to the university sector, but it was potentially a significant one since it would impinge directly on the work of every member of staff, and on the internal structures and relationships within each university.

The Jarratt Report (1985), produced by that 'too pliant and compliant . . . committee' (Elton 1988), made a number of recommendations concerning organisational arrangements in universities which it claimed would improve the efficiency of their running. Among these was included the recommendation that academic departments should become cost centres which if implemented would lead to devolution of responsibility and accountability to heads of department. Besides proffering performance criteria by which departments (and their heads) might be assessed, the report, in recommending the virtues of providing written job descriptions for heads of department, pointed to the question of the wisdom of marrying administrative and academic leadership roles in the one position. Being minded to make such a recommendation, it emphasised the need to maintain a careful balance between the two responsibilities. In effect, what Jarratt was proposing was that universities adopt a more stratified and hierarchical system of line management, a proposal which it may be said was in line with much orthodox thinking about management structures of the time. Such a structure was already in place in the University of Ulster. [. . .]

Shortly after its publication, agreement was reached between the various parties on the

*This is an edited version of an article that originally appeared in *Higher Education* in 1995.

salary rise to be awarded to university staff. Published in the 23rd Report (CVCP 1987), there was included acceptance, by the Association of University Teachers, of the establishment of staff appraisal schemes in universities. Each university was to negotiate the particular form its appraisal scheme would take.

The coincidence of the thrust of the Jarratt and the 23rd Reports towards specific lines of accountability and procedures for their enactment reflected the growing centralising concerns of the then Conservative government. The claimed benefit of these changes was that universities would, by removing surplus capacity in the system in whatever form it might take, provide better value for money to the nation. Staff appraisal would ensure that not only would every member of staff be seen to be fulfilling their job requirements, they would also actually improve their performance and thereby contribute to the raising of educational standards.

By presenting an account of a small scale piece of qualitative research into the staff appraisal scheme of the University of Ulster, I shall query the validity of these claims. In so doing I shall attempt to reveal why they are not realised, and what might be done to improve matters. Although I make no specific reference to the parallel, it may be that a retention of, or a return to, some aspects of the collegial structures which typified the traditional university, represent the kind of direction being recommended by those promoting total quality management systems. In presenting the account, I wish to draw attention to the relationship between the form which a programme of staff appraisal takes and the manner in which teaching competence is assessed. It seems that the nature of each of these and of their conjunction is not accidental: rather it seems that the same kind of conceptions and values used in devising the one are also used to devise the other. That is, each reflects and sustains the other. To put this study in context, I will first of all present two typifications of appraisal systems in order to demonstrate both how individual appraisal schemes come to have the features that they do, and secondly, to provide some insight into the complexities and issues which arise in the operation of the University of Ulster scheme. Having presented these two typifications I shall indicate how they attend to professional development through the manner in which they evaluate teaching performance.

Forms of appraisal

Most appraisal programmes in educational organisations include some kind of training, an initial meeting between appraiser and appraisee, the completion of specific appraisal documents, sometimes direct observation of practice and consultation with those with whom the appraisee works, an interview, and the writing of an agreed statement. Generally speaking, it is possible to identify two broad emphases in the forms and methods which appraisal programmes take: that which is directed towards extending and maintaining managerialist control and accountability, and that which aims at the professional development of staff. I make this distinction only to help in clarifying some of the ideas, values and issues relating to staff appraisal: in practice it is often difficult to discern.

The managerialist form emphasises a concern with 'institutional productivity and administrative convenience' (Ramsden 1992), or, as Cuthbert (1988) put it, it 'overemphasises economic considerations, economising and administrative tidiness'. While it often inherits bureaucratic stuctures and procedures, including competitive systems of reward, it uncritically accepts hierarchically defined criteria 'around a concept of good practice' (Bradley 1992). In the sense that these criteria constitute a blueprint, then, as Eraut (1992) points out, 'their validity is immediately challenged'. In this form of appraisal, primary consideration is given to assessing how the individual has contributed to the work of the organisation and to keeping formal written records of both that effort and its means of appraisal. Since the individual is essentially regarded as a functionary, it is concerned with identifying and remedying individual deficiencies in performance. Training is based on a deficit model of performance and is directed towards equipping staff with the skills needed to complete the prescribed tasks. Appraisal documents in this approach often adopt or adapt broad, sweeping, categories, and these are often supplemented by observational checklists. Since these impose limited and partial sets of criteria, they additionally serve as instruments of surveillance and control. The primary purpose of these technically devised instruments is not just to measure the degree of congruence between centrally determined policy and individual practice, but to ensure its faithful implementation. The interview is primarily concerned with establishing whether the appraisee has met, or has failed to meet, the objectives of the organisation: it asserts and reinforces dependency relationships. Follow-up is left to the appraiser, though some record indicating that the appraisal has taken place, is centrally stored. Practice in this sense is essentially replication or reproduction of behaviour according to prescribed rules and procedures: it is work as labour, following the lines of a specified blueprint. Individuals are essentially objectified in the appraisal procedure since personal views and concerns are of concern only in so far as they assist or interfere with the reproduction of managerially desired objectives. Efficiency and quality are to be assured through rigid procedures and tight forms of managerial control. Elliott (1993) explains that underlying such procedures lies the belief that the:

> power to effect change lies in systems rather than the individuals who participate in them. . . . [This belief] rests on the Parsonian view that organisational systems are constituted by a normative consensus about their aims and purposes. It is by virtue of this consensus of interest that systems have the power to shape the activities of their members. But systems constantly have to adapt to a changing environment and according to normative-functionalist theory, this is accomplished through a control centre which manages the social production of a consensus of aims and purposes – what are now fashionably called 'mission statements' – and adjust the structures to accomplish them. From a normative-functionalist perspective 'management' is the agency that enables the system to be restructured.

The professional development approach to appraisal emphasises a shared commitment to improvement: the individual shares with others ultimate responsibility, and hence accountability for, the improvement of practice. One distinguishing feature of this approach is the formal attention which it gives to the consideration of the contexts (practical as well as historical, political, and educational), in which the individual works. It recognises that 'Abilities are not attributes of individuals which exist independently . . . They are qualities of the relationship between the individual and the context in which she or he operates' (Bridges *et al.* 1986). A second distinguishing feature is the inclusion of self-appraisal. Training is directed at improving the ability of all staff to collect, interpret and discuss relevant evidence, and to translate the improved understanding, insights and judgements into action. Decisions on the focus and form the evaluation of practice is to take are negotiated and enacted collaboratively. The particular focus for each appraisal may vary in order that areas of concern may be dealt with in some depth. While self-understandings are central, observation is supplemented by the collection of relevant documentary material and the views of those whom the individual works with. It is expected that these data will often contain differing views and will generate conflicting evaluations. There is a set of ground rules to govern the collection and use of this evidence. In the interview the appraiser listens and encourages the appraisee to explore the questions and issues through consideration of the collected evidence. Individuals retain responsibility for deciding which changes to make to their practice but are to take account of others' views: these are seen to challenge, extend and enhance, but not to define. Follow-up is integrated with everyday work practices, with organisational plans and development policy, and with resource allocation. Practice involves the critical interpretation and application of professional ethics and values. Openness, trust, empathy, and critical respect are examples of the defining values of this approach. These values are recognised to represent 'ever receding standards' (Elliott 1991), whose improved realisation in practice remains the constant task: they also provide the grounds for the internal control of practice. Quality and efficiency are to be assured through commitment and support to ongoing review of current practices, individual and organisational.

Appraisal and evaluating teaching

The two contrasting models of appraisal have their counterpart in approaches to the manner in which the teaching competence of academic staff can be evaluated. Evaluation methods themselves reflect and reveal assumptions and beliefs about the nature of professional practice and about its development. Two alternative views about these are distinguishable. The first, following Schön (1983, 1987, 1991), may be called the technical or traditional, infallible expert perspective; the second, following Elliott (1985, 1987, 1988, 1989, 1991), may be called the reflective practitioner, or critical, perspective.

In the technical perspective good practice is regarded essentially as the exhibition of performance behaviours which conform to prespecified standard criteria. Practice is conceived as the efficient application of prespecified and previously acquired skills to standard recurring situations. Practice is therefore essentially the instrumental application of scientifically produced knowledge. Professionals gain their professional knowledge in formally taught and traditionally assessed courses and they learn how to apply it through periods of protected or diluted training. The courses are constructed around sets of rules grounded in psychological 'scientific' theories, which are sometimes carried into informal codes of practice. These are essentially rational-behaviouristic theories of learning which hold firstly, that practice-behaviour can be entirely shaped (guided, stimulated, motivated), by having formal plans and formal systems of external reward and punishment; and secondly, that changes in behaviour can actually be measured. What is crucial in this perspective is that teaching–learning problems which present themselves in the course of practice, are regarded as being definable in terms of the trained teacher's existing knowledge, and solvable by the application of the teacher's previously acquired skill. Each problematic situation is rendered amenable to professional expertise through being identified as congruent with some known antecedent; that is, it is recognised as being in some way stereotypical. Once categorised in this way the problem is transposed into a technical one which can be solved by applying expert knowledge skilfully. When a problem which cannot be handled in this way constantly recurs, separate research can be set up to provide certain, standardised, solutions. These in turn are taught in *a priori* fashion and become part of the professional's skilled box of tools.

Since practice is the application of general laws to specific cases covered by defined goals, it is rule bound, prespecifiable, observable-skill-behaviour which is capable of being assessed in terms of its measurable effects on whatever or whoever it is directed at. As it separates means and ends so it resembles an applied technology. What is needed in the assessment of teaching are agreed norms defining the observable characteristics of good teaching. Once produced these can be used as a blueprint to train trainees, and by a trained observer to rate teaching ability. As the student is the instrument stimulating the exercise of the teacher's skill, so the teacher's knowledge is the source of the requisite solution, and his or her skill the instrument of application. The teacher is the cause of the students' learning: teaching effectiveness is commensurate with student grades. Results are what counts. Quality from this perspective is seen in terms of fittedness for purpose and value-addedness, in terms of conformity to prespecified, standardised, criteria.

Evaluating teaching has most often been done from within this perspective: its major method is the use of student rating questionnaires. Not surprisingly these have therefore received much comment, most of which has been unfavourable. Ramsden (1992) enumerates their drawbacks: they do not meet statistical use-validity standards: they ask face-invalid questions; they 'conflate stylistic and quality measures'; they 'equate the collection of student ratings for personnel purposes with their use for diagnostic feedback purposes'; they have little effect on those who do not value student views; they prescribe minimum standards which become the average; they provide nothing which is not already known. Ultimately their use will 'trivialise the process of improvement, damage morale, and lead to a distortion of the educational system'.

From the reflective practitioner perspective, teaching is the attempt to translate into practice the moral ends of education. These in themselves are complex, and they find expression in statements of belief and value, as well as in practice. This claim, that competence is to be found *in*, and not just, *as a result of* practice, is at the heart of the reflective practitioner perspective. A good performance 'is one which calls forth abilities that are critical for success in the given context' (Bridges *et al.* 1986).

Professional knowledge resides vitally in memory and in habitual ways of working. It consists of 'structures to sustain creative thought and provide frameworks for judgement [which are] intrinsically problematical and contestable' (Elliott 1988). Eraut (1992) suggests that these structures may comprise of three kinds of knowledge: propositional, personal and process knowledge. Of these, the last seems to characterise professional performance and is itself, he suggests, constituted by five kinds of processes, namely: acquiring information, skilled behaviour, deliberative processes, giving information and controlling one's own behaviour. More holistically however, professional knowledge, as knowledge-memory recalls what has happened in the past; as value-purpose it grapples with what it intends; and as context related it depends on what is possible and on what is understood to be possible in a particular situation. Together these struggle to fuse into a form of suggestions for practical action. Action itself, embedded in these suggestions, is provisional and hypothetical: it is inherently problematic. Reflection in and on practice, and on the purposes it pursues, proceeds interactively with consideration of the context in which it occurs. Together these provide estimations of the efficacy of practice, and the grounds for improvement: caring for the values of one's practice and for one's students provides the impetus for attempting to bring it about; the context in which it occurs sets limits on what can be done. It is this personal commitment to shared professional values, and a critical attitude to one's practice, that drive the improvement process: the context provides the opportunities and constraints for it to happen. That is, practice is internally motivated and externally mediated.

Teaching is more than the formal transmission of expert, disciplined knowledge: it is both an invitation to, and a support for, independent critical learning by both the student *and* the teacher. The problems that occur in practice will in some respect be unique: they arise with the occurrence of something unexpected or puzzling. Each problematic situation will share similarities with something in the experience of the teacher, and something which is dissonant with that experience. Each will in some way, and to some extent, reveal the limits of the teacher's professional knowledge. The facts of the situation present a partially incoherent text whose meaning will arise from the interplay with the teacher's understandings and appreciations ('general hypotheses which are retrospective distillations from past experience', Elliott 1985): the problem the situation contains is to be constructed through the teacher testing the adequacy of his or her interpretations. These interpretations include possible lines of action, of implementation: they also embody the values the profession espouses. Resolving the problem involves the exercise of discretion and judgement in deciding upon and following a potentially adequate and appropriate course of action, not the following of some prescribed rule. It requires and sustains agency and autonomy, and it reveals how the 'acquisition of professional knowledge and the improvement of professional practice cannot be differentiated: each is constituted by, and constitutive of, the other' (Carr 1989). Hence practice can itself be understood to include an intrinsic dimension of learning (Winter 1989), and of invention: it is a form of research, of art, which reveals and reflects internal powers of being. In so far as it embraces all of these features, practice is a form of self-definition and determination, and therefore constitutes a form of self-professional development. Quality, in this perspective, 'is not about performing well to please one's [superiors]; still less is it about fulfilling criteria imposed by administrative agencies. It is an outcome of a duty towards oneself to be excellent' (Ramsden 1987), in terms of the internal values of the practice itself.

Evaluating practice from this perspective involves the collaborative and continuous identification and clarification of issues, problems and concerns, collecting evidence from various sources including self-monitoring, interpreting it, and judging how best to apply what it yields in practice. What evaluation cannot be, as it aspires to in the managerialist mode, is an effort to measure the congruence of the outcomes of action with a specification of its objectives. And this is so because professional action cannot be reduced to following a set of rules. [. . .]

Negotiations between management and academic staff union representatives, about the form an appraisal system should take, lasted almost two years. The major issue concerned agreeing the procedures which would ensure that staff development remained the key purpose. What was eventually agreed to, was a cyclical programme which would revolve around a biennial appraisal interview between a member of staff and his or her management superior. For a lecturing member of staff this ordinarily means that he or she is appraised by their head of department: they are in turn appraised by their dean, who is appraised by either a pro-vice-chancellor, or by the vice-chancellor.

The preparatory events to the interview were emphasised by the Pro-Vice-Chancellor,

Personnel (who led the management side of the negotiations), as of crucial importance to the success of the programme. Every member of staff is to complete an all-embracing proforma in which they detail the nature of their current academic work – teaching, research, administration, consultancies, contributions to the corporate life of the university, and relevant external activities. They are to assess their contribution to each of those areas, and they are then to indicate any area of potential into which they would like to develop. There is no specific opportunity to specify the kind of assistance or support they might need from the university in order to be able to develop in the areas they indicate, other than a section on proposals for career development and training. Completion of these proformas is to take place in the context of departmental and faculty discussions about present and future plans. [. . .] Subsequent to the appraisal interview a statement is written by the superior to which the member of staff is asked to give his or her agreement: this statement includes specific work objectives for the next two years. These form the basis of the next appraisal.

To operationalise matters, the recently established staff development unit was coopted to prepare and run appraisal training sessions for both senior and junior staff.

My research began when I made the first invitations to members of staff to give me an interview on their experience and views of the programme. The research would attempt to contribute to the improvement of appraisal through the actual conduct of the research as well as in its reporting. To realise the former aspiration [. . .] I sent each interviewee a copy of the material I had taken from their interview, and asked for agreement to my inclusion of it in the form and context in which I had presented it while I guaranteed to provide them as much anonymity as possible. Upon receiving their agreement I produced the final version of the report, a copy of which I sent to each member of staff who had given me an interview. Altogether I interviewed seventeen members of staff. In terms of occupational position, they ranged from pro-vice-chancellor, through staffing officer, dean, head of department, to senior lecturer and lecturers A and B, including two of the latter who had recently completed probation. I also interviewed a member of AUT who had been a member of the negotiating team and two members of the staff training team.

The interviews were semi-structured. With those responsible for establishing the programme I began by asking about its origins and the purposes they had in mind for it; with those involved in the negotiations I inquired about the issues debated; and with those responsible for staff training I inquired after their major concerns. Thereafter the progress of each interview depended on where the interviewee took me and how I responded to that. [. . .]

What was the major, though not altogether surprising, outcome of the investigation, was the revelation of the depth of concern of senior management with quality control mechanisms, and their lack of awareness of the consequent alienating effects on staff. Briefly put, the 'mind-set' of senior staff centred on the need for 'rational' plans to guide organisational affairs, and for assessment mechanisms to measure the congruence of outcomes with the specified objectives. Senior staff were quite clear about the need for and the nature of these plans and how they were to be achieved. The University, and each of the eight faculties, have five-year plans; departments too are expected to have their written plans; there are internal structures for managing financial control, for monitoring usage of all university facilities, and for overseeing the university's overall performance. There is a course evaluation structure in addition to the normal staff–student committee and external examiner systems. The appraisal programme was grafted onto the trunk of this administrative system. [. . .]

As the whole of university work is conducted through this formal system of administration, so the appraisal programme became a branch of it. Clearly such a state of affairs can lead to tension when differences of view are settled by committees whose remit is to maintain centrally devised, university-wide policies, rather than to deliberate on the merits of individual cases. One instance where this became apparent was in the contrast between the regard staff held of the appraisal interview itself, and that which they held for the rest of the programme.

The view of one member of staff about the appraisal interview encapsulates the positive experience of everyone I interviewed:

> it forced me to sit down and consider (a) what I was doing, (b) how I was doing it, and looking at ways in which I could improve. I also valued the opportunity of somebody taking time to sit down and talk about the work I was doing and to listen to plans that I had for my own career in the University . . . nobody had ever taken the time to ask me how I was getting on or how things were going . . . I'm aware that I have a big workload, but actually documenting it on paper just made me realise how many different areas I was feeding into, and I think I did find it a valuable exercise.
>
> (Young male lecturer, Grade B).

This statement also hints at the areas of university work which drew less favourable comments. Before moving to these, however, I would wish to emphasise the warmth with which staff recalled the face to face interview with their managerial superior. Having the formal opportunity to talk professionally about their personal work and plans, and to reflect more 'publicly' about them, had a considerable impact upon staff. That it did, reflected the need for staff to have institutional recognition of their worth, and it revealed not just the general lack of attention previously paid to it, but the more pervasive sense of being something like a cog in the machine. One member of staff expressed this feeling as being due to 'the pressure we are all under here in our everyday job'; another said staff found 'difficulty staying on course because of competing institutional demands'. A middle-aged, male head of department claimed that many staff,

> don't always see the rationale behind things – I mean I'm on many, far too many, university committees . . . but I'm not in the inner circles . . . and sometimes thinking comes out of those without perhaps being fully explained and justified . . . people are making decisions without perhaps either telling you about it or consulting you about it.

[. . .] A lecturer, Grade B, said he could not see the developmental purposes of appraisal being realised 'because of the different levels in management – the different levels of hierarchy'. Another female lecturer, Grade A, complained that, 'the institution provides virtually no support for any of the activities that you are asked to undertake'. Another youngish male head of department pointed out: 'I think one of the responses of the organisation is to try to send out more forms and more information every time something happens. I am worried about complaining about anything in case it sets off another avalanche of forms.' All in all, it seemed that the prior need for the university to service itself and its functions dominated every other concern.

What ameliorated this managerialist system of operations, in addition to the intended 'flexibility', was what a member of the staff training team referred to as 'a good deal of gentility' around the organisation. It seemed to be this feature of interpersonal relationships which ensured that centrally devised plans were acted upon rather than reacted to: in other words staff would tolerate and accept managerial control provided their views were sought.

The criticism of the University bureaucracy seemed to lie at the heart of the negative, and more neutral, accounts staff gave of the other facets of the appraisal programme. The context in which the negotiations to establish it had been held had not been good, of course – various government statements proclaiming the need for weeding out, or disciplining and retraining, incompetent staff, set the elitist and anti-egalitarian (Moodie 1988) mood. Secondly, the major training effort to prepare staff for appraisal was directed only at senior staff: the view it seems was that, given the advice from the Committee of Vice Chancellors and Principals, limited resources, the relations between management and AUT, and the bureaucratic administrative structure of the university, if senior staff were formally trained in the procedures then appraisal could be made to work. Occasional, voluntary half day training sessions were provided for junior staff.

There were, however, three other factors which bore heavily on the conduct of, and regard staff held for, the appraisal programme: the extent of the existence of the 'good practice' setting, the nature of follow-up to the appraisal interview, and the manner of evaluating teaching competence. In regard to the first of these, the reality was that there was great variation between departments in the number and type of meetings which were held, and in the existence of departmental plans. I came across no departments which held weekly or fortnightly meetings (an arrangement which the Pro-Vice-Chancellor, Personnel, believed to be widespread), although some, whose staff were in close proximity to one another, felt they had ongoing, albeit informal, discussions. While one dean could claim to have a carefully thought out and thoroughly discussed faculty plan, and to have plans for each of its departments and for every member of its staff, I interviewed staff from one department in another faculty who, despite repeated requests, had been unable to find their department's plan. In this same department there had been no departmental discussions about, nor preparations for, appraisal: indeed I discovered some staff in other faculties, who, after two years of it being in operation, had not been appraised.

It may have been unsurprising to find very little evidence of any follow-up to the appraisal interview, given the length of time it had been in existence, but what was disconcerting to find was that many junior staff did not know what was to happen to their appraisal proforma and the resulting agreed statement between themselves and their head of department. Both in fact were to remain confidential to the member of staff and to their head of department, although extracts from the latter could be used in any application for promotion (again few were aware of this).

Furthermore, there appeared to exist a considerable gulf between junior and senior staff in the expectations they held of, and the value they attributed to, appraisal. Senior staff believed they could detect beneficial effects, such as increased confidence and morale, among junior staff: they in turn, while expressing the value of talking formally to someone about their work and plans, were altogether much more uncertain of there being any good coming out of it. Such an attitude may indeed have not been without merit, since management did not have an extended view as to how follow-up, other than forming the basis of the next appraisal in two years time, was to occur. Few were aware that regular and informal reviews were expected. Monitoring of the programme itself was left to the Pro-Vice-Chancellor, Personnel, who had recently requested sight of examples of completed proformas. The purpose of this exercise was to ascertain that the appraisals had been conducted properly: it was not to consider how they might be best followed up.

Although the evaluation of teaching was not yet included in the appraisal programme, it was raised in the interviews as a matter of considerable concern. The issue was not whether or not teaching should be assessed. The problem was with the method which was being trialled. In the pilot assessment exercise, academic staffs' teaching competence is assessed entirely through student questionnaires. Each student is asked to complete a checklist. Most of them ask about the member of staff's punctuality at classes and about their speed of return of assignments: none inquire about the manner of encouraging critical reflection or independent reasoning. They pay no attention to either the physical, or indeed any other, context in which teaching occurs, nor do they inquire after the kinds of assessments which staff use. [. . .]

The most tolerant view staff expressed of this system of assessing teaching was expressed by one junior member of staff as follows: 'I think these things are important at the margins . . . they . . . emphasise one . . . the mechanistic . . . aspect of people's teaching but probably the least important one as far as I am concerned.' Other criticisms were more stringent: they included points about the indeterminativeness of the statements; the inappropriateness of their focusing only on overt teaching behaviours; of staff not seeing the completed forms; of the timing of their completion and of the unreliability of the scores. Clearly the view of teaching and learning which the checklists embraced was that of a transmission-reception process. [. . .]

Clearly the kind of appraisal system which an organisation adopts, reflects and reveals both the value system and the existing internal structures of the organisation. While these, as in the University of Ulster, interrelate in highly complex and sometimes inconsistent and unexpected ways, they do strongly influence the perceptions and expectations of staff. To the extent that the appraisal system is one effort to support the realisation of organisation aspirations, and where one of these is the promotion and achievement of quality, then the conception which is held of quality, and the structures and practices which support its maintenance and development, are important in defining and shaping staff expectations about, and understanding of, the organisation, themselves and others, and the tasks they undertake. The degree to which appraisal acts as a controlling force to ensure staff meet the organisation's functional requirements, as opposed to the degree to which it empowers staff to pursue and realise reflective educational qualities, then the more it acts to debilitate rather than to develop staff. Where appraisal concerns itself with measuring the extent to which staff have met operationally (cost-effective) defined targets (agreed to or not), and does not adequately concern itself with other values (critical intelligence for example), then the more impoverished will the contribution of staff, and hence of the organisation itself, become.

What I believe this piece of research reveals is how a formal organisational concern with attending to and promoting staff's thinking in connection with their personal work and plans (the appraisal interview), is more likely to achieve a positive contribution to the realisation of organisational goals, than is the limited and limiting production of 'rational' organisational plans, and the impersonal and imperious distribution and collation of checklists and questionnaires. When these are designed to stimulate competition among staff for the personal acquisition of scarce resources, their longer term effect will be to deter rather than to develop: they will 'encourage mediocrity, foster brooding resentment, and dampen the desire to excel' (Ramsden 1992).

The interview embodies the organisation's recognition of, and respect for, the individual's worth. The events surrounding the appraisal interview, especially the manner of evaluating teaching, reveal a more manipulative attitude and intent towards staff development. In many ways the difference between the interview and its attendant events highlights the difference between a concern for attaining quality through focusing on organisational processes, and the managerialist concern to equate quality with the hitting of prespecified targets. If quality and improvement in the reflective practitioner mode are to be preferred, then the shape and form which the appraisal interview takes ought to be expanded into other areas of university work. At the core it would seem that it is the balance between the organisation's ability and willingness to listen and respond, rather than to tell and supervise, which is crucial.

References

Bradley, H. (1992) Getting the best out of appraisal, *Journal of the Educational Research Network of Northern Ireland*, 6: 127–35.

Bridges, D., Elliott, J. and Klass, C. (1986) Performance appraisal as naturalistic inquiry: a report on the Fourth Cambridge Conference on Educational Evaluation, *Cambridge Journal of Education*, 16(3): 221–33.

Carr, W. (1989) *Quality in Teaching: Arguments for a Reflective Practice*. London: The Falmer Press.

Committee of Vice Chancellors and Principals [CVCP] (1987) *Twenty Third Report from Committee A*. London: CVCP.

Cuthbert, R. E. (1988) Quality and management in higher education, *Studies in Higher Education*, 13(1): 59–68.

Department of Education and Science [DES] (1987) *Higher Education: Meeting the Challenge*. London: HMSO.

Dockrell, B., Nisbet, J., Nuttall, D., Stones, E. and Wilcox, B. (1986) *Appraising Appraisal*. Birmingham: BERA.

Elliott, J. (1985) Teacher education and teacher quality, *British Journal of Sociology*, 1: 102–7.

Elliott, J. (1987) Teacher Evaluation and Teaching as a Moral Science, *Journal of the Educational Research of Northern Ireland*, 1: 201–18.

Elliott, J. (1988) Education in the Shadow of GERBIL. The Lawrence Stenhouse Memorial Lecture, BERA Annual Conference, University of East Anglia, Norwich.

Elliott, J. (1989) Education theory and the professional learning of teachers: an overview, *Cambridge Journal of Education*, 19(1): 81–101.

Elliott, J. (1991). 'Are "performance indicators" educational quality indicators?' Paper given at BERA Annual Conference, Nottingham Polytechnic, Nottingham.

Elliott, J. (1993) What have we learned from action research in school-based evaluation? *Education Action Research*, 1(1): 175–86.

Elton, L. (1988) The use of performance indicators in higher education, book review, *Studies in Higher Education*, 13(3): 337–8.

Eraut, M. (1992) Developing the knowledge base: a process perspective on professional education, in R. Barnett (ed.) *Learning to Effect*. Buckingham: SRHE and Open University.

The Jarratt Report (1985) *Report of the Steering Committee for Efficiency Studies in Universities*. London: CVCP.

Moodie, G. C. (1988) The debates about higher education quality in Britain and the USA, *Studies in Higher Education*, 13(1): 5–13.

Ramsden, P. (1987) Improving teaching and learning in higher education: the case for a relational perspective, *Studies in Higher Education*, 12(2): 275–86.

Ramsden, P. (1992) *Learning to Teach in Higher Education*. London: Routledge.

Schön, D. A. (1983) *The Reflective Practitioner: How Professionals Think in Action*. London: Temple Smith.

Schön, D. A. (1987) *Educating the Reflective Practitioner: Towards a New Design for Teaching and Learning in the Professions*. San Francisco: Jossey-Bass.

Schön, D. A. (ed.) (1991) *The Reflective Turn: Case Studies in and on Education Practice*. New York: Teachers College Press.

Winter, R. (1989) Problems in teacher appraisal: an action research solution? in H. Simons and J. Elliott (eds) *Rethinking Appraisal and Assessment*. Milton Keynes: Open University Press.

14 | Professional development portfolios*

DAI HALL

Introduction

By the early 1990s the world of the professional teacher was such that, for a number of reasons, there was increasing interest in the keeping of Professional Development Portfolios (PDPs) by teachers.

Firstly, Credit Accumulation and Transfer Schemes (CATS) with their explicit willingness to accredit prior experiential learning (APEL) were being developed by higher education institutions (Evans 1987, 1988; Bloor and Butterworth 1990; Hall 1991).

Secondly, it was increasingly being recognised by award giving bodies that professional development depends on a synthesis of theory and practice and that effective reflection is the key to this synthesis. (The work of writers such as Schön and Kolb in establishing an 'experiential learning cycle' had been very influential.) The implication that effective professional learning could begin in practice rather than in classroom-derived theory opened the way to formal accreditation of such learning (Boud *et al.* 1985; Land 1991).

Thirdly, INSET had reached the stage where the professionality of teachers was increasingly recognised and teachers were regularly involved in self-initiated professional development. There were increasing calls for this to be recognised by award giving institutions (Graham 1989; Chandler 1990; Mumby *et al.* 1988; Winter and Powney 1988).

Fourthly, the rationale and methodology of APEL for professionals had been developed. At least one institution (Hall 1991) had established a satisfactory method of facilitating specific portfolios for teachers and a number of education authorities were establishing programmes for helping their staff produce professional development portfolios.

---

*This is an edited version of the article 'Professional development portfolios for teachers and lecturers' that originally appeared in *British Journal of In-service Education*, published in 1994.

All the elements were in place to enable Higher Education to meet the needs of teachers in a different, more innovative way. The key to the place of the project described in this chapter was a gap in terms of delivery. The philosophy and mechanisms were in place to enable APEL to occur but there were at the time very few means of making it available to teachers within their own institutions. This then is the essence of the TRIN portfolio project.

Background

The Thames Regional INSET Network (TRIN) is a body comprising 24 local authorities in inner and outer London which enables those concerned with the development and operation of INSET to meet, continue informal co-ordination and disseminate good practice.

The University of Greenwich is one of Britain's largest teacher education institutions. Situated mainly in South East London, it is also active in INSET across all phases. It is well known for its pioneering work in Credit Accumulation and Transfer Schemes (CATS). The INSET framework has over a thousand teachers working towards more than 20 awards. Credit for prior experiential learning is a key aspect of the scheme.

As the result of pioneering work by the TRIN an investigation into the interest of advisory teachers in receiving accreditation by means of a professional development portfolio (PDP) had been carried out in 1988 by Barbara Chandler. One of its recommendations had been that the TRIN should pilot a TRIN 'professional development portfolio'. This recommendation was accepted and Thames Polytechnic was asked to undertake the work.

The portfolio project took place between September 1990 and December 1991.

Implementation

The project was, in effect, a staff development approach based on the cascade model which consisted of a number of groups of participants and three phases. It was planned that each phase should last roughly a term.

During phase 1 two experienced APEL facilitators (Michael Bloor and Christine Butterworth of Thames Polytechnic) trained a senior member of staff from each of 6 LEAs in the techniques of portfolio facilitation. The basis of the methods used by Bloor and Butterworth was described by them in 1990. The essence of this project was to establish whether techniques appropriate to the production of APEL portfolios were appropriate to PDPs.

During phase 2 (roughly January to May 1991) the 6 LEA staff facilitated the portfolios of a group of volunteer teachers in their own LEAs. The LEAs were Barnet, Barking and Dagenham, Ealing, Enfield, Harrow, and Kensington and Chelsea. The research team established contact with these groups and began to monitor their progress. Contact was also established with The Polytechnic of Central London, The Polytechnic of East London, The University of London Institute of Education, King's College, Kingston Polytechnic, The Open University, Thames Polytechnic, and The West London Institute of Higher Education.

During phase 3 (roughly May to December 1991) a number of interviews were conducted with the LEA facilitators and their portfolio groups. These meetings took place in April, May and June 1991. The views of the HE institutions and employers were also sought.

Information in five key areas emerged from the project.

The nature of a professional development portfolio for teachers and lecturers

A professional development portfolio is a collection of material, made by a professional, that records, and reflects on, key events and processes in that professional's career.

The main characteristic of a PDP that distinguishes it from a professional diary or record of achievement is the stress it places on *reflection*. Being reflective about an experience and relating that experience to other aspects of the person's professional life is fundamental to three important aspects of PDPs:

- They can assist the process of learning itself by helping the individual move from the 'concrete experience' to the 'abstract conceptualisation' aspect of the experiential learning cycle.
- They can assist in helping individuals through the 'active experimentation' phase of the experiential learning cycle.
- Reflective writing *can* make it possible for a portfolio to attract accreditation.

A second important distinguishing characteristic is *structure*. PDPs are much more than chronological records of events; they are organised around themes or types of activity.

It is clear that individuals undertake the keeping of PDPs for a wide variety of reasons. It is possible to discern several broad categories of purposes for the portfolio:

- to assemble a career record,
- to assist in application for promotion or new jobs,
- to reflect on the past,
- to be challenged academically,
- to formalise key experiences,
- to celebrate achievement,
- to help to plan for the future,
- to help to acquire new skills,
- to see what it is like,
- to gain recognition (seek accreditation?),
- to be able to judge its value and effectiveness (particularly for appraisal and/or staff development), and
- to be able to use the experience to help and encourage others.

This project did not represent what might become the 'normal' working of a PDP support system. This is because it was concerned more with helping experienced professionals *retrospectively* to assemble portfolios of their careers to that point. A 'normal' system would be more likely to be concerned with enabling people to learn the techniques so that they could then keep portfolios that recorded things *as they happened* and for the rest of their career.

All participants were asked to suggest which groups of teachers would benefit most from portfolios. Generally it was recognised that most enthusiastic teachers would benefit from and enjoy portfolios but that the longer and more varied career a person had had the harder was the catching up.

Two main groups were, however, identified most frequently as being good targets for portfolios. These were inductees and those approaching new responsibilities.

Interestingly, several people suggested that the 'less enthusiastic' teacher would not benefit. As a worker in teacher education I am intrigued by this response. I would have thought that, if learning to keep a portfolio is as inspirational as some of the replies suggest, then these are the very people with the most to gain.

Interesting also is the suggestion of using a portfolio with inductees. It is worth pointing out the view of Anna Kendall, the Kensington and Chelsea portfolio facilitator. She had been appointed specifically in order to support inductees (50 of them in 1990/91) and had chosen portfolios as a key aspect of this support. However it became clear early on that the very first year of practice was not the time to introduce the notion of a reflective diary or anything like it. Instead the year was spent (among other things) introducing young teachers to the skill of writing reflectively through addressing professional issues of immediate interest. The desire for a portfolio then emerged naturally as the teachers entered their second year.

The potential benefits of professional development portfolios for individual teachers and lecturers

There is little doubt that generally the participants in the project were of the opinion that portfolios and portfolio production were of benefit to those who kept them.

The most outstanding benefit identified was that of learning to be a reflective professional. This is possibly the most important discovery of the project. The enthusiasm of the portfolio producers that was encountered during the meetings of April, May and June 1991 is difficult to over-stress and was largely based around the work they had done on learning to think and write reflectively.

The importance of the reflective process in becoming and remaining a professional has been described by (among others) Schön and Kolb. It forms the core thinking behind many courses of teacher education. What is particularly gratifying is to find so many teachers in so many different situations supporting the theories and claiming better practice as the result of portfolio counselling.

A general view of the project participants was that *through improving reflectivity* in teachers a portfolio can improve the pupils learning. They were also clear that effective counselling was as important as the portfolio itself.

A number of other benefits were also identified:

- It helps professionals focus on their career and think pro-actively about their intentions.
- By reflecting on the achievements of the past a portfolio can boost a professional's confidence and alter the way he or she approaches the future. People can become more organised and structured in their work.
- People can become more effective managers.
- Portfolios can help people prepare applications for new jobs and promotion.

- Many people were of the view that a portfolio would enable a teacher to approach an appraisal interview in a positive way; to set the agenda for themselves rather than merely responding to the interviewer.
- A well supported portfolio counselling system could help teachers become more effective by helping them use their strengths to improve their practice.

The potential benefits of professional development portfolios for local education authorities and institutions

In many ways it is difficult to separate the benefits to employers of teachers from the benefits to teachers themselves. It seems fairly clear that anything that makes teachers more effective is of benefit also to their employers as well as to their own students. It is therefore possible to claim that all the advantages set out above also apply in this section.

In addition, a number of aspects of the project emerged that should be of specific interest to employers of teachers. Perhaps the most important evidence that LEAs can perceive advantages in portfolio systems is the fact that *all* LEAs that participated in the project are implementing and resourcing follow up projects.

A very important suggestion is the view that properly organised and resourced portfolio systems can, through the creation of a supportive atmosphere for teachers, improve teacher retention.

There were two components to this view:

- A well organised portfolio system can put both teachers and their employers into a position where each has a *realistic*, well informed view of affairs in the LEA/institution and of the relationship between the individual and their institution.
- Teachers will remain where they are supported and a portfolio system can be a very effective way of making teachers feel supported. Teachers who feel good about themselves will feel good about their employer, especially if the employer is funding the portfolio system.

Participants in the project identified a number of other potential benefits for employers of portfolio systems:

- It could form the basis of a rational system of appraisal. It would focus the appraisal process on the individual's progress and needs and go some way to remove the anxiety that currently exists.
- It could form the basis of a more rational system for selection and promotion (at the same time promoting equality of opportunity). Present systems rely on application forms, references and interviews. These all have well documented shortcomings. How much more rational will be a system based on an on-going carefully documented reflection on practice available (with the agreement of the owner) in an accessible form.
- It is also important not to neglect the equal opportunities aspects of PDPs. There was a clear view that, because they were truly supportive of the individual, portfolios would be helpful to those who were disadvantaged by traditional systems of appointment and promotion.
- It could result in more effective use of the INSET budget. The essence of the argument is that if all teachers were reflective professionals they would make better use of INSET activities and experiences. They would learn more effectively. Thus money spent on

portfolio counselling would be repaid by better use being made of all other aspects of INSET spending.

- In addition to this it is possible that professional development based on reflective analysis of practice might prove more effective (and more cost effective) than courses as a means of delivering INSET.

Outline guidelines on the development of support systems for professional development portfolios for teachers and lecturers

One of the most important findings to emerge from the project is what can be learned about ways to support people learning to produce their portfolios.

The majority of participants were very clear that counselling is an essential element in the portfolio process. A number of specific aspects of the support were identified as valuable.

Just as becoming a reflective professional is the most important benefit of producing a portfolio, *learning how* to think and write reflectively was considered to be the most important aspect of the counselling support.

The most important work in this area is that of Bloor and Butterworth, who developed a training and counselling package at Thames Polytechnic whose aim is to develop these reflective skills. The underlying principle of the processes in the package are derived from the 'reflective learning cycle', developed by David Kolb, and the importance of reflection as both a key to professional learning and as a source of evidence that learning has taken place. The methodology is to establish an understanding in the writer of the components of reflective writing and of their own skills in these components and to develop areas of less strength. There is no doubt that the LEA participants in the project found this approach valuable.

At Kensington and Chelsea (where the project worked with 50 inductees) the process of developing reflective writing and thinking skills was considered so important that large amounts of time and energy were given over to it. Much can be learned about this from the carefully designed series of activities orientated around issues of immediate concern to the participants and building one upon another. The activity of the counsellor was well supported by the LEA and it is quite possible that the success of the scheme (all inductees remain in the LEA and many remain keen to continue to meet into their second year) is due to the care with which the programme was designed and implemented.

A key aspect of effective counselling is the creation of a supportive environment in which learning can take place. This is particularly important in an area such as portfolio production where individuals need to be prepared to share their experiences and understanding. Almost impossible to separate from this is the importance of peer support and the pooling of ideas. The idea of the development of the counsellor into a 'critical friend' and the group into a group of 'critical friends' seems particularly important.

It is appropriate to distinguish two kinds of portfolio counselling support. Much of the project was concerned with support for those learning to write reflectively and starting to produce a portfolio. However, during the project it became fairly clear that continuing support would be needed if employers and teachers were to obtain the full benefits of portfolios. This support may well require different skills from those involved in developing portfolio production in the first place (induction) and may be delivered by a different person. One model might be for the induction counselling to be carried out by a person from outside the counsellee's institution and the continuing support to be local, and available on an 'as required' basis. The two counsellors would probably need to liaise.

Accreditation of professional development portfolios towards Higher Education awards

The response to the questionnaire to institutions of Higher Education was one of the few disappointing aspects of the project (5 questionnaires were returned from a total of 10 institutions). Despite this there are a number of ways in which the project can contribute to an understanding of the relationship between professional learning and higher education awards.

Of the 5 institutions replying 3 are in a position to give credit for prior learning and two are able to give credit for portfolios. There is no doubt that a great deal of work needs to be done before there is general acceptance by higher education of the potential for awarding portfolio based credit.

One important understanding that can be obtained from the project is that there is a difference between a professional development portfolio and an APEL portfolio (that is a portfolio prepared specifically in order to establish a claim for Accreditation of Prior Experiential Learning). The essence of the argument is that professional development portfolios differ from APEL portfolios in that they are not compiled in order to articulate a particular claim for credit towards a particular award. Rather they are general collections of material recording the compiler's experiences over a prolonged period, possibly an entire career. Bloor and Butterworth are clear that there are three differences between the two processes:

- An APEL portfolio focuses a narrow, often carefully selected, range of activity whereas a PDP ranges across a whole career.
- In a PDP the choice as to which experiences are focused on is made by the individual. In an APEL portfolio this choice will be strongly influenced by the institution from which credit is being sought.
- An APEL portfolio is aimed at accreditation towards a particular award. The counsellor knows clearly the standard that is required and the writer will be working towards fairly explicit criteria.

They feel that the general, wide ranging, nature of the process that will lead to PDP production will pose particular difficulty for PDP writers. They suggest that writers may have great difficulty deciding when to stop writing and may experience dissatisfaction with their portfolios because they will lack the depth of an APEL portfolio. This is not to say that depth cannot be achieved through a PDP but that it may be difficult to do so.

These views were certainly borne out by the project. Relatively few people acknowledged having completed their portfolio, and dissatisfaction was expressed at the difficulty in coming to terms with the appropriate depth and criteria.

This difference between a general purpose personal document on the one hand and a specific, carefully documented, claim on the other may well be unbridgeable. This is borne out by the reaction of the Thames Polytechnic representative to the portfolios. Despite acknowledging the high quality of the portfolios the Thames respondent felt it would be difficult to award credit to the portfolios as they stood. It was difficult to relate the learning evidence in the essentially linear, fragmented, structure of the PDPs to the institution's need for writing in depth on a small number of clearly identified themes.

Another, potentially greater, difficulty in this area is that not only does an APEL claim need to be specific but this specificity will vary from institution to institution and possibly from course to course. This implies that if a person writing a PDP feels that they *may, one day*, want to claim HE credit they will need to know which institution (and possibly which award) they may go for. This is clearly quite impracticable.

In order for this not to be the case it might be that Higher Education will need to come together to agree a set of common inter-award and inter-institutional criteria for accreditation. These criteria will then need to be communicated to PDP facilitators so that they can be borne in mind by portfolio producers.

These differences between a PDP and an APEL portfolio need not prevent a PDP contributing to accreditation. The skill of writing reflectively is a key to both. The important thing abut this is that the *skills* developed in order to create and maintain a PDP as well as the *document* itself could form a general purpose basis out of which a specific document could be developed whenever the owner wishes.

Conclusion

The findings of the project were very significant. It is clear that effective, well resourced and teacher centred portfolio production can energise teachers in a very positive way that can improve their performance and their relationships with their employers.

Perhaps this is best illustrated by two quotations from participants:

> The project interested me and I wanted to learn more but I did not have clear and precise expectations before it started. If there was one general overall expectation it was that the process could make a teacher a better professional. My involvement has confirmed this expectation.

> It has been an interesting and valuable experience for me. In the future I can see it as being a matter of course for all people at the start of (or before) their careers to begin such a compilation of useful and valuable material – whether in teaching or any other career/job. I can see it being a much more realistic and fair way of appointing people to position/promotion than an application form, interview and reference in the future – not to replace those entirely but to act as solid evidence for claims made, say by those shortlisted for jobs.

References

Bloor, Michael and Butterworth, Christine (1990) Realising human potential, in *Aspects of Education Technology*, Vol. XXIV.

Boud, David, Keogh, Rosemary and Walker, David (1985) Promoting reflection in learning: a model, in Boud, Keogh and Walker (eds) *Reflection: Turning Experience into Learning*. London: Kogan Page.

Chandler, Barbara (1990) *Feasibility Study of an Accreditation Scheme for Advisory Teachers across the TRIN Network*. Informally published by Thames Regional INSET Network.

Evans, Norman (1987) *Assessing Experiential Learning*. Further Education Unit.

Evans, Norman (1988) *The Assessment of Prior Experiential Learning*. CNAA.

Graham, Jim (1989) Professional development portfolios and their implications for portability in modular schemes, *British Journal of In-service Education*, 15(1) Spring: 45–50.

Hall, David (1991) Credit where it's due – INSET by Credit Accumulation at Thames Polytechnic, *NASD Journal No. 25*, June: 40–5.

Kolb, David and Fry, Donald (1975) Towards an applied theory of experiential learning, in C. Cooper (ed.) *Theories of Group Processes*. New York and London: Wiley and Sons.

Land, Ray (1991) 'Rationale for a PGCE'. In a validation document for a course at Thames Polytechnic.

Mumby, Stephen, Ogilvie, Chris and Sutton, Ruth (1988) INSET and records of achievement – where do we go from here? *British Journal of In-Service Education*, 14(2): 18–23.

Schön, Donald (1983) *The Reflective Practitioner – How Professionals Think in Action*. New York: Basic Books.

Winter, Richard and Powney, Janet (1988) Teacher education and the 'accreditation of individual learning', *Journal of Further and Higher Education*, 12(3): 54–61.

15 | The development of staff*

FERGUS O'SULLIVAN, KEN JONES AND KEN REID

Two aspects of staff development

John Robinson has been teaching for five years. He is energetic and enthusiastic. He enjoys teaching his subject (mathematics) and the pupils seem to enjoy his lessons. Being fairly new to the profession, he has been able to adapt quickly to the demands of GCSE, information technology and other developments. He entered teaching having taken a one-year PGCE course. His competence in his subject is not questioned. He does, however, feel that he would like to know more about different styles of teaching and learning, especially the cross-curricular application of mathematics. He has become interested in integrated pre-vocational courses but has no background or specific skills in this field. He is an excellent form teacher and has taken on the extra responsibilities associated with being an assistant head of the fifth year. The head of year has recently advised him to look for a pastoral post in another school. His head of department has suggested he applies for a head of mathematics post elsewhere. There seems to be little prospect of either of these two career options being open to him at his present school in the near future.

Headway Comprehensive is a split-site school located in the suburbs of a large conurbation. Years 7–9 are accommodated in the old grammar school building; one mile away, years 10 and 11 occupy what used to be the local secondary modern school. Staff commute during break and lunchtime; pupils remain on site for all lessons. A recent Ofsted report has highlighted deficiencies in a number of areas:

- the curriculum needs to be reviewed; it does not adequately represent the interests of all pupils; cross-curricular work is lacking;

*This is an edited version of Chapter 1 in *Staff Development in Secondary Schools* published in 1990.

- teaching styles are over-didactic;
- there is a need to update syllabuses in geography and French;
- there is insufficient communication with parents;
- teachers in the school tend to be insular, tending to gravitate to their departments or school bases whenever they can;
- extra-curricular activities are few;
- there is little to stretch the more able pupils; and
- although discipline and public examination results are generally good, there is an overemphasis on the academic to the detriment of individual pupils' personal qualities.

The headteacher needs to come to terms with these criticisms quickly. She has designated a deputy head to act as staff development coordinator in the school. She has also approached three heads of faculty (science, humanities, creative subjects) to form a staff development committee, working under the staff development coordinator. Their brief is to utilise school-focused INSET funding to tackle these and related issues.

The two examples given above indicate the wide interpretation that can be placed on the term 'staff development'. In the first example, it is an individual member of staff who is motivated to pursue some form of professional development; in the second, the whole staff need to become involved. [. . .]

What is staff development?

This chapter will focus on three key issues related to staff development. First, we begin by asking what is staff development and what does the term mean? Second, we consider how staff development works in practice. Third, we introduce the notion of the staff development cycle and discuss the various stages in this operation.

Staff development and professional development

Teachers are in the business of education. They are now perceived to be 'facilitators of learning' rather than didactic founts of all knowledge. It follows that teachers themselves should adopt this philosophy of lifelong learning in their own professional activities. This process of learning is individualistic and personal. A higher degree in the philosophy of education may, or may not, help a head of year to deal more effectively with pupils and parents. However, it may not begin to show signs of practical application for perhaps three or four years after the course has been completed. It may never be used in any direct practical sense. It must, however, develop the thinking, learning and reflective processes of the individual.

   We will begin this chapter by distinguishing between *personal professional development* and *staff development*. The distinction is a real one. A teacher is employed as a member of staff in a school. The school has an ethos, aims and objectives, and staff have a corporate responsibility to pupils and the community as a whole. The teacher, as a loyal member of staff, may hold different values to the teacher as an individual. That is not to say that the individual's values and requirements are any less important than those prioritised by the staff at the school as a whole.

   In the ideal world, there would be sufficient time and resources for teachers to follow their own professional educational interests, as well as give a full commitment to the school. However, we are not yet at this stage and may never get there. Until then, demands on time and resources have to be prioritised. One of the most sensitive roles of the headteacher and staff development coordinator (SDC) is, therefore, to balance the teacher's individual needs and the school's requirements of them as a member of staff. It is crucial for reasons of morale, if not for the preservation of some professional status in teaching, that *teacher* professional development is not lost in the mechanistic institutional programmes of development of a school's *staff*.

The term 'staff development' has been defined in a number of ways. Matheson (1981) defined it as: 'the activity of staff training, that is a conscious institutional approach intended to improve the capability for staff to fill specified roles, particularly in relation to teaching'.

Several aspects of staff development follow from this definition. First, it is concerned with a range of staff training activities, irrespective of whether they are voluntary or mandatory, in-school or externally based, knowledge or skill based, of personal or school interest and, finally, related to curriculum-led staff development schemes or otherwise.

Second, the definition emphasises the need for a conscious school approach to staff development. This means there should be an agreed policy statement about the aims and obligations of the individual and school towards staff development. In order to succeed in involving staff, the school's first task is to create the right climate for school-wide staff development to take place. Without a credible, creative, positive environment for in-service training and staff development, very little will work. What is on offer must be perceived by staff as being an acceptable part of a coherent school plan.

Carroll *et al.* (1986) suggest that the first action every headteacher should take, with regard to his or her school, is to check that the institution has:

1 a clearly articulated policy on staff development;
2 a programme for implementation;
3 a realistic budget;
4 a senior member of the management team designated as responsible for staff development;
5 widely accepted procedures for job review and career development;
5 suitable accommodation and facilities for staff development and in-service training;
7 integrated approaches to academic and non-academic support staff, reflected in staff development provision;
8 a procedure for regular evaluation of the staff development programme in terms of its outcomes for both staff and students;
9 agreed and efficient procedures for disseminating information relating to staff and curriculum development;
10 ease of access to development and training opportunities for part-time staff; and
11 a staff development policy and programme which positively promote good equal opportunities practices.

Third, the definition implies the need for:

1 regular reviews in the light of curriculum development plans;
2 the availability of funds and opportunities for staff to undertake staff development both inside and outside school and school time;

3 the setting up of structures and procedures for collating staff needs into a coherent plan for staff development; and
4 acceptance and support from senior management and union(s) for staff development.

Without all these, the job of SDCs in schools will be severely restricted, and this will impede staff development progress. Moreland and Withington (1987) suggest that teachers in schools should ask themselves six initial questions in relation to staff development. These are:

1 Why is staff development seen as important in the school?
2 In what ways are staff development needs made known in the school?
3 What are the criteria for the assessment of priorities in staff development?
4 What are the range of opportunities available within staff development?
5 What is the availability of resources to support such activities?
6 What are the responsibilities of those staff involved in encouraging, supervising and providing staff development?

Fourth, Matheson's definition assumes that staff development leads to staff improvement. In other words, people are better at their jobs as a result of their staff training exercises. If this really is to be the case then the following processes should occur:

1 pre-course activity – to investigate needs;
2 post-course (follow-up) activity – to support the person in putting their new found skills and knowledge into operation;
3 ensuring the best use of new or updated knowledge for (a) the individual and (b) the school;
4 evaluation and feedback; and
5 where necessary, retraining (either for role evolution or movement).

Therefore, procedures should be available for feedback, support, dissemination and aiding career development.

Moreland and Withington advise schools to establish their own staff development committees to assist and work with the SDC in organising and coordinating staff development. They suggest that having or acquiring these skills will help in the processes of:

● helping staff to learn and develop;
● helping staff to solve performance problems; and
● helping staff to anticipate needs, problems and formulate policies and action plans.

In turn, SDCs need support and encouragement from their headteacher and colleagues if they are to succeed with:

● curriculum-led staff development;
● a publicly agreed staff development policy;
● systematic procedures for deciding staff development priorities; and
● institutional support for their own role as a staff developer.

Alternative definitions and ideas on staff development abound. Some theorists use the term interchangeably with in-service teacher education, considering it to be 'any training activity that helps teachers improve [their] teaching skills' (Sparks 1984).

Dillon-Peterson (1981) sees staff development in terms of organisational development and improvement. As such, it provides the basis for school improvement which, in turn, leads to maximum personal growth and a better atmosphere for effective school change.

Vaughan (1983) considers staff development to be the vehicle by which recent research into teaching effectiveness can be used to make a difference in schools. Hence, it is allied closely to the teacher-as-researcher concept (Hopkins 1985).

Southworth (1984) suggests that staff development is adult education. Therefore, he argues that it should be aimed at enriching the teacher's understanding of his/her tasks and activities which go beyond simply improving performance.

Wideen (1987) takes a particular perspective on staff development. He 'places teachers at the centre of any improvement effort and assumes that the work of the teacher, and the visions that teachers have about improving their work, provide the starting point'. He sees collaboration, collegiality and mutual adaptation as necessary ingredients in any school improvement plan. He puts value on the differences among teachers and schools and the uniqueness which results. He views single-minded policy and managerial perspectives of school reform with scepticism. We agree with him. At the same time, we cannot ignore the earlier definition constructed by Matheson, which, in a narrower sense, focuses on the training needs of teachers in a 'knowing and doing' occupation.

Communication

Critical to effective staff development are good communication systems. This is not as easy as it sounds. Communication is complex and in many schools ineffective. Thus, the task of the SDC is two-fold. First, to get hold of information coming into the school. Second, to disseminate this information by passing it onto colleagues as appropriate.

An effective communication system can be established in the following ways:

1 By designing and negotiating with senior management in the school a system for communicating information about staff and curriculum development.
2 By ensuring that the SDC's name is on the list of all external agencies. Note that some headteachers are reluctant for staff to receive external information and mail directly. Vital information can be blocked in this way. Direct access to *all* information relating to staff development activities is a necessary condition of effective management of staff development by the SDC.
3 By devising a checklist of staff and curriculum development materials which it would be helpful to receive. Ensure these materials actually reach the SDC.
4 By making sure that the school is part of any electronic mailing system. This may be delegated to another member of staff who can be relied upon to download relevant information.

Dissemination

Ways of keeping colleagues up to date with staff development and INSET provision include the following:

1 A staff development notice board.
2 Close liaison with the librarian.
3 Good relationships with the senior management team, heads of year and house. Opportunities to attend appropriate meetings to listen and/or speak as necessary.
4 Close liaison with the person in charge of the school's resources. This will help facilitate the development of good communication systems. It can also ease the load on the SDC.
5 A regular in-house staff development bulletin. This bulletin should provide

information on courses, conferences, meetings, etc. It could contain articles on curriculum change. It might provide feedback from courses and conferences which staff have attended.

6 A representative in each subject/year who is designated to receive and publicise staff development materials.

7 A record of all staff interests so that they can receive the relevant information. Sub-mailing lists and networks of staff with particular interests and/or areas of expertise will probably need to be established.

8 A staff development feature in any school news-sheet, governors' report, broadsheet to parents.

9 Ensuring that staff who have attended courses and conferences are given a feedback form. Feedback forms should be kept simple and are easily devised. They should be kept in a ring binder as a reference in the library, staff development workshop or staffroom – or in all three places.

10 Ensuring that staff development progress reports feature regularly as an item in staff meetings.

Hence, there are several approaches to disseminating information to colleagues in school. There are also several methods. These include: printed materials in the form of newsletters or pamphlets; advice-giving on the telephone or through correspondence; organised conferences or one-day sessions gatherings with 'speakers'; courses/events which occur more than once with tutors/speakers/experts involved; consultancy – providing problem-solving advice; workshops – normally 'active learning' sessions and problem-orientated.

Some first principles for school-focused staff development

- Staff development should be *managed*: it must be coordinated, structured, planned and publicised;
- it may be coordinated by one person or by a staff development team;
- it may, depending on philosophy, be a managerial/training approach to enhancement of skills and changing of attitude, or a counselling approach focusing on individual professional development. It may be seen as a continuum along which both these aspects are met;
- it should address *needs*: LEA, school, individual teacher, pupil;
- it should be based on a clear needs-identification process – needs are identified and analysed to determine priorities;
- it should be *democratic* – involving 'ownership' of the programme with *all* staff participating in the identification and analysis processes;
- needs should be school focused – related directly to pupils through curriculum development or, indirectly through staff or management effectiveness;
- conflict of individual and school needs should be avoided. Clarification of procedure is important from the outset (purpose of the programme, levels of funding, criteria for prioritisation, etc.);
- the staff development programme should be coherent (i.e. elements should be connected and developmental);
- it should be perceived by staff as having relevance to practice;

LIBRARY , UNIVERSITY COLLEGE _____

- it should involve staff in active learning processes;
- it should use strategies which may be replicated with pupils;
- it should recognise and utilise existing staff expertise;
- it should involve a variety of activities;
- it should involve a variety of venues;
- in-house provision for whole staff or for interest groups should be balanced, with provision for individual staff attending courses elsewhere;
- feedback should be 'contractual' for staff who are given support from school INSET funds to attend courses (as a minimum through a written report; preferably through a feedback training exercise involving interested staff);
- programmes should fully utilise available resources (funding, time, expertise);
- programmes should aim to be cost effective;
- staff development should be evaluated;
  by the provider/trainer/coordinator,
  by the participants, and
  where appropriate, by the pupils;
- evaluation should address (amongst others):
  effectiveness of INSET in terms of pupil outcomes,
  cost effectiveness,
  short- and long-term benefits, and
  suitability and effectiveness of delivery;
- results of the evaluation should be fed back to participants; and
- evaluation feedback should form the basis of the next stage in the process of staff development.

The staff development cycle

The process outlined above relates to the staff development cycle (Figure 15.1).
  The staff development cycle can be broken down into six stages. These are:

1 the identification of staff needs;
2 the analysis of staff needs;
3 the creation and design of the SD programme in response to the data gathered and analysed;
4 the carrying out of the SD programme;
5 the monitoring of the programme and, crucially,
6 the evaluation of the programme.

Although the idea of a 'cycle' is easy to translate into practice, the reality needs to be much more complex. Evaluation, for example, needs to be considered at each stage and not left until the 'final' part of the programme. It must be remembered that individual professional development will need to be planned in conjunction with, but often independent of, the school-focused staff development programme. A key task of the SDC is to manage compatibility of school and individual teacher requirements.

Staff development programmes may be designed to fit in with the financial year from April to March. Teachers think in terms of the academic year from September to July. In combining these two, it is very easy for the system to become rigid and overstructured. As stated above, each stage in the staff development cycle is a process in itself and, although

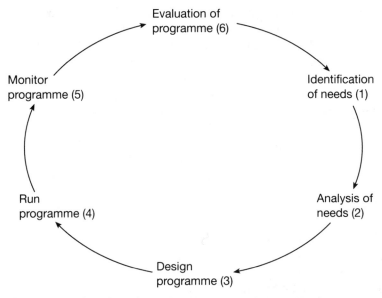

Figure 15.1   The school-focused staff development cycle

it must be formally planned, will not necessarily occur at the same time each year. The identification of needs or INSET requirements, for instance, will take place formally (perhaps by interview) at the least busy time (often the summer term) but this may be too late to organise INSET activities for July. The informal process of needs identification will take place throughout the year. Thereafter, the SDC will be in touch with staff, encouraging and listening to their requests at all times. It is these activities which make the SDC's role more time-consuming than is appreciated by many headteachers.

Identification of training and professional development requirements

We need to distinguish at this point between staff development as *training*, and staff development as continuing professional *education*. Jinks (1979) defined a training need as: 'A gap between the knowledge, skills and attitudes required in a job, and the knowledge, skills and attitudes of the person carrying out the job.'

It is questionable whether 'training' is an appropriate word for activities which try to change attitudes. In a professional setting, the development of a professional approach must grow by persuasion or personal insight.

Staff development as continuing professional education is less easy to define. It is personal, individualistic and often unquantifiable. It fits into the concept of teaching as an art rather than teaching as labour or as a craft. Some professionals take issue with the use of the term 'needs' in this context. It may suggest a 'deficit approach' to staff development, i.e. What does the teacher need to perform better? It often implies solutions to problems rather than a reflective approach to what is, after all, an extremely complex interaction of personal relationships between human beings involving the teacher, as facilitator of learning, and the pupil as learner. In the development of management skills, the leader maximises the contribution of the other members in the team.

In the following section we will look briefly at identifying the training requirements of teachers. Moreland and Withington (1987) suggest that a training need is defined

through a comparative analysis of what is required to perform a job well and the current extent to which an individual possesses those necessary characteristics. This training need is then turned into a learning need that the individual ought to satisfy in order to become better able to perform their job.

INSET linked to subject-based GCSE courses was undertaken, for example, very much in a training mode. For most teachers it focused on classroom skills and techniques – the practicalities of teaching to a new examination system, the philosophy of which was already determined.

Eight questions should be asked when identifying the training needs of staff in a school. These are:

1 Who should be involved in the training programme?
2 What do staff need training in and/or about?
3 How many individuals are affected by each need?
4 What kind of training is required to meet each need?
5 What are the standards/methods/procedures to be followed for each need?
6 When and how should the training be completed?
7 What will be the costs of the training?
8 What will be the benefits of the training?

Design of programme

When considering the design of the programme it is important to remember that staff development *per se* has two important functions: improvement of performance in the person's present job; and preparing people for future opportunities, responsibilities and tasks.

It must also take into consideration the intrinsic requirements of teachers – the need to stand back and take a broad, reflective look at the process of education in schools rather than the practice of teaching.

There are a host of possible ways of organising training courses/sessions within the staff development programme. Courses can be conducted utilising one or some of the following activities. These include:

- external short courses (non-residential or residential);
- in-school short courses organised by the SDC, other staff, headteacher, external agency *et seq.*;
- external or internal one-day (or less), one-off conferences/seminars/workshops;
- contracted training/consultancy programmes;
- attendance on degree/certificate/diploma or other award-bearing programmes;
- job enrichment schemes (expanded responsibilities/talks/roles, etc.);
- job rotation;
- private study or sabbaticals;
- open learning methods or flexistudy;

- correspondence courses/distance learning/distance learning materials;
- case studies and 'incidents';
- film, television, video sessions;
- lectures;
- discussions held by 'experts';
- coaching/on-the-job training;
- 'junior'/assistant/'pupil' training (understudying a role);
- special briefs/assignments, often with fixed timescales;
- written reports;
- research projects;
- evaluation schemes;
- internal and external secondments;
- problem-solving and decision-making exercises;
- industrial or commercial links/joint ventures/secondments;
- simulations and games;
- role play, and
- self-help staff development meetings ('quality circles').

The above list offers a very wide range of staff development activities. For different needs and circumstances, a mixture of methods/approaches will be used. Good staff development programmes will utilise a variety of approaches, concepts and formulae. Whichever method is appropriate will vary in time for differing members of staff, and will depend upon their needs, inclinations, the topic or issue, the nature of their subject, the work of their department, year or section as well as the way the SDC presents the information/ideas to them.

Staff development is a two-way process. Individual staff, through discussions with colleagues (headteachers, heads of department/year, etc.) should take important decision-making roles in terms of their own requirements and progress. In this connection, staff development review procedures are vital, whether related to appraisal exercises or otherwise.

It is important to note at this point, however, that the nature of evaluation and the criteria on which it is based should be discussed fully *before* the programmes/activities are run.

Summary

The terms 'staff development', 'INSET' and 'professional development' are frequently used as if they mean the same thing. Professional development is, in fact, much broader and refers to the individualistic and personal process of continuing professional education. Staff development, on the other hand, relates to the development of an individual teacher as a member of staff in a particular school, or to the development in some way of the whole staff of a school. A wide variety of definitions and interpretations of staff development exist. Effective staff development will usually be formally managed by an SDC and an elected staff development team. Emphasis is placed on good communication and active dissemination of information. Staff development programmes in schools are ideally built on a number of first principles. They should be seen as forming a continuing process rather than disjointed stop–start provision. The model of the staff development cycle is commonly used to outline the stages in the process.

Although evaluation is commonly placed as the final stage, it should occur throughout and should be considered in conjunction with the needs identification stage.

References

Carroll, S., Fairless, H., Graessle, L. and McQuade, P. (1986) *The Staff Development Manual,* Volume 2: *Staff Development in Action.* Lancaster: Framework Press.

Dillon-Peterson, B. (1981) *Staff Development/Organization Development* (1981 Yearbook). Washington: ASCD.

Hopkins, D. (1985) *A Teacher's Guide to Classroom Research.* Milton Keynes: Open University Press.

Jinks, M. (1979) *Training.* London: Blandford Press.

Matheson, T. (1981) quoted in N. Moreland and T. Withington (1987) Market Research for PICKUP, Unit 2, Module 1, in FEU/PICKUP (1987) *Project Report – Staff Development Programme.* York: Longman for the FEU.

Moreland, N. and Withington, T. (1987) Market Research for PICKUP, Unit 2, Module 1, in FEU/PICKUP (1987) *Project Report – Staff Development Programme.* York: Longman for the FEU.

Southworth, G. W. (1984) Development of staff in primary schools, *British Journal of In-Service Education,* 10(3): 6–15.

Sparks, D. (1984) Staff development and school improvement: an interview with Ernest Boyes, *The Journal of Staff Development,* 5(2): 32–9.

Vaughan, J. (1983) Using research on teaching, schools and change to help staff development make a difference, *Journal of Staff Development,* 4(1): 7–23.

Wideen, M. F. (1987) Perspectives on staff development, in M. F. Wideen and I. Andrews (eds) *Staff Development in School Improvement.* London: The Falmer Press.

Index